D0948720

LONDON

CITYSCOPES: a unique overview of a city's past as well as a focused eye on its present. Written by authors with intimate knowledge of the cities, each book provides a historical account with essays on the city today. Together these offer fascinating vignettes on the quintessential and the quirky, the old and the new. Illustrated throughout with compelling historical images as well as contemporary photos, these are essential cultural companions to the world's greatest cities.

Titles in the series:

Beijing Linda Jaivin

Berlin Joseph Pearson

Buenos Aires Jason Wilson

Chicago: From Vision to Metropolis Whet Moser

London: City of Cities Phil Baker

Madrid: Midnight City Helen Crisp and Jules Stewart

Mexico City: Cradle of Empires Nick Caistor

New York Elizabeth L. Bradley

Paris Adam Roberts

Prague: Crossroads of Europe Derek Sayer

San Francisco: Instant City, Promised Land Michael Johns

CITYSCOPES

London

City of Cities

Phil Baker

REAKTION BOOKS

For Nancy

Published by Reaktion Books Ltd
Unit 32, Waterside
44–48 Wharf Road
London N1 7UX, UK
www.reaktionbooks.co.uk

First published 2021
Copyright © Phil Baker 2021

Printed and bound in India by Replika Press Pvt. Ltd

A catalogue record for this book is available from the British Library
ISBN 978 1 78914 218 1

p. 6: 30 St Mary Axe (informally known as 'the Gherkin') rising over the church
of St Andrew Undershaft, City of London; p. 7: view from St Paul's Cathedral dome
looking west; p. 8 (top): woman trooper, Royal Horse Artillery, at Horse Guards,
Whitehall; p. 8 (bottom): Victorian sculpture of Boudicca by Thomas Thornycroft,
Westminster; p. 9: Edith Cavell Memorial, St Martin's Place; p. 10: neo-Gothic interior,
St Pancras Renaissance Hotel; p. 11: Regency Terrace, Regent's Park; p. 12 (top):
James Smith & Sons umbrella shop, New Oxford Street; p. 12 (bottom): Cecil Court,
aka Booksellers' Row; p. 13 (top): Electric Cinema, Notting Hill; p. 13 (bottom):
the Cast Court, V&A; p. 14 (top): 'ghost' advertising signage in Redcross Street,
Bermondsey; p. 14 (bottom): Regent's Canal, Islington; p. 15 (top): Columbia Road
flower market; p. 15 (bottom): looking south at the Millennium Bridge; p. 21: 'Burlington
Arcade as it was in 1828', an engraving by T. H. Shepherd; p. 165: Turbine Hall, Tate Modern;
p. 233: Leadenhall Market.

Contents

The Tower of London, showing the White Tower, in an illuminated manuscript from the late fifteenth century.

Prologue

I talo Calvino's novel *Invisible Cities* is a catalogue of cities: cities of desire and memory; cities of commodities (caviar, astrolabes, amethyst); cities of rubbish; cities of kite flying, and injustice, and old postcards. Slowly you realize all these cities are really the same city – Venice, in Calvino's case – in all its angles. London is like the city in Calvino's book; it is a city of cities, vast and various enough to reflect back whatever the viewer projects onto it. It is a gracious and civilized hotbed of squalor, crime and vice; a city enriched by multiculturalism and ruined by mass migration; and a giant Babylonian factory of oppression, designed to respect the individual and produce happiness.

Writing around 1190, a chronicler named Richard of Devizes has an unsavoury description of London:

> All sorts of men crowd there from every country under the heavens. Each race brings its own vices and its own customs to the city. No one lives in it without falling into some sort of crimes . . . Whatever evil or malicious thing that can be found in any part of the world, you will find in that one city.

For Dr Johnson on the other hand, in 1777, 'When a man is tired of London he is tired of life.' It is possible to be tired of both, as more than a few Londoners have discovered, and to be tired of seeing Johnson's endlessly repeated quote, but there is a less well-known observation on the same subject from Johnson's friend and biographer James Boswell:

> how different a place London is to different people . . . A politician thinks of it merely as the seat of government in its different departments; a grazier, as a vast market for cattle; a mercantile man, as a place where a prodigious deal of business is done . . . a dramatick enthusiast, as the grand scene of theatrical entertainments; a man of pleasure, as an assemblage of taverns, and the great emporium for ladies of easy virtue.

But to the thinking person, says Boswell, what is really striking is that it includes 'the whole of human life in all its variety, the contemplation of which is inexhaustible'.

Seen as gigantic and awe-inspiring throughout its history, London was the modern world's first great metropolis. Through the nineteenth and early twentieth centuries it came to seem like a great grimy monster, housing around one-fifth of Britain's population and inhaling thousands of commuters every morning before exhaling them again every night. Even when it was small by modern standards, London was not only relatively large – Renaissance London was twelve times larger than any other city in Britain – but its subjective vastness was increased by its labyrinthine quality. Unlike New York on its grid, or Paris after it was rebuilt by Haussmann, London's growth was organic and unplanned, with its density increased by the convolution of smaller streets: 'if you wish to have a just notion of the magnitude of this city,' Johnson told Boswell in the 1760s,

> you must not be satisfied with seeing its great streets and squares, but must survey the innumerable lanes and courts. It is not in the showy evolutions of buildings, but in the multiplicity of human habitations which are crowded together, that the wonderful immensity of London consists.

London's immensity is diverse, without the more unified ambience of Paris or Venice. It is made up of distinct districts in a coral reef-like conglomeration of 'villages' (which some districts, like Stoke Newington or Knightsbridge, were, but which has taken on a life of its own as a metaphor). Hampstead, Whitechapel,

Knightsbridge, Camden, Pimlico and the rest are distinct in architecture, atmosphere and people; where the Londoner lives will tend to shape their life. London is further diverse in its ethnicity: already in the nineteenth century it was said to have more Irish than Dublin and more Jews than Palestine.

For all that, London has an intense identity, from the Victorian capital of empire to the swinging London of the 1960s. Sometimes the idea outlives the reality: pinstripe is not as popular as it was, never mind bowler hats, yet they still keep their place with red double-decker buses – London livery and street furniture tends to be red – classic phone boxes, pillar boxes, Guardsman's jackets, black taxicabs and Victorian street lamps, all accompanying more obvious monuments such as Big Ben.

These images multiply even as London becomes international, along with an enduring idea of London as an essentially Victorian city with dark Gothic undertones. Late nineteenth-century writers such as Arthur Conan Doyle and Robert Louis Stevenson have left an image of the imperial metropolis as a place of foggy, gaslit mystery. London's past has often been violent, and London's squalor and darkness have been romanticized to an extent almost unique among cities, with tourist attractions like the Chamber of Horrors – formerly the most celebrated part of Madame Tussaud's waxworks – and the London Dungeon.

At the same time, amid the grime, the image of old London has something cosy about it, as in London Fog raincoats, an American brand, and the idea of clubland or Sherlock Holmes-era decor, with its old bookcases and Chesterfield sofas.

'The mind has its West End and its Whitechapel,' wrote Victorian novelist Robert Hichens, and London's variety and striking contrasts have long made it a city that cries out to be investigated, whether out of fascination or social concern. 'We had but to go a hundred yards off and see for ourselves,' said Thackeray guiltily after reading Henry Mayhew's revelatory *London Labour and the London Poor* (1851), 'but we never did.' Much of what the explorers found in this fragmented and mysterious city was bad, like the world of Margaret Harkness's documentary novel *In Darkest London* (1889).

Others concerned themselves with pleasure, or history. Together they have generated a vast literature: the major bibliography, by Heather Creaton, only covers London to 1939 and has almost 22,000 entries, most of them written and published within the city, like a great organism conscious of itself. London has been investigated in the work of such writers as James Greenwood, Thomas Burke, the great Geoffrey Fletcher and, more recently, Iain Sinclair, in an endless stream of titles such as *East of Aldgate*, *The London Spy*, *The Wilds of London*, *Low Life Deeps*, *London: A Pilgrimage*, *Night Side of London*, *Wonderful London*, *Ghosts of Literary London*, *Off the Track in London* and *Curiosities of London Life*. London is a place that demands to be explored.

HISTORY

London spires and buildings, from a 1497 edition of *Caxton's Chronicles of England*.

1 In the Land of the Dagenham Idol

London has its mythic origin as the 'New Troy', in a tale involving the giants Gog and Magog, who can be found in the Guildhall. For over five hundred years figures of Gog and Magog have been paraded through the streets in the Lord Mayor's Show. They were originally Gogmagog, a British giant, and Corinaeus, the foreign giant who defeated him: Corinaeus came to Britain, so the story goes, with Brutus. Brutus, descended from Rome's mythical founder Aeneas, was a refugee from the fall of Troy. With the help of his champion giant, Brutus founded New Troy as the capital of Albion. As time went by, the name of Corinaeus was forgotten and the name of Gogmagog split to cover both of them. The tale can be found in the history of Geoffrey of Monmouth, writing in 1136, and its larger significance for Geoffrey would be that it links Britain (London in particular) to Troy and Rome. And it all happened, according to him, at the nicely round date of 1000 BC.

What was really going on at 1000 BC, and earlier, is not so clear. There was plenty of life in the prehistoric Thames Valley – remains of crocodiles, rhinoceroses and hippopotami have been found (at Islington, Greenwich and Trafalgar Square), and superstitious Victorians used fossilized sharks' teeth, dug from the London clay and even older, as a remedy against cramp. Coming into human times there were mammoths. It is often said there was nothing at the site of London until the Romans built Londinium, but there were certainly people, who already had settlements but not durable buildings. Julius Caesar describes the Thames Valley area as 'thickly studded with homesteads'.

The beliefs of the earliest Britons are not known. The most remarkable surviving object is the 'Dagenham Idol', a piece of British tribal art. It is about 4,300 years old, pre-dating Stonehenge by a thousand years, and was found buried with the skeleton of a deer; they may have been an offering to the gods. Like the gods, the river was a presence from the earliest times. When ancient skulls were found in the Thames at Battersea, in what one Victorian antiquary called a 'Celtic Golgotha', they were first thought to come from a battle between the Romans and Britons, but they are too early. They may be a sacrifice to the river itself.

By the time the Romans arrived, Britain was in the hands of Celts, originally from Gaul. The British Celts were a farming people for whom warfare was a source of status involving the taking and displaying of heads; the reputation of the islanders as savages disturbed the Roman troops when embarking for Britain, and they had to be entertained by comedians to keep morale up before boarding ships. The Celts fought with chariots, minted coins, made pottery and even glass, and had a strong aesthetic sense; no one who sees their sword shapes or the British Museum's Battersea Shield – with its curvilinear decorations, akin to the 'Celtic' element in Art Nouveau – could think of them as simply primitive.

The Dagenham Idol: 4,300-year-old London tribal art.

The first Romans landed in 55 and 54 BC, but found little to interest them in the Thames Valley marshland. The Roman settlement came after the larger Roman invasion of AD 43. It was Roman practice to leave tribal kings in place as clients of Rome: the kings gained an ally against non-client tribes in return for paying taxes, but there was discontent with high taxation, brutal treatment and land-grabbing.

Resentment flared up with the Iceni revolt of AD 60, leading to the worst ever bloodshed on British soil. The Iceni were an East Anglian tribe; when their king died his people were ill-treated by the local Roman governor. When his widow Boudicca complained, she was flogged and her daughters raped. In revenge she led her people to sack the towns of Camulodonum (Colchester, the capital), London and Verulamium (St Albans). The governor of Britain, Suetonius Paulinus, tried to evacuate the civilian population, but it was too late: the Iceni slaughtered them, beheading, hanging, burning and crucifying. The historian Tacitus put the total death toll at 70,000.

This was also the first of the city's recurrent great fires, and one of the worst. Archaeologists have found three distinct layers of burned earth: from the Blitz, the Great Fire of 1666 and the Iceni revolt. Boudicca, with knives on her chariot wheels, became a folkloric British heroine: the Victorians liked her as an image of a strong queen, and put a statue of her by the Houses of Parliament.

The town Boudicca destroyed was a small trading centre, but it was rebuilt on a grander scale. The Roman city occupied the area that is now the City financial district, ringed by a wall. Ludgate, Newgate, Aldersgate, Cripplegate, Bishopsgate and Aldgate all take their names from the main gated entrances (Moorgate came later). Inside was a barracks, amphitheatre, forum, a great basilica (where Leadenhall Market is now), baths and temples, and all the celebrated amenities of Roman life, like mosaic and underfloor heating.

Tacitus writes cynically that Londinium's baths and banquets seduced the Britons 'into assimilation and to thinking of [these] novelties as civilization, when really they were only features of enslavement'. To make the warlike and disorganized Britons 'pleasurably inured to peace and ease', he writes, the governor Agricola

> gave private encouragement and official assistance to the building of temples, public squares and private mansions . . . Furthermore he trained the sons of chiefs in the liberal arts

Tattooed ancient Britons as the Georgians imagined them, in a print from 1804.

    . . . [so that] in place of distaste for the Latin language came a passion to command it. In the same way, our national dress came into favour and the toga was everywhere to be seen. And so the Britons were gradually led on to the amenities that make vice agreeable – arcades, baths, and sumptuous banquets.

As for vice, the baths became mixed until public decency became a concern and the emperor Hadrian – who visited London in AD 122 – restored segregated bathing. Roman London was strikingly mixed

N

Found in the Thames, the Battersea Shield from around 200 BC.

in other respects, with an international population: gravestones and fabric fragments show a city with inhabitants from Greece, Germany and Spain, who might have owned clothing from the Silk Road or China. Various religious cults flourished, including that of Isis, a goddess originally from Egypt, and Mithras, a bull-slaying god originally from Persia; a temple of Mithras was unearthed in the 1950s (and is now open to the public). It is likely that the new cult of Christianity also had some presence.

Roman London had its greatest days around the second century and then declined, until in 410 the legions were recalled from Britain to defend a crumbling Roman Empire. The departure of the Romans was followed by the poorly understood period that used to be known as the 'Dark Ages'. Literacy and building in stone disappeared, along with the money economy, as people reverted to barter.

When invading Angles and Saxons arrived from Germany, the remaining Romanized Britons asked Rome for help, but none came. Over the next two centuries the Anglo-Saxons took over the London area, but made little use of the Roman buildings, which they seem to have regarded with awe. A Saxon poem calls them 'enta geweorc', 'the work of giants'.

The main Anglo-Saxon settlement was 'Lundenwic', on the north bank where Covent Garden and the Strand are now: the Strand was then a literal strand, in the sense of a riverbank path. The suffix '-wick' means a trading town, and by the eighth century Lundenwic

Mithras, a deity popular with Roman soldiers, here depicted slaying the bull in a white marble relief, now in the Museum of London.

was described by the Venerable Bede (673–735), an early historian, as 'a trading centre for many nations'. But the British Isles suffered Danish and Viking raiding in the eighth century, in one case with a force of over three hundred ships coming up the Thames, and Lundenwic had to be abandoned. The Saxons made a new stronghold in what they called Lundenburgh – '-burgh' means a fortified town – within the walled area of the old Roman city, and the old Lundenwic leaves its name, as 'old wick', in Aldwych.

London was in the kingdom of the East Saxons, but much of Britain was now under the Danes. London itself fell under Danish control in the 880s, and its return to Saxon rule in 886 under King Alfred is commemorated by the simple Alfred Plaque on the north bank of the Thames, near St Paul's.

London – not the Saxon capital, which was Winchester, but still an important city – was further fought over in the ninth and tenth centuries. The Saxon king Aethelred the Unready made London his capital, but he was displaced by Viking raiders and driven abroad. He came back, in alliance with King Olaf of Norway – commemorated in churches with the name of St Olave – and recaptured London. The nursery rhyme 'London Bridge is falling down' originates in a Norse poem, and is believed to refer to British and Norwegian forces destroying the bridge by burning it and pulling it into the river.

The Vikings returned, and Aethelred's son Edward had to share power with King Canute, who became sole king upon Edward's death. The Saxons were restored in 1042 with Canute's stepson Edward the Confessor. Meanwhile Christianity had become established in London among both Saxons and settled Danes (a cathedral of St Paul had been built in 604 by Aethelbert, King of Kent, England's first Christian king). When Edward the Confessor began building Westminster Abbey on Thorney Island, Westminster, in the eleventh century, moving his seat of power westwards out of Lundenburgh, he paved the way for the enduring three-way division of London into western 'Westminster' (the royal and administrative centre), the eastern 'City' (the commercial centre) and 'Southwark' (a more unruly South Bank district associated with pleasure and entertainment).

Gog, in the Guildhall; one of the two legendary giants of London, the other being Magog.

After Edward the Confessor's death, the Saxons elected Harold as king, but Edward's cousin Duke William of Normandy claimed the throne, leading to the Norman invasion of 1066. The Norman Conquest created a two-tier society, with effects that can still be felt in the English language and class system. Words of Saxon origin tend to be simpler and describe, for example, livestock rather than products: Saxon cow, swine and deer, compared with Norman beef, pork and venison. Parliament comes from the French *parler*, to talk, while its Saxon forerunner, the 'moot' (related to meeting), survives in 'a moot point': a point for debate. The Normans introduced surnames to Britain, and almost a thousand years later people with 'distinguished' French-sounding names of Norman origin, such as Mandeville, Granvill or de Courcy, are still wealthier and longer-lived than people with trade surnames such as Smith or Cooper. The class glamour of the Norman name is captured in the character of Fitzwilliam Darcy in Jane Austen's 1813 novel *Pride and Prejudice*.

William was crowned at Westminster Abbey, consecrated just the year before, and the Normans reinforced their grip by building the Tower of London, starting with the White Tower, towering over the surrounding land at 27 metres (90 ft) high, and white because it was built from French Caen stone. Norman rule survived a fever epidemic, and a fire in 1087 that burnt down St Paul's Cathedral. With its densely packed wooden houses, and even wooden chimneys, London was plagued by fire. One of the earliest chroniclers, William Fitzstephen (*c.* 1140–1191), wrote, 'The only two inconveniences of London are the excessive drinking of some foolish people, and the frequent fires.'

London exerted power over the monarchy in an uneasy symbiotic relationship. The semi-independent status of the City was recognized by the creation of the office of mayor around 1193 (in tune with the new order, the word is from the French *maire*), and further formalized in 1215 – shortly before Magna Carta – by the Charter of King John recognizing the right of Londoners to elect this mayor themselves. The mayor and sheriffs are still elected by liverymen of the City Livery Companies, trade guilds with their origins in the twelfth century.

The City financed the monarchy and funded its wars, with London's Jewish community, who had come over with the Normans, playing a leading role as money lenders. They are remembered in City place names such as Old Jewry, EC2, an area which, with its synagogue, was ransacked by a mob in 1262 with over five hundred deaths. There were recurrent anti-Jewish riots, often sparked by rumours of fire-starting or child sacrifice, as well as resentment at the lending of money at interest. This was banned by anti-usury laws in 1275, putting Jews in a difficult position because they were forbidden to earn a living by joining livery guilds. In 1291 Edward I expelled them altogether, and their financial role was taken over by Lombard bankers from Italy – as in Lombard Street, EC3 – whose symbol of three golden spheres is the origin of the pawn shop sign.

Public disorder was widespread in medieval London, with the apprentices often at the centre of it. Westminster and the City fought in 1222, after a wrestling match, and the ringleader of the City crew was executed. Apprentices of the Goldsmiths and Tailors livery companies clashed in 1267, leading to deaths and subsequent hangings, and the City fell under mob rule from September to November 1326 when supporters of Queen Isabella, estranged wife of the widely hated Edward II (murdered the following year), released prisoners from the Tower and attacked Lombard houses.

The stained glass and choral music of the Church must have been a transcendent contrast to the hardness of daily life. London was heavily ecclesiastical in this pre-Reformation period, and religious orders have left their mark on place names, buildings and institutions, with Carthusians at Charterhouse, and an Augustinian community at St Bartholomew's (giving rise to St Bart's Hospital, founded by the monk Rahere). St Mary Spital (as in Hospital, becoming Spitalfields) and Mary Bethlem (later Bedlam, for the insane) also had church origins, and Blackfriars Monastery has given its name to a district, a bridge, an underground station and a magnificent Art Nouveau pub, the Black Friar.

The Church tried to alleviate the sickness and poverty of fourteenth-century London – over fifty desperate people were killed in a 1322 stampede for alms at the gates of the Black Friars

– but it was all but powerless when the Black Death arrived in 1347, killing over half the population of around 80,000: the bishop of London could only attempt to bury the victims, while the abbot and 27 monks died at Westminster.

Public disorder reached new heights with the Peasants' Revolt of 1381, sparked by a tax imposed without regard to income – the same issue that caused the London poll tax riots in 1990. The peasants had a touching faith in the young King Richard II, and believed he would help them if he heard their case. Led by the charismatic Wat Tyler, believed to have been a roof tiler from Kent or Essex, they marched on London, opened up the Fleet and Marshalsea prisons, raided the Tower of London, and beheaded the archbishop of Canterbury. Finally they met the king, first at Mile End and then at Smithfield, where the rebels had camped on Clerkenwell Green. And it was there that the mayor, William Walworth, suddenly stabbed Tyler and brought the revolt to an end.

Tyler had led the peasants with the help of a priest named John Ball. Ball is associated with the rhyme 'When Adam delved and Eve span [that is, Adam dug the earth and Eve spun wool] / Who was then the gentleman?' (meaning a man living comfortably without working) – a question revived in Victorian times by the Pre-Raphaelite William Morris, in his novel *The Dream of John Ball* (1888). Another reformer whose ideas were popular in London around this time was John Wycliffe; his followers, the Lollards, translated the Bible into English around 1380, but were repressed, with burnings being held at Smithfield. Meanwhile William Caxton, working with more respectable aristocratic patronage, succeeded in printing some Bible verses in English, along with English-language literary works such as Chaucer's *Canterbury Tales*, and Malory's *Morte d'Arthur*. Caxton's *Chronicles of England*, printed by Wynkyn de Worde in 1497, contain the first known printed image of London.

Recovering from the Black Death, London flourished with a new prosperity and at least relative order, but lawlessness was still widespread: Chaucer was robbed twice in one day in 1390. The notorious Tyburn gallows had been set up in 1388, near today's Marble Arch (Oxford Street, the main route to it, was formerly known as

Tyburn Road and Tyburn Way). One of the first people hanged there was former mayor Nicholas Brembre, charged with murder and treason, who allegedly planned to rename London as Little Troy.

Merchants were growing rich and City prosperity was consolidating: the Guildhall was a magnificent building by the 1400s. One of its benefactors was Dick Whittington, the mayor, a man with interests in textiles and finance whose life bears little resemblance to the pantomime character. The image of Whittington as the poor boy coming to London to seek his fortune seems to have arisen centuries later, appealing to the perennial dream of London as the place where luck changes and the streets are paved with gold.

There was further revolt with the Jack Cade rebellion in 1450, which is fictionalized in Shakespeare's *Henry IV, Part Two*. The rebels executed several prominent figures including the Lord High Treasurer, but were stalemated at London Bridge; they were then tricked with a promise of pardon, before being killed.

The strangest detail of the Cade revolt is the role of the London Stone, a large rock, possibly a Roman milestone, that used to be at St Swithin's church. It was once so famous that when Cade touched it with his sword, he could announce himself 'Lord of the City'. It figures in Shakespeare and in William Blake, who believed it was a druid altar and made it the centre of Golgonooza, his mystical London. Since then it has fallen into obscurity and sits retired behind a metal grille at 111 Cannon Street, opposite the station, in what was once a bank and is now, at the time of writing, a branch of W. H. Smith.

2 Brutal but Golden

When Richard III – villain of Shakespeare's play, popularly remembered for having his nephews strangled in the Tower of London – was killed in battle in 1485 at Bosworth Field, ending the Wars of the Roses, the crown passed to Henry VII, first of the Tudors. The new dynasty presided over a golden age for London, remembered for the culture of the English Renaissance, the beginnings of the British navy and British Empire, and the personal cult of Queen Elizabeth as 'Gloriana'. It was so golden, in the national memory, that a revival of its half-timbered architecture took place in the 'Tudorbethan' style of the late Victorian period, continuing through to the 1920s and 1930s. Some relatively original half-timbered building can be seen at Staple Inn, beside Chancery Lane station (restored in the 1890s): a survivor of what the Victorians treasured as 'Old Holborn'.

London's population more than doubled from around 75,000 in 1500 to around 200,000 a century later (and it would double again by 1650); many of these people lived in rapidly spreading suburbs that were little more than shanty towns. It was a period of social and cultural change, defined by the Protestant Reformation and the dissolution of the monasteries under Henry VIII. Henry's reign was one of considerable grandeur, during which he built Hampton Court Palace and Whitehall Palace – in its day the largest in Europe – but the lack of a male heir led him into six marriages and conflict with the pope, who refused to annul his first marriage to Catherine of Aragon. She fared better than Anne Boleyn and Catherine Howard, both beheaded at Tower Hill.

Old London Bridge in 1616, by Claes Visscher, with traitors' heads on pikestaffs just visible over the gate.

Henry's break with papal authority coincided with a larger movement of Protestantism in Europe. He made himself head of the new Church of England and enforced an English Reformation, with the dissolution of monasteries and religious orders. Gold ornaments were melted, robes were burned to get the gold thread out, and stained glass windows were smashed for the lead.

The dissolution changed the landscape of London, previously dominated by religious institutions. The Cistercian abbey at Tower Hill became a bakery for ship's biscuits, and the Savoy Hospital for the poor became a glass factory. It sealed the end of medieval London, as a transition began to a time of secular aristocratic wealth, but it left the sick and destitute uncared for. In the face of all too obvious need, Henry refounded a few institutions on less ecclesiastical lines, notably St Bartholomew's and St Thomas's (now the hospitals Bart's and Thomas's).

When the Catholic Queen Mary – married to King Philip of Spain, remembered for the Armada – came to the throne in 1553, the situation was reversed: now Protestants were burned at Smithfield.

But then Queen Elizabeth was crowned in 1558, and persecution switched back to Catholics. Protestant and Catholic atrocities added to London's violent and brutal culture in the sixteenth and seventeenth centuries: this was noticed by foreign visitors, and as late as 1661 a German traveller counted twenty heads stuck on poles on Tower Bridge.

Bear-baiting, bull-baiting and horse-baiting with dogs were popular. Elizabeth enjoyed bear-baiting, and theatre performances were prohibited by the mayor on baiting days, so as not to compete: actors caused 'great hurt and destruction of the game of bear-baiting and such like pastimes which are maintained for her Majesty's pleasure'. There was more hurt and destruction in 1583 when scaffolding collapsed at the Paris Bear Garden, Bankside, killing spectators.

The violence of Elizabethan society coexisted with one of the highest literary cultures the world has seen, including Christopher Marlowe (*Dr Faustus*), Ben Jonson (*Volpone*) and Shakespeare. Marlowe was killed in a tavern in 1593, apparently after a dispute over the bill (there are murkier theories involving Elizabethan espionage), and in 1598 Jonson killed an actor in a duel. Like baiting, plays were popular with all levels of society, and the poorer members

Surviving Tudor architecture at Staple Inn, Holborn.

of the audience had standing space as 'groundlings'. Notable theatres included the Boar's Head (1597) and the Globe (1599, particularly associated with Shakespeare): the latter is now recreated, close to its original site.

Theatre, baiting and prostitution were all centred south of the river in the Southwark area, consolidating the triangular structure of royal west, financial City and licentious South Bank. Partly as a consequence of the dissolution, with the increased number of beggars and itinerant poor making their own living in the streets, there was a large Elizabethan underworld, preserved in the work of educated 'low-life' writers such as Thomas Nashe, Thomas Dekker and Robert Greene, recording a world of 'coney-catching' (swindling the gullible) and 'apple squires' (pimps), along with astrologers and fortune tellers. Ben Jonson's 1610 comedy *The Alchemist* details the chaos when Lovewit leaves his house in Blackfriars – just across the river from the badlands of Southwark – in charge of his servant Face, who soon invites Subtle, a fake alchemist and astrologer, and Dol Common, his moll, and they set about fleecing the unwary. For all that, it is no less remarkable how relatively law-abiding most of Elizabethan London seems to have been, with a self-policing system of guild officials, watchmen and beadles. The underworld was exaggerated by the low-life writers of the day, who can be seen as early examples of London's long tradition – with Defoe and *Moll Flanders*, the *Newgate Calendars*, Penny Dreadfuls, Victorian mysteries, the Sherlock Holmes stories, and much more – of crime writing.

These were pre-Enlightenment times; modern and yet not. Queen Elizabeth's adviser Dr John Dee (1527–1609), who lived at Mortlake, practised astrology, alchemy and conversation with angels (the 'scrying stone' that he and his assistant Kelley allegedly used for this, a black obsidian mirror, can be seen in the British Museum), as well as studying mathematics and navigation. Dee was an early advocate of Britain's maritime expansion – the term 'British Impire' [*sic*], later to be enormously resonant, first appears in his writing – and he thought Britain had a particular claim to North America, based on the idea that King Arthur had travelled there. It has been suggested that he partly inspired the figure of Prospero in Shakespeare's *The Tempest* (1611), and more recently H. P. Lovecraft, writing in 1927, credited him with translating his own fictional *Necronomicon*.

The great chronicler of London, John Stow, catches the changing Elizabethan city in transition in his masterpiece *The Survey of London* (1598). For the first time, this was not a compendium of dubious tales about Brutus, Arthur or Troy, but an on-the-ground guide to the city. Despite his monumental achievement, Stow ended in poverty: at the age of 79 he was granted a licence to beg in the street. By way of belated compensation, in one of London's many odd ceremonies, his statue at the church of St Andrews Undershaft, in Aldgate, now has the quill in its hand changed every three years after a special church service.

London was also being impressively surveyed for the first time in maps. There had been extraordinary panoramic bird's-eye views, such as Wyngaerde's *Panorama* of around 1540, but the first true printed map is generally said to be the 'Copperplate' map from the second half of the sixteenth century. Two of the original copper plates are in the Museum of London. It was printed on the Continent around 1560, and a reduced woodcut version known as the Agas map or *Civitas Londinum* was popular – not as a ready

The older St Paul's, which stood from Norman times until the Great Fire.

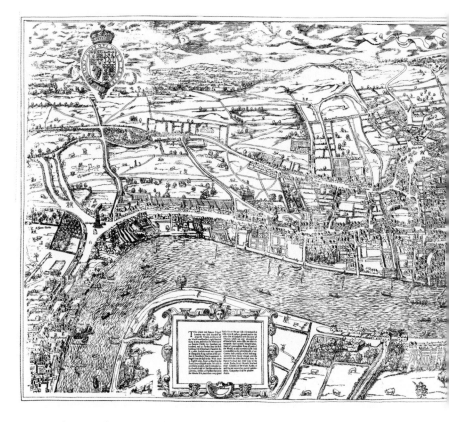

reference for use on the streets, but as a wall ornament – from about the same time.

London was becoming a popular destination for foreign visitors, and sights included the Tower of London; Cheapside – then the city's main thoroughfare – with its fountains and luxury shops, including goldsmiths; the Guildhall and its statues of Gog and Magog; the old St Paul's Cathedral, which had rooftop views; Westminster and Whitehall Palace; and the Royal Exchange, which had around 150 shops on the upper floor above a piazza, including apothecaries, armourers, clothiers, and booksellers with maps and guidebooks. This original Royal Exchange (the present one, the pillared building near Bank tube station, is Victorian) was formally named and opened by Elizabeth in 1570 with a herald and trumpet. It was the creation of the wealthy merchant Sir Thomas Gresham,

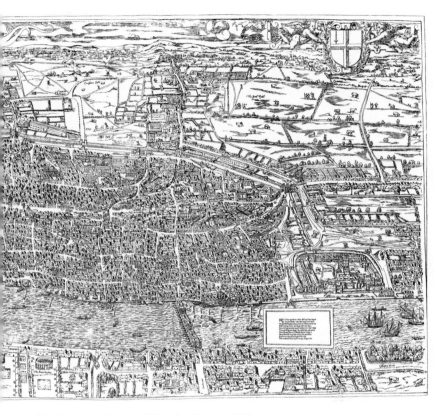

Woodcut map of London, *Civitas Londinum*, c. 1560.

and incorporated grasshopper decorations, from his coat of arms; this is also the origin of the great golden grasshopper which now hangs above Lombard Street.

Elizabeth was succeeded by the Stuart King James I in 1603. Hopes of greater religious tolerance were destroyed by the 1605 Gunpowder Plot, when Catholic conspirators packed a cellar under the Palace of Westminster – now more popularly known as the Houses of Parliament – with barrels of gunpowder. The planned explosion, building collapse and fire would have murdered the entire parliament along with the king and queen. Instead, the conspirators ended with their heads displayed on pikes and, far from greater tolerance, Britain's religious divide was enshrined with 'Guy Fawkes' (or 'Bonfire') Night.

The golden grasshopper in Lombard Street, from the 16th-century emblem of Sir Thomas Gresham.

James's son Charles I was Protestant, but was married to a French Catholic, and his style of Protestantism tended to the High Church. Together with his belief in the divine right of kings to rule (in effect as God's emissaries), this caused tension with Low Church factions, so-called Puritans, increasingly found among the ascendant merchant classes. The king's conflict with Parliament led to the Civil War from 1642 to 1645, in which London was strongly parliamentary: support for Charles was stronger in rural areas. On failing to take London, when his army retreated from Turnham Green, he established an alternative capital at Oxford, but without the nation's central powerhouse of London his cause was doomed.

Charged with treason, the king was executed on the morning of 30 January 1649 on a scaffold outside Banqueting House, the Inigo Jones building on Whitehall opposite the Horse Guards. He wore two shirts, so as not to shiver from cold in case it was mistaken for fear, and made a dignified speech, although it was almost impossible to hear; it ended on 'remember'. In contrast to the often rowdy behaviour at executions, the crowd – whatever their individual feelings about monarchy – flinched and groaned when the axe came down.

Charles was regarded in some quarters as a royal martyr, and a small book purporting to be written by him, the *King's Book* or *Eikon Basilike* (literally the King's Image), became a clandestine best-seller after his death. Britain still has a divided attitude to the monarchy, but it is deeply imbricated in London, not only in its palaces but in its institutions and rituals, like the distribution of Maundy money at Westminster Abbey, and in peculiar offices such as the Royal Ravenmaster, Queen's Swan Marker and Queen's Remembrancer – who appoints a jury of goldsmiths for the Trial of the Pyx at Goldsmiths Hall, where he presides at the Horseshoe and Faggot Cutting Ceremony. Perhaps most ornate of all is the world of the College of Heralds, and its officers such as the Garter King of Arms and the four 'Pursuivants' (a rank just below Herald) named Blue Mantle, Rouge Croix, Rouge Dragon and Portcullis.

Cromwell's Puritan government proved unpopular. Theatres were closed and the celebration of Christmas suppressed as 'trappings of popery and rags of the beast' (presumably the Beast 666, from the Book of Revelation). Holly and mince pies were banned, and shops ordered to open as normal on 25 December. Cromwell grew increasingly autocratic, and in 1653 dismissed parliament to rule as 'Lord Protector'. The diarist John Evelyn described Cromwell's funeral in 1658 as 'the joyfullest funeral that I ever saw', and a new

The Le Sueur statue of King Charles I as depicted in a painting by Joseph Nickolls, *c.* 1746.

parliament invited Charles's son back from exile in Holland to rule as Charles II.

The equestrian statue of Charles I by Hubert Le Sueur, which stands at the southern end of Trafalgar Square, was also restored. A Holborn metalworker had been entrusted with its destruction, but instead hid it, and it was re-erected in its present position. Horse and king stand on the site of the original Charing Cross (the last of the crosses that Edward I placed to commemorate the funeral cortège of his wife Eleanor: hence Charing Cross, from *chère reine*, 'Dear Queen'). This spot is the official centre of London from which distances are measured, and every year on 30 January the Royal Stuart Society lays a wreath there.

Cromwell's body was exhumed and decapitated but there were relatively few reprisals, and many men who had held offices under Cromwell retained them under the restored monarchy. One of the exceptions was Major-General Thomas Harrison, who had signed the king's death warrant. He was hung, drawn and quartered at Charing Cross, during which he displayed no fear, first forgiving his executioner and later punching him in the head. The diarist Samuel Pepys went to see the execution, and thought Harrison was 'looking as cheerful as any man could do in that condition'.

In an almost inevitable reaction against Puritanism, Restoration society was elegant, corrupt and amoral. When a desperado named Colonel Blood tried to steal the Crown Jewels from the Tower in 1671, Charles II was so charmed by his audacity that he not only pardoned him but awarded him land; it has even been suggested (by Winston Churchill, no less) that the king may have had a financial interest in the theft.

The theatres reopened, and a new theatre culture took hold that was both more risqué and more socially exclusive than before, with no place for the 'groundlings' of Elizabethan times. Restoration comedy featured fops, bawds and naive rustics, and the central theme was scheming intrigue, sexual or financial. The aristocratic indecency of the time is exemplified by the poet John Wilmot, Earl of Rochester (1647–1680), subject of Graham Greene's classic short biography, *Lord Rochester's Monkey* (1974).

The population continued to expand, and monstrous growth was becoming intrinsic to London's identity. For most people London was an overcrowded, unhealthy city, and subject to regular outbreaks of plague. Back in 1500 plague had killed around 20,000 people, and there had been several plagues since. But in 1665 came the outbreak remembered as the Great Plague, first taking hold in the poor quarter of St Giles, where Centre Point is now. Within a year it had killed around one in five Londoners. Affected houses had a cross painted on them and were forcibly sealed for forty days, by which time the inhabitants had usually died. Carts travelled the city with cries of 'Bring out your dead!', grass grew in the streets, and cats and dogs were slaughtered as possible carriers (making the problem worse, because it allowed the city's rats – the real carriers, with plague fleas on their feet – to multiply unchecked). There is a vivid account of plague-struck London in Daniel Defoe's *Journal of the Plague Year*: all the more remarkable because Defoe wasn't there, but reconstructed it sixty years later. The victims were disproportionately the poor, in the overcrowded shanty suburbs, but there must have been a sense of random death striking all around: in a moment worthy of a horror film, Pepys was travelling in a hackney carriage when he realized his driver was becoming delirious.

With winter the plague abated, and by the spring of 1666 it was finished, but London's troubles were not over. Fires were commonplace (the Globe Theatre had burned down in 1613, and London Bridge – then covered in houses – was half destroyed in 1633), so when on 2 September 1666 the lord mayor, Sir Thomas Bludworth, was notified of a fire starting in Pudding Lane, he was not impressed: 'a woman might piss it out,' he said, and went back to bed.

Five days later 400 streets had burned, with the destruction of around 14,000 houses, leaving 100,000 people homeless. Pigeons had flown singed and burning from eaves, stone masonry exploded in the heat and molten lead poured from church roofs. The stones of St Paul's Cathedral 'flew like grenados', reported John Evelyn, 'the Lead mealting down the streetes in a streame and the very pavements of them glowing with fiery rednesses, so no horse, nor man, was able to tread on it'. Pepys sent his wife to safety in

Wren's Monument to the Great Fire of London: the world's tallest stone column.

Woolwich and buried his rare Parmesan cheese in the garden, under a terrible sky: '[how] horridly the sky looks, all on a fire in the night, was enough to put us out of our wits; and, indeed, it was extremely dreadful, for it looks just as if it was at us, and the whole heaven on fire.' He continued to have nightmares about burning buildings.

The king joined in the firefighting, and explosives were used to bring down buildings ahead of the fire. Finally it was over. Only nine people are believed to have died, but the destruction to the city was colossal, including St Paul's, the Royal Exchange, over fifty livery company halls and 87 churches. It destroyed an area between the Tower of London and 55 Fleet Street. It was accidental, but Catholics were blamed: a Frenchman with mental problems, one Robert Hubert, confessed to starting it and was hanged.

Puritans saw the plague and fire as punishment for the vices of the Restoration, and John Evelyn was reminded – less judgementally, more in terms of images – of both Sodom and Troy. But London rose again, more stone-built and more splendid. The 'over-sailing' of buildings – the typically Tudor look, where wooden buildings jut forward with each storey and lean towards each other over narrow streets – was banned, and minimum street widths were specified. Polymath architect Christopher Wren built the Monument, at 62 metres (202 ft) the highest standing stone column in the world, completed in 1677 and finally topped with a gilt bronze urn of flames; earlier designs for the summit had included a statue of the king, and a phoenix. In due course parliament would pass an Act for the Building of Fifty New Churches in the Cities of London and Westminster, which would give full expression to the genius of Wren and his colleague Nicholas Hawksmoor.

Meanwhile Charles had died. His brother James II briefly tried to reintroduce absolutist monarchy on the old Stuart model, but he was displaced by the so-called Glorious Revolution of 1688, when William and Mary were invited from Holland to the throne. It was a further step in the direction of more tractable, powerless, constitutional monarchy. The Glorious Revolution brought in the so-called 'long eighteenth century', from 1688 to around 1815. It was the era of Hogarth and Grub Street, Chippendale and Dr Johnson, the South Sea Bubble and the craze for tea-drinking; the era in which London would become the planet's predominant city, 'the emporium of the world'.

3 'All that Life Can Afford'

London was still split by royal and religious factions. When William (of William and Mary) died in 1702, after his horse stumbled on a molehill in Richmond Park, the Jacobites – supporters of the rival James II line – drank toasts to 'the gentleman in the velvet waistcoat'. William was succeeded by Queen Anne, and when she died – with no surviving heir, despite fourteen births – there was Tory and Catholic support for another Stuart, her half-brother James: 'James III', as he would like to have been, but 'the Old Pretender', as he was fated to remain.

Instead Anne was succeeded by George I, who came from Germany in 1714. The Bill of Rights, restricting the power of William and Mary, had already been a key stage in the world's first constitutional monarchy. There was a further move in this direction when King George – who spoke little English – left the running of the country to his parliament and chief minister. Without the king taking the lead, the chief minister became head of the government: Robert Walpole became the first prime minister.

The Royal Society (more fully the Royal Society of London for the Improving of Natural Knowledge) had been founded in 1662, consolidating a new spirit of rationalism, scientific enquiry and religious tolerance. Early members included Hans Sloane (whose personal collection became the basis of the British Museum), philosopher John Locke and poet John Dryden. Isaac Newton was president for twenty years, although he was as concerned with alchemy as with the optics and gravity he is remembered for; Bloomsbury economist John Maynard Keynes called him not a scientist in the post-Enlightenment sense, but rather 'the last magician'. However scientific, or not, it might have been, the Society included old Royalists and Puritans together, putting their religious differences aside for a shared interest in 'the new Philosophy or Experimental Philosophy'.

It is another Royal Society member, Christopher Wren, who is remembered for rebuilding London after the Fire. He originally envisaged a more orderly plan, but his churches had to take their place in a city that remained organic and relatively chaotic. He was buried in St Paul's Cathedral, his own work, under a plain slab; the wall above says, 'Lector, si monumentum requiris, circumspice' ('Reader, if you want to see his monument, look around'). His monuments can be seen across London, including Chelsea Hospital, for army pensioners, and churches such as St Bride's, off Fleet Street – its pillared tiers the model for the classic wedding cake design – and St Magnus the Martyr, Lower Thames Street, its interior described in T. S. Eliot's *The Waste Land* as 'inexplicable splendour of Ionian white and gold'.

Wren was assisted in the church project by Nicholas Hawksmoor, an architect who went beyond the Baroque of the time to include

Royal Society meeting in Crane Court, off Fleet Street, with Isaac Newton in the chair.

a more alien and antique use of pyramids, obelisks and massive porthole-like windows sunk through stone. This monumental quality gives his baroque–Gothic churches a darker, heavier power than most Christian architecture, as in Christ Church, Spitalfields.

Speculative building continued alongside the new churches, and London was shaped by developers like Nicholas Barbon (1640–1698) as well as by aristocratic landowners who built squares such as Cavendish Square, Hanover Square and Bedford Square, now the last intact Georgian square. Relatively intact Georgian streetscapes of a humbler kind – built slightly earlier, but typical of eighteenth-century London – can also be seen at Goodwin's Court in Covent Garden, and Little Green Street in Kentish Town, the setting of London rock band the Kinks' 1966 video for 'Dead End Street'.

London's East End/West End split was being consolidated by these aristocratic squares; the West was becoming established as the place for persons of quality, with fashionable areas such as Pall Mall, Jermyn Street and St James's Square. The abiding image of

The present St Paul's Cathedral (built 1675–1710) is still new in this 1720s painting, with bare land around it.

The steeple of St Bride's Church, off Fleet Street: the inspiration for the classic tiered wedding cake.

Georgian life is one of clichéd graciousness, like the animal grace of the cabriole leg on furniture, which looks as if it might start hoofing the floor and dancing a jig. Powdered wigs were popular for gentlemen, having come into royal court circles from France with the Restoration (they are recalled in the wigs of judges and barristers). The wig craze lasted until a tax on wig powder in 1795, and William Hogarth satirized it in his engraving *The Five Orders of Periwigs* (1761), like the five orders of classical columns, neatly combining wigs with Neoclassical architecture.

Alexander Pope's mock-heroic poem *The Rape of the Lock* (1712) brought finely tuned ridicule to bear on an aristocratic women's quarrel over a lock of hair. Literary culture flourished, high and low, and Pope satirized the bad poetry of the time in *The Dunciad* (1728). The idea of 'Grub Street' literary production and journalism took its name – according to Dr Johnson, compiling his *Dictionary* (1755) at Gough Square – from a small street near Moorfields inhabited by hack writers (now renamed Milton Street). The *Daily Courant*, generally regarded as the first truly regular newspaper, appeared in 1702, and there were more miscellaneous periodicals like the

Inside a coffee house, in London's thriving 17th-century coffee house culture.

Gentleman's Magazine; *The Times* came later (as the *Daily Universal Register*), in 1785.

There was a strong coffee-house culture (the first coffee house in London had appeared in the 1650s in St Michael's Alley, off Cornhill, 'At the Sign of Pasqua Rosee'). Coffee houses such as Don Saltero's and the Cocoa Tree were places for exchanging political and financial news: Lloyd's of London, insurance brokers, began in 1688 as Lloyd's Coffee House. Tea drinking was a newer and more domestic activity, with Twining's tea shop – still there at 216 Strand – founded in 1706; Tom Twining had previously run Tom's Coffee House. Initially expensive, tea became a fashionable drink for the upper and middle classes.

Like Twinings, Floris perfumers (1730), Hamley's toyshop (1760), Paxton & Whitfield cheesemongers and Hatchard's book-shop (both 1797) are surviving monuments to eighteenth-century shopping. The fun-loving side of eighteenth-century London was also at play in its public pleasure gardens – more like funfairs than parks – which were open day and night, the most famous being Vauxhall. They attracted a wide range of people into a cultivated leisure ambience that had previously been restricted to the *bon ton*, with music and dancing, spa waters, and spectacles such as balloon ascents.

Eighteenth-century London could be a fun-loving, highly civilized and substantially well-to-do place, but it was also a society with no safety net, built over an abyss. Banking had allowed monarchs and governments to run on debt, but this privilege was not extended to ordinary individuals. They risked being sent to debtors' prisons, often for trivial sums; there were several hundred debtors in Marshalsea prison, Southwark, where many starved to death, and in 1716 there were 60,000 debtors imprisoned nationally. Thousands more joined them after the picturesque-sounding South Sea Bubble of 1720. The South Sea Company had been founded in 1711, to trade with Spanish America, and caused feverish over-excitement among the investing public: shares increased tenfold shortly before the company crashed, with widespread and often tragic ruin.

The sedan chair – a booth-like box in which a better-off individual could be carried between two men (this, not committees and boards, is the source of the 'Chairmen' in pub names, like the

Vauxhall's famous pleasure gardens, a site for romance and even balloon ascents, as it was in the mid-18th century here depicted in Canaletto's *The Grand Walk, Vauxhall Gardens*, 1751, oil on canvas.

Two Chairmen in Westminster and the Crown and Two Chairmen in Soho) – was a characteristic transport of the times, offering protection not just from mud and rain but more criminal hazards. Poverty was everywhere: the street cries of old London ('Sweet lavender!', 'Hot peas!', 'Sweep!') were a superficially attractive aspect of this, and a subject of nostalgia and sentimentality in the late nineteenth and early twentieth centuries, when they appeared on plates and cigarette cards. Meanwhile street crime was epidemic: Robert Walpole complained that one was 'forced to travel at noon as if one was going into battle', and in 1751 Henry Fielding, novelist and Bow Street magistrate, noted 'the great irregularity of . . . buildings [and] the immense number of lanes, alleys, courts and bye-places . . . in which a thief may harbour with as great security, as wild beasts do in the deserts of Africa or Arabia'.

Law and order was breaking down, with the old system of watchmen and beadles unable to cope. Jonathan Wild, a criminal remembered in John Gay's *Beggar's Opera* (1728), became head of a syndicate capable not only of 'restoring' stolen property, or selling it back to its owners, but seemingly of rooting out wrongdoers and bringing them to justice, with Wild enjoying the title of 'Thief-Taker General'. He was hanged in 1725.

Draconian punishments failed to solve the problem: towards the end of the seventeenth century there were fifty offences punishable by hanging, but by the end of the eighteenth century there were over two hundred. The law was hard on petty theft, and people were hanged for stealing handkerchiefs, although the existence of so many hanging offences allowed judges to make a frequent show of mercy: many wrongdoers were merely transported to Australia for life. Prison conditions were vile, and Newgate prison, which stood where the Old Bailey is now, became a byword for hellishness: Charles Dickens later said it had a 'horrible fascination'.

Newgate went further into the collective consciousness with the popular *Newgate Calendar*, c. 1773–1866, which recorded notorious crimes, feeding the public appetite for sensational literature and effectively making heroes of figures like Jack Sheppard, a burglar who escaped from prison four times. There was a carnival atmosphere around his hanging in 1724, with around 200,000 people – one-third of the population – turning out to see him taken to Tyburn.

When the actor David Garrick asked Dr Johnson to name humanity's greatest pleasure, the answer was 'fucking', and the second was 'drinking'. Along with poverty and crime went vice, a massive industry in Georgian London. Prostitution became a problem in the pleasure gardens after their respectable fashionability had faded, and in 1786 the *Universal Daily Register* estimated that one-sixth of London's population were 'Rakes or Whores'. *Harris's List* – an annual guidebook to prostitutes, particularly in the Covent Garden area, with addresses, physical characteristics and specialities – was a widely available bestseller, running from 1757 to 1795. Successful prostitutes could become wealthy celebrities, the mistresses and even wives of noblemen, or simply successful businesswomen, like 'Mother' Jane Douglas, 'the Empress', who ran a brothel at the King's Head Tavern on Euston Road with uniformed footmen and an aristocratic clientele; she was the model for Mother Cole in John Cleland's pornographic novel *Fanny Hill* (1748). Moll King, who ran a coffee house with a dubious reputation in Covent Garden, built a row of houses in Hampstead with her profits. But for most sex workers it was a life of disease and degradation: Boswell was a user of prostitutes in St James's Park, noting (on a not untypical night in 1763) 'She who submitted to my lusty embraces was a young Shropshire girl, only seventeen, very well-looked, her name Elizabeth Parker. Poor being, she has a sad time of it!'

Dan Cruickshank, in his *Secret History of Georgian London* (2009), has shown how vice shaped the city; he estimates around one in five people were involved. Certain specialities of the time have died out: the large silver or pewter platter being carried into the room in plate III of William Hogarth's *Rake's Progress* (1735) is a wink to the once popular practice of a woman displaying herself while sitting on a plate. There was also a thriving queer subculture, with meeting places for flamboyantly effeminate men known as Molly Houses, but it was a hazardous life: sodomy was a hanging offence. One of the more picturesque erotic scenes of the period took place in Mrs

Hogarth's classic 18th-century engraving on the evils of drink, *Gin Lane*, set near present-day Centre Point.

Charlotte Hayes's establishment at King's Passage, off King Street, St James's. Captain Cook's expedition had arrived at Tahiti in 1770, and brought back reports of its beautiful, near-naked and supposedly liberated inhabitants, so Mrs Hayes threw a 'Tahitian Feast of Venus'. We could see her fantasy South Sea Island theme as a bizarre premonition of Tiki culture, although there are aspects of the night that don't deserve to be celebrated, with girls as young as eleven, and members of parliament among the clients.

Crime and vice were fuelled by gin, which was cheaper than beer: Fielding's 1751 essay 'An Enquiry into the Causes of the Late

Increase in Robbers' describes this 'diabolical' spirit as producing 'a new kind of drunkenness'. It was

> the principal sustenance (if it may be so called) of more than a hundred thousand people in the metropolis . . . the intoxicating draught itself disqualifies them from any honest means to acquire it, at the same time that it removes the sense of fear and shame and emboldens them to commit every wicked and desperate enterprise.

One in four houses in St Giles was said to sell gin, and with gin, unlike beer, women drank alongside men, giving it a reputation as a woman's drink. In 1734 a woman named Judith Dufour left her two-year-old son in a workhouse, but unfortunately a couple of days later she collected him again. He now had on new, workhouse-issue baby clothing, which she was able to sell – after strangling him – to raise one shilling and fourpence and buy gin.

Hogarth's *Gin Lane* print of 1750 (almost contemporary with Fielding's 'Enquiry'; they were friends) shows a slum, but unlike a Dickensian slum it is devoid of sentimentality, and the black humour has lasted better. The pawnbroker, the undertaker and the gin shop are all doing well – but the other buildings are crumbling, and a wall has fallen away to reveal a man hanged inside. Various characters are up to no good or making fools of themselves, and a man is chewing a dog's bone, much to the annoyance of the dog. In the foreground sits a drunken, scabby mother, obliviously letting her child fall head-first off some steps. The scene is St Giles – Hawksmoor's St George Bloomsbury can be seen in the background, with its distinctive steeple inspired by the mausoleum at Halicarnassus (one of the 'seven wonders' of the ancient pagan world). *Gin Lane* contrasts with the health and prosperity of its companion print, *Beer Street*, but *Beer Street* is not as funny.

Hogarth was the great visual chronicler of the age, in narrative series – almost graphic novels – such as *The Rake's Progress*, *The Harlot's Progress* and *The Four Stages of Cruelty*, as well as one-off tableaux such as *The South Sea Bubble*. He was at the centre of a

An avid crowd viewing prints at Piercy Robert's print shop, Holborn: the man with no legs is probably a naval veteran.

visual print culture that bloomed as the century went on, but his moral stance became less fashionable and his work gave way to a new generation of more frantic and luxuriant caricatures (caricature being something Hogarth disliked – he saw himself as being in the business of social criticism and novelistic 'character') that dealt with topical personalities, politics and fashions rather than deeper-seated social evils. Thomas Rowlandson and James Gillray were at the forefront of satirical caricature when prints were an immensely popular medium, with around 20,000 published between 1770 and 1830, along with their younger and more Dickensian contemporary George Cruikshank. Looking at the window displays of print shops such as Darly's on the Strand was one of the pleasures of London, and prints could be hired for the evening in albums as well as bought. It was a medium capable of an idiosyncratic peculiarity all its own, and a print such as *Top and Tail* (1777), published just north of Oxford Street and supposedly drawn and engraved by 'Mr Perwig' and 'Miss Heel', belongs to a sophisticated metropolitan culture.

With an increasing spirit of humanity, eighteenth-century London was in various ways trying to clean its act up. The last burning of a woman guilty of counterfeiting coins, Catherine Murphy – men were hanged for the same offence – took place as late as 1789, by which time it seemed anachronistic; burnings were abolished in 1790. More in tune with the new spirit was Captain Thomas Coram's establishment of the Foundling Hospital in 1739 (it moved to Coram's Fields in 1745), where babies could be left anonymously. Viewing the mad ceased to be public entertainment at Bedlam in 1770, and in 1772 the Society for the Relief and Discharge of Persons Confined for Small Debts was established to get debtors out of prison: in its first fifteen months it freed nearly a thousand people.

Popular politics continued to throw up riots, largely unchecked by the 1715 Riot Act (as in 'reading the Riot Act'), which allowed the army to attack rioters after a magistrate had read the Act and given them a chance to disperse. There were High Church Riots, Corn Riots, Mug-house Riots, Election Riots, 'No Popery' Riots, Gin Riots, Liberty Riots and more.

The blues: life's troubles personified as blue devils in this 1823 print by George Cruikshank, later to illustrate Dickens.

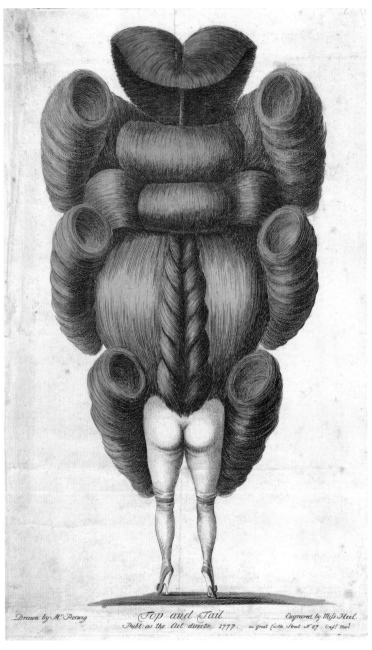

Top and Tail, a bizarre print from 1777, published just off Oxford Street and satirizing the excesses of hair fashion.

King Mob at work: Newgate prison burns during the 1780 Gordon Riots.

These disturbances were dwarfed by the Gordon Riots of 1780, vividly described in Dickens's *Barnaby Rudge* (1841), when about 50,000 people – initially driven by anti-Catholic bigotry, stirred up by Lord George Gordon – rampaged for a week. The lord mayor (Brackley Kennett, a former brothel owner) declined to act, 'lest I bring the mob to my own house', but rioting was finally ended by soldiers. As many as 850 rioters were killed, but not before they had destroyed the Clink, Marshalsea and Newgate prisons, burning them down and releasing the inmates, and attacked the Bank of England, defended by City militia. They might have done more damage had they not broken into a Catholic-owned gin distillery on Holborn Hill, where 'hundreds . . . risked their lives by dashing down into the cellars through the raging flames with pails and jugs, bowls and even pig troughs'.

The idea of the mob – from the Latin *mobile vulgus* (fickle multitude), suggesting that the common people were liable to move unpredictably – was crowned with the title 'King Mob', supposedly found daubed on the wall of Newgate: the prisoners had been freed by order of 'His Majesty, King Mob'. This anti-monarch, the spirit of disorder, is a spectre who has never gone away.

Atkinson Grimshaw's *Reflections on the Thames*, 1880, showing the newly built Embankment.

4 City of Dreadful Delight: The Nineteenth Century

The nineteenth century was London's monster century, when everything people had long been saying – that it was vast, splendid, criminal, sooty, full of foreigners, expanding out of control, labyrinthine – came more true than ever. Now it seems the archetypal London era: the gaslit city of Sherlock Holmes and Dr Jekyll. Towards the end of it Henry James, living near Piccadilly, could write, 'It is difficult to speak adequately or justly of London. It is not a pleasant place; it is not agreeable, or cheerful, or easy, or exempt from reproach. It is only magnificent.' For all its foggy, brutal vastness, said James, for him it was still 'the most possible form of life', and it had everything: 'the most complete compendium in the world'. All in all, he said, it was 'the dreadful, delightful city'.

By 1800 London had almost a million people. Early in the century it was already starting to have the wonders of a world city, including what seems to be the first Indian restaurant: in 1807 'Dean Mahomet's Hindostanee Coffee House' opened at 34 George Street off Portman Square. 'Here', said his advert, 'the Nobility and Gentry . . . may enjoy the Hoakha [that is, hookah pipe, or shisha], with real Chilm tobacco, and Indian dishes, in the highest perfection, and allowed by the greatest epicures to be unequalled to any curries ever made in England.'

London was now a metropolis, a new Babylon. In 1800 Thomas De Quincey first encountered 'the city – no! not the city, but the nation – of London. Often since then, at distances of two and three hundred miles or more from this colossal emporium of men, wealth, arts, and intellectual power, have I felt the sublime expression of her enormous magnitude.' Thinking of cattle being driven towards London from the north made him think of a pulling force: 'A suction so powerful . . . [it] crowds the imagination with a pomp to which there is nothing corresponding upon this planet.'

The anonymity of a big city was still a relatively new experience – Wordsworth wrote of 1790s London in his autobiographical poem *The Prelude* (1799) that 'The face of everyone / That passes by me is a mystery' – and it was possible not only to get lost but to lose another person, as never before. After running away from school, De Quincey writes in his *Confessions of an English Opium-eater* (1821), he became friends with a child prostitute named Ann, and when he left town to borrow money they arranged to meet again on the corner of Great Titchfield Street, thinking it would be safer than 'the great Mediterranean of Oxford Street'. But when he returned Ann was not there, and he never found her again, or knew what had happened to her: 'If she lived, doubtless we must have been in search of each other, at the very same moment, through the mighty labyrinths of London.'

London was so vast it seemed a kind of nature. De Quincey claims to navigate by the stars in his nocturnal rambles, and felt he was encountering terrae incognitae, like those unknown, uncharted spaces on old maps marked 'Here be Dragons'. Contemplating the vastness of London could offer sensations of urban sublimity to compare with the more traditional sublime – a sensation of the awesome and limitless – experienced by the Romantics with mountains or thunderstorms or stars. Watching the sun rise from Westminster Bridge, Wordsworth writes, 'Never did sun more beautifully steep / In his first splendour valley, rock, or hill; / Ne'er saw I, never felt, a calm so deep!' Wordsworth's poem has no human detail, and there is a more engaging reply to the rural sublime from his friend Thomas Lamb, declining his invitation to the Lake District:

> I don't much care if I never see a mountain in my life. I have passed all my days in London, until I have formed as many and intense local attachments, as any of your Mountaineers can have done with dead nature. The Lighted shops of the Strand and

Fleet Street, the unnumerable trades, tradesmen and customers, coaches, waggons, playhouses, all the bustle and wickedness round about Covent Garden, the very women of the Town, the Watchmen, drunken scenes, rattles; – life awake, if you awake, at all hours of the night, the impossibility of being dull in Fleet Street, the crowds, the very dirt & mud, the Sun shining upon houses and pavements, the print shops, the old Book stalls, parsons cheap'ning books, coffee houses, steams of soup from kitchens, the pantomimes, London itself a pantomime and a masquerade . . .

The Romantics were wary of London, and Shelley's lines are more typical: 'Hell is a city much like London – / A populous and a smoky city' (nose-diving into an excruciating comic rhyme: 'There are all sorts of people undone, / And there is little or no fun done.'). The exception is William Blake. He was born in London: the font where he was christened, with its marble Adam and Eve, can still be seen in the church of St James's, Piccadilly (with its extraordinary Grinling Gibbons woodcarvings), and he lived here almost all his life, mainly on South Molton Street and Fountain Court (now a grim alley off the Strand, beside the Savoy, and not to be confused with the Fountain Court in Temple). Blake's London is not only a place of suffering, with its 'Chimney-sweeper's cry' and 'youthful Harlot's curse', but a visionary landscape with an infinite possibility for transformation: the new Jerusalem.

After almost continuous war since the 1790s, Napoleon was defeated in 1815. He was a fascinating figure to many people in Britain, and around half a million visited an exhibition of his personal effects, from his carriage to his soap, at Bullock's Museum on Piccadilly. The government also bought Canova's giant nude statue of him as Mars the Peacemaker and presented it to the Duke of Wellington (it is in Apsley House, Wellington's residence at No. 1 Piccadilly). With Napoleon gone, the Pax Britannica began. With Britain as the world's prime power and global policeman between 1815 and the First World War, there was a sense of London as capital of the world.

The Adam and Eve font where William Blake was christened, at St James's Church, Piccadilly.

The Continental-style elegance of London's first arcade, built by John Nash and G. S. Repton, 1816–18.

The victory sealed the Regency period's confidence and its almost Continental elegance. The architect John Nash devised Regent's Park to be not only a park but a garden suburb, with terraces and crescents: by the time it was completed in 1830 it had also gained a zoological garden which became London Zoo. This relatively distant development had to be linked to the West End by a new thoroughfare, Regent Street – a colonnaded street modelled on the Parisian rue de Rivoli, although nothing of Nash's original building remains except the church. London also gained several Paris-style arcades, including the Royal Opera arcade (Nash and Repton, 1816–18) and Burlington Arcade.

Georgian architecture had been brick-built, but Regency architecture was transformed by stucco facing, like icing on a cake. The conspicuous leisure and status culture of late Georgian and Regency London included dandyism (along with duelling and ruinous gambling). True dandyism was perfectionistic but relatively austere, in a reaction against the foppish culture of over-dressed

eighteenth-century 'Macaronis', much ridiculed in the prints of the day.

Foremost among the dandies was George 'Beau' Brummell, born in Downing Street in 1778; a man much occupied with tying the faultless cravat and perfecting the 'cut' – the art of not acknowledging people while having obviously seen them. Friendship with the young Prince of Wales, the future George IV, led to a commission in the 10th Royal Hussars, which Brummell resigned rather than go with the regiment to Manchester, a place he considered too dreary. Living in Mayfair he became the arbiter of taste, and favoured dark jackets with a waistcoat and plain boots.

Brummell was praised by Byron, who said he would rather be Brummell than Napoleon, and later celebrated by Oscar Wilde and Baudelaire. His lasting legacy is London-led style. Paris is the capital of women's couture, but London is still the capital of gent's tailoring (returning from the States nearly two centuries later, punk impresario Malcolm McLaren said, 'In LA, I was just terribly surfed out, but walking the streets of London it just seemed far more comfortable to be conscious of Savile Row and a good old-fashioned suit'). Brummell's influential dandy taste for perfect but relatively plain, dark tailoring can still be seen in the dinner jacket and the now global classic man's suit.

The dandy was only one type of the man-about-town, which included the beau, the buck and the Corinthian. Being a beau was less about good looks and more about cutting a dash or having presence, while the buck had connotations of being rakish and 'fast' as well as well dressed, and the Corinthian had further connotations of sport, such as boxing. Pierce Egan's best-selling adventures of Tom and Jerry – *Life in London; or, The Day and Night Scenes of Jerry Hawthorn Esq. and Corinthian Tom* (1821) – followed a couple of bucks on the town, with a sense not just of rakish adventuring but exploring, and seeing how the other half lived. But unlike the more socially concerned explorations later in the century, it was essentially slumming, and the same is true of George Smeeton's factually based low-life explorations, *Doings in London; or, Day and Night Scenes of the Frauds, Frolics and Depravities of the Metropolis* (1828).

London roughly doubled in size and population between 1800 and 1830, from around one million to approaching two million, making forays into unknown London worlds increasingly possible. As usual, the population was swelled less by births – given the appalling infant mortality rate – than by migration, and there was a great influx of Irish labour working on railways and canals: canal diggers were 'inland navigators', or 'navvies', a word which makes an early appearance in Pierce Egan's 1829 boxing book, *Boxiana*.

When a baby was christened Alexandrina Victoria in 1819, no one could have known her name would give the world a monumental adjective, conjuring up a mental picture of some kind for almost everyone. When Victoria came to the throne in 1837, the Victorians looked back on their immediate predecessors without affection. After the Regency and the reign of George IV, not to mention the Restoration, and the more distant medieval days of streets like 'Gropecunt Lane', the Victorians brought a new respectability to public morality. Their dislike of the recent past went with idealizing Greece and Rome (with classical architecture) and the Christian Middle Ages (with Gothic revival architecture), and these styles made a claim for Victorian culture as the heir to these civilizations.

The new Gothic – like the slightly later Pre-Raphaelite movement, which looked back to an ideal quattrocento past, and the Victorian cult of King Arthur – was an implicitly moral and Christian style. The Houses of Parliament had burned down in 1834, and the new building designed by Charles Barry (with Augustus Pugin providing further Gothic decoration) has been described by Ian Nairn as 'like the Gothic Revival itself . . . a vast hallucination, set down in Westminster to bewitch and enchant'. The effect of its rather ecclesiastical style has been to create something like a cathedral of democracy.

Much of the city the Victorians inherited from their predecessors was crumbling, and the physical fabric of low nineteenth-century London was often rotting eighteenth-century London. The now picturesque Bedfordbury was a particularly notorious example, depicted by Charles Manby Smith in *The Little World of London* as Lagsmanbury ('the resident population consists of a low class of labourers, chiefly Irish . . . and a predator class, still lower, who never work'); George Augustus Sala described it as 'a devious, slimy little reptile of a place'. Newman Passage in Fitzrovia now has a distinctly nineteenth-century feel (and a picturesquely sinister one: it was known as 'Jekyll and Hyde Alley' to 1940s Fitzrovians, and was chosen as a backdrop for murder in the 1960 film *Peeping Tom*), though it was built in the 1740s; Dickens uses it as the spot for Mr Turveydrop's somewhat shabby, down-at-heel academy of dancing and deportment in *Bleak House* (1853).

Some of the worst slums or rookeries were older, including derelict aristocratic houses now occupied by several families to a room: a Thomas Beames wrote that 'in the dingiest streets of the metropolis are found houses, the rooms of which are lofty, the walls panelled, the ceilings beautifully ornamented . . . the chimney-pieces models for the sculptor. The names of the courts [rookery courtyards]

Brickwork is everywhere in this claustrophobic view from Gustave Doré's illustrations to Blanche Jerrold's *London: A Pilgrimage* (1872).

remind you of decayed glory – Villiers, Dorset, Buckingham . . .' The Victorians made major attempts to erase some of these slums in the 1840s and 1850s (even as new ones were arising in the East End), and they drove New Oxford Street though the former slum of St Giles in 1845.

If London often feels like a Victorian city, it is because it is: much of it was built during Victoria's early life and subsequent reign. Piccadilly Circus arrived in 1819, formed by the new Regent Street meeting Piccadilly, and the current Trafalgar Square was begun in 1830, on the site of former stables (a plan for a 22-storey pyramid on the site, by a Colonel Trench, remained unbuilt). Nelson's Column was built in 1839–42, and the statue added in 1843. The British Museum Reading Room, its great blue dome like the cranium of intellectual London, was built into the former museum courtyard in the 1850s. Big Ben, originally just the name of the bell, became a working addition to parliament in 1859. The Embankment was built around 1870 on what had been a rotting river-front of wharves and warehouses, re-envisioned in massive granite with lion-head mooring rings, dolphin lamps and cast-iron camel benches.

The Great Exhibition of 1851 was a landmark in the Victorians' sense of themselves, set up in Joseph's Paxton's Crystal Palace – a gigantic purpose-built greenhouse in Hyde Park – and displaying wonders of manufacture from around the world: it had 100,000 exhibits and around 15 kilometres (10 mi.) of stands. Between May and October over six million people visited, including a woman of 84 who had walked from Cornwall. As many as 800,000 people bought season tickets and visited regularly.

One effect of the exhibition was to highlight the poor state of British design and manufacturing, thereby providing the stimulus to create the Victoria and Albert (V&A) Museum. The exhibition's Royal Commission obtained land in South Kensington to continue the exhibition's aims and extend 'the influence of Science and Art upon Productive Industry': the South Kensington Museum, fore-runner of the V&A, was opened by Queen Victoria in 1857.

Victorian modernity was striking: news of victory at Waterloo was carried by a man on a horse, but by the 1850s there was a

The Great Exhibition of 1851, a Victorian wonder attracting over six million visitors.

transatlantic cable to America. The Victorians introduced pillar boxes, telephones, bowler hats, omnibuses, postage stamps, Christmas crackers, department stores, disinfectant, typewriters, anaesthetic and underground trains. The world of the Sherlock Holmes books was for the most part newly built, including St Pancras Hotel (1872), the Criterion Bar in Piccadilly (1874), Liverpool Street station (1874), Victoria Street (running through a former slum and completed in the 1880s), Aldgate station (1884) and New Scotland Yard (1890).

'Cleopatra's Needle', the Egyptian obelisk on the Embankment, is a more peculiar testimony to Victorian modernity. Brought to Britain with some difficulty – it weighs 186 tonnes, and was almost lost at sea – in a specially designed, cigar-shaped metal vessel called the *Cleopatra*, it reached London in 1878 to be met by cheering crowds and celebratory cannon fire. When it was finally set up, with a plaque to the men who died transporting it, the Victorians buried a pyramid-inspired 'time capsule' under this already 3,500-year-old object, for the people of some distant future to find. In sealed jars it included the morning's newspapers, a razor, Bibles in different languages, photographs of twelve good-looking English women, a man's dark suit, some coins and *Bradshaw's* railway guide. It is hard to imagine such a confident gesture, with its historical perspective and its mixture of grandiosity, modesty and wit, being made in any previous era. As H. V. Morton wrote in the 1920s, the most ancient monument in London stands over this capsule like an 'old hen, waiting for Time to hatch it'.

By now London was truly vast. A syndicated newspaper piece from the mid-1880s, headed 'The Greatest City in the World', told readers that London had a population of five million and 12,800 kilometres (8,000 mi.) of streets, with around 64 kilometres (40 mi.) of new streets opened every year. In 1883 there were over 22,000 houses added, 'thus forming 368 new streets and one new square, covering a distance of 66 miles and 84 yards', to which our anonymous writer adds, 'It is difficult to form any mental picture from these figures.' Attempting to convey this sublime vastness, they specify 1,000 ships in port every day, and yearly figures of 38,000 drunks before the magistrates, 56 million omnibus passengers and 298 million letters delivered. More than that, it was a world city: its five million included two million 'foreigners from every quarter of the globe', with more Irish than Dublin, more Jews than Palestine and more Roman Catholics than Rome.

By the late Victorian era London had grown into its role as capital of the world. Henry James observed that this was lucky for Britain, as if the city and the nation were only incidentally connected: 'It is a real stroke of luck for a particular country that the capital of the human race happens to be British.' It was the centre of the greatest empire the world had ever seen, and possibly the most benevolent, at least in relative terms. But for all that far-flung glory, things were far from well at home.

In the words of MP Will Crooks, the same sun which never set on the Empire never rose on the dark alleys of East London. The imperial capital, or in the words of William Morris 'the horrible muckheap in which we dwell', was a place of poverty, filth and disease, where even towards the end of the century 55 per cent of infants in the East End died before the age of five. And those were ordinary, everyday deaths in a statistic only fractionally raised by the additional scandal of 'baby-farming', where a woman would take babies off their mother's hands for cash – often permanently, notionally to raise them to adulthood – and frequently keep them in appalling conditions and/or murder them, so that dead babies were found floating in the Thames. A number of women were hanged, including 'the Finchley Baby Farmers' Amelia Sach and Annie Walters – working as late as 1903 – who accounted for dozens of infants between them, and Amelia Dyer, who may have killed as many as four hundred.

Outbreaks of cholera were common and killed thousands of people in poorer and overcrowded districts. In 1849 *The Times* published a letter with over fifty signatures:

> Sur,
> May we beg and bessech your proteckshion and power. We are Sur, as it may be, living in a Wilderniss, so far as the rest of London knows anything of us . . . We live in muck and filthe. We aint got no privez, no dust bins, no drains, no water splies, and no drain or suer . . . The Stench of a Gully-hole is disgustin. We al of us suffer . . . and if the Colera comes Lord help us.

Cholera was thought to be caused by foul air or 'miasma', but in 1854 Dr John Snow argued that it was caused by sewage-contaminated water: he traced an outbreak to a public pump in Broadwick Street, Soho, and removed the pump handle. Snow's theory was controversial, and a writer in *The Times* complained, 'We prefer to take our chance with cholera than be bullied into health.' Snow died with his discovery still not universally accepted, but it is commemorated by Soho's John Snow public house.

The Thames was filthy, and one of the by-products was 'Thames Butter', a trade name for sewage fat gathered from the mud: despite a couple of scare stories, this was not for spreading on toast but for candles and soap. Pollution came to a head in the summer of 1858 with the so-called Great Stink, when the windows of parliament had to be hung with sheets soaked in lime chloride. The problem continued until Joseph Bazalgette's monumental sewer system, a wonder of Victorian engineering with 2,100 kilometres (1,300 mi.) of sewers (and a polychrome Gothic pumping station at Crossness). The worst of the problem was over before an 1892 writer in the *Medical Press and Circular* suggested introducing crocodiles – branded with the city seal to prevent theft – into the Thames to eat filth. Fortunately this idea was never adopted.

With the city's ever-growing population and high mortality rate, disposal of the dead was a long-established London hygiene problem. Small churches appeared to be sinking because the churchyards around them were rising with bodies, and, with churchyards full, bodies increasingly had to be disposed of in burial grounds. Perhaps the most famous is Bunhill Fields (from Bone Hill Fields, although the name is older and seems to be a coincidence): inhabitants include Daniel Defoe and William Blake.

Bodies were also interred under the floorboards in chapels, with a resulting stench for the churchgoers above. The Enon Chapel in Clare Market, Holborn, was a particularly notorious case in the 1830s: children at Sunday school grew used to the distinctive flies and called them 'body bugs'. The chapel passed to new management in 1844 as a low dancing saloon, which tried to capitalize on its contents by advertising 'dancing on the dead'. Finally a local surgeon and philanthropist, George Walker, bought it and set about re-interring bodies in Norwood cemetery; it was alleged that the greedy former minister, a Mr Howse, had stashed as many as 12,000 under the premises.

From the 1830s, action was taken to provide adequate cemeteries, and in 1837 Kensal Green opened: it was the first of the General Cemetery Company's 'Magnificent Seven' (including Highgate,

Abney Park and Brompton). Its high boundary walls and secure catacombs were a response to the outbreak of 'body-snatching' by 'Resurrection men' – the theft of bodies for black-market sale for medical dissection. A spiked gate was added to Bunhill Fields for the same reason, and London's narrowest house – 10 Hyde Park Place, 0.9 metres (3 ft) wide – was built to block access to St George's Churchyard.

The magnificent cemetery at Highgate was opened in 1839, with its Egyptian columns and Egyptian Avenue designed by the versatile Stephen Geary, who also designed gin palaces. In contrast to the picturesque, horror-film-style decay into which Highgate had fallen by the 1960s and '70s, and its current wealth of trees and density of monuments, it began as a lawn park, popular for picnics; the popularity of the cemetery parks for leisure helped inspire the growth of London's ordinary park spaces.

The General Cemetery Company was joined in the 1840s by the competing London Necropolis Company, who built the enormous, park-like London Necropolis at Brookwood, then the largest cemetery in the world, and still the largest in Britain today. It had its own railway, the Necropolis Railway, with its own London Necropolis station next to Waterloo: one-way tickets were issued for coffins, with a very Victorian social gradation of first, second and third class.

Victorian mourners were provided for by Jay's Mourning Warehouse on Oxford Street (established in 1841). The Victorians were made very conscious of death by the mortality rate and the omnipresence of death and bereavement in families, with sentimental and afterlife hopes; by the mourning of Victoria after the death of Albert; and perhaps even by the new amenity of the beautiful graveyards themselves. One of the strangest manifestations was the fear of being buried alive. This led to bells that could be rung from below, and telephone devices, but even those are not as strange as what may be London's most curious grave, dating back earlier to 1809: the 'Floating Coffin of Pinner' is a tomb in mid-air, sticking through a tower structure built to support it. It houses a William Loudon and was erected by his son, John Claudius Loudon, a cemetery designer.

Seemingly not about fear of being buried alive in this case, what Loudon Senior is doing up there remains a mystery.

Unlike sewage and corpses, London has been more ambivalent about smoke, soot and fog. It had long been sooty (two centuries earlier, when Newcastle was blockaded during the English Civil War and coal consumption fell, John Evelyn had recorded that London orchards 'were observed to bear such plentiful and infinite quantities of fruits, as they never produced the like either before or since'). Dickens described the sooty smoke as 'London ivy', wreathing and draping the buildings it seemed to cling to. By Victorian times, houses were so sooty that a French visitor thought they were 'like chimneys turned inside out', and this griminess is a part of the peculiar cosiness of the image of nineteenth-century London.

Smoke turned what might have been clean mist into the notorious London fog, said to have killed seven hundred people in a single week in December 1891. With visibility down to 1 metre (3 ft), it was also associated with accidents, robbery and a hazardous intimacy. Weeks could go by without sunlight, as George Gissing recorded in January 1888. London fog was mostly a sulphurous yellow but it

Claude Monet, *Waterloo Bridge, Grey Day*, 1903, oil on canvas.

could be grey or even orange, and the expression 'pea-souper' for a thick fog came not only from its appearance but its choking texture; if you were unlucky you could swallow it. 'The fog appears . . . slowly, like a melodramatic ghost,' wrote German visitor Max Schlesinger in 1853, and Nathaniel Hawthorne wrote

> I went home by way of Holborn, and the fog was denser than ever, – very black, indeed, more like a distillation of mud than anything else; the ghost of mud . . . So heavy was the gloom, that gas was lighted in all the shop windows; and the little charcoal furnaces of the women and boys, roasting chestnuts, threw a ruddy, misty glow around them.

It was so thick that on getting home he found it had somehow got into his drawing room. 'And yet,' he adds, 'I liked it. This fog seems an atmosphere proper to huge, grimy London.'

Monet visited London several times around the turn of the century, specifically to paint fog: 'What I love more than anything in London is the fog; without the fog London wouldn't be a beautiful city.' H. G. Wells's novel *Love and Mr Lewisham* (1899) recalls 'thick fogs, beautiful, isolating grey-white veils, turning every yard of pavement into a private room. Grand indeed were those fogs, things to rejoice at mightily.' London fog was unique, said a *Times* editorial, like 'London gin or London wit. And Londoners are secretly proud of it.'

The most famous description of London fog is at the opening of Dickens's *Bleak House*, where it takes on a metaphorical dimension for the hopeless legal obfuscations to come in the plot. There is smoke, and soot, and almost prehistoric mud, and

> Fog everywhere. Fog up the river, where it flows among green aits and meadows; fog down the river, where it rolls defiled among the tiers of shipping and the waterside pollutions of a great (and dirty) city . . . Fog creeping into the cabooses of collier-brigs; fog lying out on the yards, and hovering in the rigging of great ships . . . Chance people on the bridges peeping over the

parapets into a nether sky of fog, with fog all round them, as if they were up in a balloon, and hanging in the misty clouds.

London's enduringly nineteenth-century quality is as much about writing as buildings. In the words of the later Victorian novelist George Gissing, 'London as a place of squalid mystery and terror, of the grimly grotesque, of labyrinthine obscurity and lurid fascination, is Dickens's own; he taught people a certain way of regarding the huge city.' Dickens created an enduring London of the mind filled with eccentrics, urchins, virtuous poor, kindly gentlemen, repressive, swindling authority figures, and lucky or unlucky chance encounters. It is poky and grimy, pivots on contrasts, and has a distinctively dense descriptive texture, as in this passage from *Sketches by Boz* (1836):

> The filthy and miserable appearance of this part of London [by Drury Lane] can hardly be imagined by those (and there are many such) who have not witnessed it. Wretched houses with broken windows patched with rags and paper: every room let out to a different family, and in many instances to two or even three, fruit and 'sweet-stuff' manufacturers in the cellars, barbers and red-herring vendors in the front-parlours, cobblers in the back; a bird-fancier on the first-floor, three families on the second, starvation in the attics, Irishmen in the passage, a 'musician' in the front kitchen, and a char-woman and five hungry children in the back one – filth everywhere . . .
>
> You turn the corner. What a change! All is light and brilliancy. The hum of many voices issues from that splendid gin-shop which forms the commencement of the two streets opposite.

Balanced between sentimental warmth and social abyss, Dickens's writing offers dangerous squalor and cosy good cheer in equal measure, around a central outrage at social conditions. In 1824 his father had been imprisoned for debt in Marshalsea prison, Southwark, and the twelve-year-old Dickens had to work in a boot polish factory, Warren's Blacking Factory by Hungerford Stairs, below

Charing Cross on the rotting pre-Embankment riverside. He still had nightmares about it as an adult.

The 1842 Parliamentary Commission into the Employment of Children in Mines and Manufactories shocked the public, and children's employment in mines was eventually prohibited, but not without a struggle in which colliery-owning peers such as Lord Londonderry fought against reform in the House of Lords. Londonderry, who owned a vast mansion on Park Lane, argued that education beyond the age of ten was unnecessary, because by then people knew all they needed to know. He published an open letter on child labour, devastatingly reviewed by Dickens, who remembered him a few years later when reviewing a book about ghosts. The author argued her case too strongly, wrote Dickens, and this reminded him of Londonderry: just as no character witness at the Old Bailey ever knew a better man than the prisoner in the dock, so

> that sage statesman, Lord Londonderry, when it was suggested that the occupation of a trapper (a little child who sits alone in the dark, at the bottom of a mine, all day, opening and shutting a door) had something dreary in it, could conceive nothing jollier than 'a jolly little trapper', and could, in fact, recognize the existence of no greater jollity.

The extent of poverty was the festering open secret of nineteenth-century London (and England: Benjamin Disraeli's 1845 novel *Sybil; or, The Two Nations* was about the 'two nations' of rich and poor since the Industrial Revolution), and one of the many words London has given the world is 'slum'. Originally an informal, slangy word meaning a room – so around 1820, a modest house might be said to have a front and back slum – it seems to have slipped to its modern sense via run-down back rooms and lodgings. There was a particularly squalid area near Westminster Abbey, termed 'The Devil's Acre' by Dickens (including what is now Old Pye Street), and in 1850 Cardinal Wiseman described it:

> Close under the Abbey of Westminster there lie concealed labyrinths of lanes and courts, and alleys and slums, nests of ignorance, vice, depravity, and crime, as well as of squalor, wretchedness, and disease; whose atmosphere is typhus, whose ventilation is cholera; in which swarms a huge and almost countless population, nominally at least, Catholic; haunts of filth, which no sewage committee can reach – dark corners, which no lighting board can brighten.

Wiseman was widely quoted, and the word slum was launched on its modern career.

London poverty was given non-fictional treatment by Henry Mayhew in his extraordinary, multi-volume *London Labour and the London Poor* (1851). Mayhew had been to a London the middle classes had never seen, and brought back (in the words of Thackeray) 'A picture of human life so wonderful, so awful, so piteous and pathetic, so exciting and terrible, that readers of romance own they never read anything like it; and that the griefs, struggles, strange adventures here depicted exceed anything that any of us could imagine.'

Here were people so ignorant that one boy had heard of a place called England but didn't know what part of London it was in. Here were people who made a living from scavenging in sewers (they were 'toshers') or collecting cigar butts, or dog excrement. Here was a girl of eight who got up before four every morning to buy watercress, and hawked it on the streets crying 'Four bunches a penny, water creases!' She had 'lost all childish ways', wrote Mayhew, and was 'in thoughts and manner, a woman. There was something cruelly pathetic in hearing this infant . . . talking of the bitterest struggles of life.' 'All my money I earns,' she told him, 'I puts into a club and draws it out to buy clothes with.'

Some of Mayhew's most extraordinary material was devoted to the underworld of 'Those That Will Not Work', including a variety of specialized begging-letter scams such as Decayed Gentleman, Distressed Scholar and Author's Wife. But life in the metropolis was hard even for those that would work, with jobs like making wooden raspberry pips for fake jam, cited as an example of sweated female labour in Sylvia Pankhurst's book *The Suffragette Movement* (1931).

Colonial and expeditionary metaphors came naturally when exploring the other London. Poor children who often slept rough were known as 'street Arabs', and in 1885 a Christian building society said the East End was 'as unexplored as Timbuctoo'. Mayhew described himself as a 'traveller in the undiscovered country of the poor' about whom his middle-class readers knew less than about 'the most distant tribes of the earth'. George Sims, in *How the Poor Live* (1883), offered

> a book of travel . . . into a dark continent . . . as interesting as any of those newly-explored lands which engage the attention of the Royal Geographical Society – the wild races who inhabit it will, I trust, gain public sympathy as easily as those savage tribes for whose benefit the Missionary Societies never cease to appeal for funds.

The Salvation Army had its origin in the 'Christian Mission for the Heathen of Our Own Country' and, following Stanley's explorations in Africa, and the publication of *In Darkest Africa*, General Booth of the Salvation Army wrote *In Darkest England* (1890). Stanley had brought back 'a terrible picture' of life in Africa, said Booth, and 'The lot of a Negress in the Equatorial Forest is not, perhaps, a very happy one, but is it so very much worse than that of many a pretty orphan girl in our Christian capital?'

The enormous inequalities between rich and poor led to vice on a grand scale: the Victorian sexual underworld has been the subject of many books. Dostoyevsky visited in the 1860s and left a vivid account of central London nightlife, where he said the masses were to be seen on a scale unmatched anywhere in the world. He had been told that half a million men, women and children thronged the streets on Saturday nights, and went out to see the West End: 'At every step you come across magnificent public houses, all mirrors and gilt';

Great jets of gas burn in meat and food shops, brightly lighting up the streets. It is as if a grand reception were being held
for those white negroes. Crowds throng the open taverns and
the streets. There they eat and drink. The beer houses are dec-
orated like palaces. Everyone is drunk, but drunk joylessly . . .

In the Haymarket area he saw prostitutes 'swarm by night in their
thousands', and 'mothers who had brought their young daughters,
girls who were still in their early teens, to be sold to me. Little girls
of about twelve seize you by the hand and ask you to go with them.'

Crusading journalist W. T. Stead shocked readers with a four-
part prostitution exposé in the *Pall Mall Gazette*, 'The Maiden Tribute
of Modern Babylon' (1885). It was written in a lurid, sensational style
– the public were queuing to buy it by the final issue – but based on
solid research: in the course of it, Stead bought (not hired tempo-
rarily) a thirteen-year-old girl from her mother. This exploit helped
raise the age of consent to sixteen, and earned him a six-month
prison sentence.

Stead met a brothel-keeper from the Mile End Road who told
him that he had courted young women outside London in all
manner of disguises, sometimes dressing as a clergyman, and made
them believe he wanted to marry them: 'I bring her up [to London]
. . . then I contrive it so she misses her last train.' Another way of
getting 'maidens' was by 'breeding them', he said – and there were
networks of men who bought options on the female children of
prostitutes, often combined with threats – so 'When they get to be
12 or 13 they become merchantable . . . you may get as much as £20
or £40 . . . In the East End, you can always pick up as many fresh
girls as you want. In one street in Dalston you might buy a dozen
. . .'

One of the most notorious documents of Victorian sexuality
is *My Secret Life*, by 'Walter' (his identity is still unknown). Over
a million words, originally running to 4,200 pages in eleven volumes (privately and clandestinely published circa 1888–95), it is the
record of an obsession. Fog, for example, is 'propitious to amatory
caprices'; 'Timid men get bold and speak to women', and prostitutes

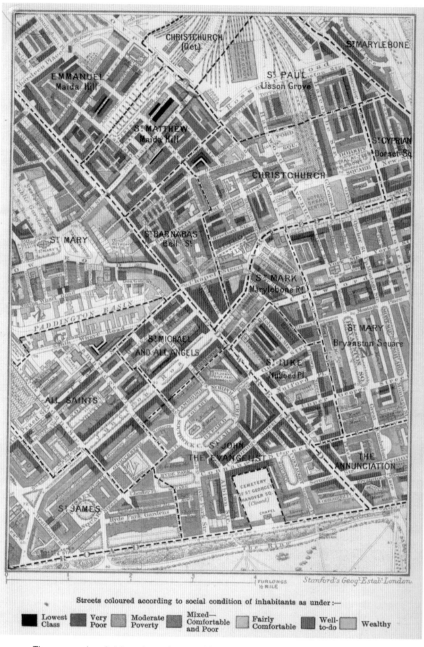

Streets coloured according to social condition of inhabitants as under :—

| Lowest Class | Very Poor | Moderate Poverty | Mixed—Comfortable and Poor | Fairly Comfortable | Well-to-do | Wealthy |

The geography of rich and poor in one of Charles Booth's pioneering 'poverty maps', ranging from comfortably wealthy to the semi-criminal 'lowest class'.

told him they did particularly good business, 'especially those who are regular nymphs of the pavé, and who don't mind exercises in the open air'. Walter estimated that he had 'fucked something like twelve hundred women'. Almost none of these women are of anything like his own class: it is the sexual safari of a man who was able to use his social inferiors as if they were in a gigantic brothel.

In his own inglorious way, Walter could be placed in a long tradition of urban exploration, along with Ned Ward's *London Spy* (1687–1709), Pierce Egan's Regency slumming, Stead's undercover enquiries and Blanche Jerrold's *London: A Pilgrimage* (1872). Jerrold set out to visit London in general but his book is memorable for its descriptions set in the lower reaches – like 'the flaring public house lamp – hateful as the fabled jewel in the loathsome toad's head' – and the teeming density of Gustave Doré's hellish illustrations, where realistic overcrowding meets artistic delirium.

A monumental contribution to this tradition, ranking with Mayhew, was made by Charles Booth's seventeen-volume *Life and Labour of the People of London* (1891–1902). A Liverpool ship owner (not to be confused with William Booth of the Salvation Army), Booth was sceptical about reports that one-quarter of Londoners lived in poverty, but on investigating – and initially hoping to disprove this alarmist figure – he discovered the reality was more like one-third.

Booth made 'poverty maps', a detailed street-by-street guide analysing London into seven colour-coded grades, from gold ('Upper-middle and upper classes') down to dark blue ('Very poor. Casual, chronic want') and black ('Lowest class. Vicious, semi-criminal'). It is sometimes striking how close these contrasts are, barely a stone's throw away from each other, but overall it is very clear that things get worse going east. The maps started to appear in 1891, the same year J. H. Mackay wrote, 'The East End of London is the hell of poverty. Like one enormous black, motionless, giant kraken, the poverty of London lies there in lurking silence and encircles with its mighty tentacles the life and wealth of the city.'

The City financial district had become less residential, depopulating at night, and on the far side of it lay the slums. When Portuguese historian Oliveira Martins visited in 1895, the policeman guarding him said, 'This is no longer London. London ends with the City. This is the East End.' Even in daylight, said the policeman, it would be unwise to come here, among people who were unaware even of Hyde Park: 'They are born and they die here.' Arthur Morrison, a local boy who had escaped, wrote in his novel *A Child of the Jago*, based on the Old Nichol slum, that 'the whole East End was a wilderness of slums: slums packed with starving human organisms without minds and without morals, preying on each other alive.' On a lighter note, the same novel has a smug bishop who sets out on a fact-finding mission to the east: he is just congratulating himself on discovering it's not so bad, when he realizes his watch is missing.

What this kind of writing obscures is the fact that thousands of relatively poor people did manage to live decent lives. Not all poor women were dragged into prostitution; not all working-class men were violent alcoholics. The lurid accounts and pessimistic estimates of reformers – of 80,000 streetwalking women in London, and 1,000 brothels on Shadwell's Ratcliff Highway – obscured the fact that in many ways London was improving since Georgian times, with a growing 'respectable' working class.

London was divided not only by economic inequality but by class culture, supposedly stronger in England than anywhere else in the world. Cockney culture had its own languages: back slang, such as 'yob' for 'boy', was associated with market porters and was used to keep conversations private from overseers and customers, as first noted by Mayhew. Back slang has equivalents in other languages, but Cockney rhyming slang, which seems to have developed around the 1840s, is more singular and has a charm of its own: to be drunk was 'elephant's trunk', and bread was 'Uncle Fred'. In its full development the second word is elided, so 'bees in your sky' was money in your pocket, from 'bees and honey' and 'sky rocket'. Words slipped and bounced around, so 'aris', for backside, comes from 'bottle and glass' (arse) moving to bottle and then to Aristotle. With some Veras and trout you can roll a cigarette ('Vera Lynns', skins or cigarette papers; and 'salmon and trout', snout or tobacco).

Rhyming slang is still going, but with something self-parodic and tongue-in-cheek about it: drugs are persians, from Persian rugs, and if it's all gone a bit Pete Tong (a well-known English DJ), then things have gone wrong.

No less distinctive, in its way, was the fate of the aspirate H: uneducated people 'dropped their aitches', leaving the first H off words (''urry up'), so a desire for genteelism and an uncertainty about spelling led to a corresponding tendency, among the respectable London working class, to put aitches on where they didn't belong, as if to be on the safe side ('Hadelaide 'obson').

Safety and the chance of respectability increased in the nineteenth century with the foundation of a relatively modern police force, after the older systems of 'hue and cry', watchmen and 'Bow Street Runners' (founded by Henry Fielding in the 1740s). The Metropolitan Police was founded in 1829 by Sir Robert Peel, and any resemblance to the army was deliberately played down by dressing them in blue rather than red, avoiding old memories of gunfire and bayonets after the reading of the Riot Act. They carried a truncheon and a loud rattle, later replaced by a whistle, and originally wore 'pot hats' of strong leather, looking like top hats in old photos.

The early police were resented. When a policeman was stabbed to death in 1833 during a political disturbance at Coldbath Fields, Clerkenwell, the coroner's jury brought in a verdict of 'justifiable homicide'. An anonymous donor sent medals to the jury, and on the anniversary of the verdict there was a boat trip, celebratory cannons and a banquet hosted by Sir Samuel St Swithin Burden Whalley, MP for Marylebone. After a toast to 'The people, the only source of legitimate power', the jurors were presented with a silver cup 'as a perpetual memorial of their glorious verdict of "justifiable homicide" on the body of Robert Culley, a policeman who was slain whilst brutally attacking the people when peaceably assembled in Calthorpe Street on the 13th May 1833'.

Gradually the police won the public's respect and the city became safer, although there was ambivalence. The music hall song, 'If You Want to Know the Time, Ask a P'liceman' is said – by historian C. H. Rolph, himself a former police officer – to have been

amusing to its original audience because the police had a reputation
for taking watches from drunks.

Despite incidents such as Coldbath Fields, political disorder
never reached the revolutionary scale it did on the Continent. Queen
Victoria survived eight assassination attempts, but they were all of
the lone lunatic variety (and when Prime Minister Spencer Perceval
was assassinated in 1812, it was by an unhinged individual with a
grudge). There was a more radical plot to murder a prime minister
in 1820, when the Cato Street conspirators planned to assassinate
Lord Liverpool and his entire cabinet, with the head of the home
secretary to be cut off for display. They were hanged, but they had
surprising public sympathy.

For all the magnificence of the Victorians' new parliament
buildings, only one in seven men had the vote. Chartism, a movement demanding the vote for all adult males, peaked in 1848 with a
rally on Kennington Common, followed by a march to parliament to

A collage-like frenzy of bill-sticking in John Orlando Parry's early Victorian painting
A London Street Scene.

present a national petition with an alleged five million signatures. In response they were met with volunteer Special Constables – 80,000 of them – 4,000 regular police guarding the Thames bridges, and a military presence at the Bank of England, with cannons ready. In the event the march was stopped at the bridges and the petition was taken by cab to parliament, where many of the signatures were found to be fake. This was very different from events in France and Germany in the same year, 'the Year of Revolutions'. Agitation for a wider vote continued as the century went on, although democracy was not the universally positive word it has since become: when Edward Pease (later to be a founder of the socialist Fabian Society) attended a South Bank socialist meeting in 1880, he describes a meeting of 'characteristically democratic men with dirty hands and small heads, some of them obviously with very limited wits'.

Fear of revolution was matched by fear of crime. London was swept by waves of panic about street crime, with 'garrotting panics' – where street robbers strangled their victims – breaking out in 1856 and 1862. Member of Parliament Hugh Pilkington was choked and robbed of his watch after leaving the House of Commons, leading to the Garrotting Act and more ingenious responses such as spiked collars to defeat would-be throttlers. *Punch* published numerous cartoons on the subject, but it was no joke for the rising but embattled middle classes, butt of the *Punch* cartoons (and stigmatized as suburban for the amusement of *Punch*'s more 'clubland' audience: an 1863 cartoon of two men walking back-to-back was captioned 'Brown and Jones return home to the Suburbs, with safety, taking front and rear rank alternately'). Feeling himself distinct from both the toff and the proletarian, and not carrying a sword like earlier generations, the middle-class man could escalate his umbrella or cane to a swordstick. James Smith and Sons umbrella shop – founded in 1857 and still there on New Oxford Street – did a good trade in such items.

The garrotting menace faded, to be replaced in the 1890s by talk of Hooligans, or criminal youth gangs. The word comes from the London Irish but its exact origin is disputed; suggestions include a rough Lambeth family called Houlihan, an individual named Hooligan and a music hall song. By 1899 it was established enough for Clarence Rook to write a novel, set just south of the river, *Hooligan Nights*.

Iron was the great material of the Industrial Revolution, but as the century progressed the crucial material was paper. Newspapers were big business (Victorian writer Walter Bagehot compared London itself to a giant newspaper: 'Everything is here, and everything is disconnected') and there was also a vast amount of unregulated advertising: a painting from the 1830s, John Orlando Parry's *A London Street Scene*, already shows the density of bills and posters on a wall. 'Advertising is to business what steam is to machinery – the great propelling power' was a Victorian business maxim, and some of the patent medicine ads now seem unforgivable. The *Christian Glowworm*, published on Farringdon Road, carried an advert announcing 'DO NOT LET YOUR CHILD DIE! READ FENNING'S EVERY MOTHER'S BOOK, sent post-free for eight stamps.' Fenning's book maintained that 'In London alone almost twenty-five thousand children die every year who have not attained ten years of age. But who is to be blamed for this? The mothers? The doctors? Certainly not their all-wise Creator.' Readers were told whooping cough – a potential killer, for which there was no effective treatment before antibiotics – would 'always' be cured by Fenning's Whooping Cough Powder. And it was the mother's responsibility: she should become her 'Child's only Doctor', to ensure 'the safety of the little earth angel that nestles in your bosom and the preservation of the small loved ones who lisp you Mother'.

Cheap printing technology and increasing literacy made London a world leader in sensational gutter papers and proto-'true crime' periodicals such as the *Tell-tale* and the *Terrific Register* (1823–5), packed with murder and every kind of horrible novelty from cannibalism to spontaneous human combustion; the young Dickens was a great reader of the *Terrific Register*. A mass readership loved sensational stories, like the giant hogs reported in the sewers of Hampstead. Giant eels were a popular early Victorian subject (even the *Times* in October 1852 reported a giant conger – 'an immense reptile' – in the Thames mud, captured and exhibited), but eel stories faded in the 1850s: it has been suggested this was because the growth of empire offered more interesting material and wider horizons.

The public were excited by the Tichborne Claimant, in its day the longest case in legal history (not surpassed until the 1990s). Wealthy gentleman Sir Roger Tichborne drowned at sea in 1854, but the story shifted from sad to ludicrous in 1865, when a man named Arthur Orton claimed that he was Tichborne, rescued by a passing ship and returned to claim his fortune. He had a remarkably fair hearing, given that he was a butcher from Wapping, unable to speak French (Tichborne's first language) and prone to lapse into London speech habits (referring to 'a clerk in Holy Horders'). He had passionate supporters among the newly literate poor, and his name survives – via the dwarfish comedian Little Tich, from Little Tichborne – in the use of the word 'titchy' to mean small.

The *Illustrated Police News*, a lurid shocker said to be the worst paper in Britain, was founded in 1862. It fed an appetite for sensation and reading about crime, contributing to what Judith Flanders has called the Victorian 'invention of murder'. This built on the earlier tradition of the *Newgate Calendar*, coming up to date with Victorian 'penny bloods', known slightly later as 'penny dreadfuls', including such works as *Varney the Vampyre* and *The String of Pearls*, the latter launching Sweeney Todd, the Demon Barber of Fleet Street. The fictional Sweeney Todd, often believed to be real, shows the blurred boundaries between penny dreadfuls and sensational crime stories. Real cases took on the quality of Gothic shockers and *guignol* melo-dramas (like the case of Maria Marten, or the Red Barn Murder), while a fictional folkloric creation such as Spring-heeled Jack, who seems to have started in the 1830s, triggered sightings and panics over half a century, leading to an 1886 dreadful called *Spring-heel'd Jack, the Terror of London*.

Reality overtook fiction in 1888, with Jack the Ripper and the 'Autumn of Terror'. Between August and November five women were night-marishly butchered in Whitechapel and Spitalfields; the murderer was never caught, but the theories have been endless, and the public panic – fanned by the press – was unprecedented. The police had to deal with 1,200 letters a week, many from cranks, and themselves handed out 80,000 leaflets in the Whitechapel area. Meanwhile women formed self-protection groups, armed with knives and hat-pins – mercifully they never caught anyone, since it would probably have been the wrong man.

There have been over a hundred suspects suggested, the serious ones – including Montague Druitt, and American Dr Francis Tumblety – being outnumbered by suggestions such as Lord Randolph Churchill, painter Walter Sickert, poet Ernest Dowson, Dr Barnardo and Lewis Carroll. Conan Doyle's theory, with Holmes-like ingenuity and logic, was that the murderer must be a woman – and therefore so unsuspected that she was effectively invisible – while George Bernard Shaw said the crimes must have been the work of a social reformer drawing attention to conditions in the East End.

One result, remembered by M. V. Hughes in her memoir *A London Girl of the Eighties* (1936), was that professional men suddenly stopped carrying bags of the Gladstone or 'doctor's bag' type, because the Ripper had been reported to have one. In fact he almost certainly didn't, nor a top hat, nor a cloak – the most plausible sighting says he looked like a sailor. But the Ripper is part of a vague, clinging image of London as a foggy, gaslit place with top hats, capes, carriages and house railings. It seems to date to the 1880s, and the stories (and film sets) chiefly responsible are Stevenson's *Dr Jekyll and Mr Hyde* (1886, with notable films in 1920, 1931 and 1941), overlapping by association with the Ripper case; the Sherlock Holmes stories (first appearing in book form in July 1888); and Wilde's *Picture of Dorian Gray* (1890).

Alfred Hitchcock's first major film, *The Lodger* (1927), was based on the Ripper and subtitled *A Tale of the London Fog* – although in fact there was no fog on the Ripper nights, just as there is little mentioned in the Holmes stories. But the idea of it goes with the territory: an editor of Walter's *My Secret Life* has written that even with a map of the time it is difficult to recreate his journeys, let alone trace his home address: 'The seeker finds himself left in the middle of the street with, as it were, a Victorian fog descending and Walter's cab disappearing round a corner.'

The Sherlock Holmes stories epitomize another aspect of London, as the capital of crime and detective writing. The increasing anonymity of nineteenth-century London – the mystery in every face that Wordsworth saw – made this possible, as in the labyrinthine world of G.W.M. Reynolds's *Mysteries of London*, an immensely popular serial that began in 1845. It was modelled on Eugene Sue's *Mysteries of Paris* (1843), but excelled it with elements of the penny dreadful, Gothic shocker and social tract (it has also been described as a work that 'out-Dickenses Dickens').

Big cities generate mysteries. The Pre-Raphaelite painter John Everett Millais was with a couple of friends, one of them the writer Wilkie Collins, when they saw a woman running, seemingly in distress. Collins ran after her, and discovered:

> She was a young lady of good birth and position, who had accidentally fallen into the hands of a man living in a villa in Regent's Park. There for many months he kept her prisoner under threats and mesmeric influence of so alarming a character that she dared not attempt to escape, until, in sheer desperation, she fled from the brute, who, with a poker in his hand, threatened to dash her brains out. Her subsequent history, interesting as it is, is not for these pages.

Collins liked a sensational mystery, and it is no coincidence that he wrote *The Moonstone* (1868), a detective-type novel (sometimes described as the first detective story, and certainly early). Mystery is an urban genre, and Raymond Williams has written of Holmes:

> Conan Doyle's London has acquired, with time, a romantic atmosphere . . . the fog, the gaslight, the hansom cabs, the street urchins . . . London in the Sherlock Holmes stories becomes again the city of 'labyrinthine obscurity and lurid fascination' [George Gissing on Dickens]. Indeed, the urban detective, prefigured in a minor way by Dickens and Wilkie Collins, now begins to emerge as a significant and ratifying figure: the man who can find his way through the fog, who can penetrate the

intricacies of the streets. The opaque complexity of modern life is represented by crime.

It is in keeping with this that Mr Hyde has five bolt-holes in different parts of the city, and London topography figures among Sherlock Holmes's peculiar hobbies: 'I should just like to remember the order of the houses here. It is a hobby of mine to have an exact knowledge of London.'

More than just mystery, the vastness of a city like London is a vast potential. Almost anything could happen, not all of it bad. French geographer Elisée Reclus wrote in the 1860s, 'We propose that immense cities such as London are saturated with exoticism; they have the capacity for infinite intrigue, pleasure and terror equal to the jungle, the deep ocean, the desert and the cosmos.'

5 'Beacons of the Future': Late Victorian Era to 1918

Charity was as quintessentially Victorian as their sense of death and the afterlife, and many newer charities – such as the Asylum for Deaf and Dumb Females, the Shoeblack Society Homes and the Temporary House for Lost Dogs (Battersea) – joined older nineteenth-century charities such as the City Truss Society for the Relief of the Ruptured Poor. Larger charitable initiatives included Barnardo's boys' night shelters, and later Barnardo's Homes and Lord Shaftesbury's 'Ragged Schools'. Shaftesbury is commemorated by the statue at Piccadilly Circus, popularly known as Eros but in fact the Angel of Christian Charity, shooting an arrow into the ground in a 'shaft burying' pun.

Public libraries and art galleries, like the charitably funded Whitechapel, were coming into being, and there is a more idio-syncratic manifestation of late Victorian decency in Postman's Park, EC1, where in 1900 the artist G. F. Watts consecrated a wall of plaques to commemorate acts of heroism and self-sacrifice: 'Harry Sisley of Kilburn, drowned in attempting to save his brother after he himself had just been rescued, May 24 1878.' Despite the occasional bathetic caption – of the 'tried to save her friend from a raging inferno, while wearing a highly inflammable dress' variety – it still brings a lump to the throat.

Many middle-class women were involved in active charity, including Sylvia Pankhurst, Beatrice Webb, Annie Besant and Olive Malvery, an Anglo-Indian woman who came to London to study music but gave it up to volunteer in the East End, documenting conditions there in books such as *The Soul Market* (1906).

One of many plaques commemorating extraordinary public heroism in Postman's Park, EC1.

There were more sensationalistic accounts in F. C. Masterman's *From the Abyss* (1902) – this time in south London, among the 'denizens of another universe of being' – and Jack London's *People of the Abyss* (1903). Both seem to regard their subject with the same horror as that in H. G. Wells's *The Time Machine* (1895), when Wells imagines the evolution of a future species of degraded, subterranean 'Morlock' workers. But the tide was turning: 'outcast' London was less outcast – the Ripper case had been a wake-up call to deal with East End conditions – and society was becoming more integrated. The Old Nichol slum, Morrison's 'Jago', became Arnold Circus, with a bandstand on the green space in the centre. It was built in the red-brick, Queen Anne revival style, like the Millbank estate behind Tate Britain, a style associated at the time with social progress.

Along with better housing, the great integrating factor was education. Schooling was compulsory after the 1870 Education Act, and schools were being built all over London, as Holmes points out to Watson in 'The Naval Treaty'. When their train goes past Clapham Junction, Holmes comments on the cheering view and Watson thinks he must be joking ('the view was sordid enough'), but Holmes explains:

'Look at those big, isolated clumps of building rising up above the slates, like brick islands in a lead-coloured sea.'

'The Board-schools.'

'Light-houses, my boy! Beacons of the future! Capsules with hundreds of bright little seeds in each, out of which will spring the wise, better England of the future.

Patriotism was another integrating force. Britain was the centre of a mighty empire. However, as Linda Colley shows in *Captives* (2002), it was an empire precariously and hazardously acquired, at times almost in self-defence: the lines in 'Rule, Britannia!' asserting Britons 'never, never, never shall be slaves' reflected anxieties about British subjects being captured for slavery by Barbary pirates.

But by Queen Victoria's Golden Jubilee in 1887, and even more so her Diamond Jubilee in 1897, as Colley writes, it was an empire 'reimagined as inexorable and inevitable', with an extraordinary parade of British and empire troops through London, and Victoria in her carriage. She wrote in her diary:

A newly built Arnold Circus in 1901, on the site of what had been London's most notorious slum, the Old Nichol; it was crowned with a bandstand shortly after.

A never to be forgotten day. No one ever, I believe, has met with such an ovation . . . passing through those 6 miles of streets . . . The crowds were quite indescribable and their enthusiasm truly marvellous and deeply touching. The cheering was quite deafening and every face seemed to be filled with joy.

All this Victorian triumph was dented by the Boer War, in which 22,000 British soldiers died. The major event in public consciousness was the siege of Mafeking, where an outnumbered British garrison of soldiers and trapped civilians held out from October 1899 to May 1900, eating their horses and printing their own currency and stamps. The conflict was followed avidly in the press, and when Mafeking was saved there was jubilation on the streets. Trafalgar Square was damaged by celebratory bonfires, and 'Mafficking' (to celebrate wildly) became a verb.

The exultant side of being a late-Victorian Briton can be seen in a boys' paper of the time, *Chums*. Along with ripping yarns, empire adventure and educational features, the paper was interspersed with

Queen Victoria's Diamond Jubilee procession, passing just north of Trafalgar Square.

cartoons and drawings, some of which defy parody, like 'The Joy of Life' in August 1900: a female elephant, wearing a spotty dress, is jumping up and down on her hind legs while waving a Union Jack with her trunk.

The sort of men who steered the empire – the officer class – had a home from home in the world of the gentleman's club. While the public house had grown more proletarian in the nineteenth century, and was no longer the tavern any traveller might use, the West End club had become part of being a solidly upper- or upper-middle-class man. They were long established – White's was founded as White's Chocolate House in 1693, making it older than the Bank of England – but after a more dissolute existence in eighteenth-century and Regency times, when they were associated with gambling, they came into their own in the Victorian era. White's, Boodles, Brooks, the East India, Travellers, Oriental and many others clustered around the Mayfair, Piccadilly and St James's areas, and were part of Britain's image abroad: Phileas Fogg, in Jules Verne's *Around the World in Eighty Days* (1873), is a member of the Reform Club, site of his 'eighty days' wager. Club members were cocooned in a comforting world of leather armchairs and discreet, butler-like club servants, and White's has been described by its historian, Percy Colson, as 'an oasis of civilisation in a desert of democracy'.

Like the 1960s, the 1880s and especially the 1890s were times of social flux and change. The idea of 'the Nineties' calls up a world of decadence, aesthetes, peacock feathers and Aubrey Beardsley, with absinthe drinking at the Cafe Royal and idling on chaises longues. Meanwhile the Arts and Crafts Movement – socially committed, related to Pre-Raphaelitism and urging a return to simple craftsmanship – combated the more extreme tendencies of 'art for art's sake', and John Ruskin criticized James McNeill Whistler's aestheticized and almost abstract painting of Thames-side Cremorne Gardens, *Nocturne in Black and Gold: The Falling Rocket*, as 'a pot of paint flung in the public's face'. It led to a court case which Whistler won, only to be awarded a derisory farthing in damages.

Symbolist poet Arthur Symons – firmly in the aesthetic camp, wondering in his *London: A Book of Aspects* (1908) why ordinary people on Edgware Road had to exist, and 'why they take the trouble to go on existing' given their vulgarity and lack of beauty – saw a city made strange by gaslight in his poem 'London', where 'Men as trees walking loom through lanes of night / Hung from the globes of some unnatural fruit.'

Oscar Wilde aestheticized the Thames in his poem 'Symphony in Yellow' (1889), bringing out 'aesthetic' green and yellow colours; a few years earlier, Gilbert and Sullivan parodied 'art for art's sake' aestheticism in their comic opera *Patience* (1881), with its 'Greenery-yallery, Grosvenor Gallery' young man. For Wilde the Thames fog was 'like a yellow silken scarf' and the river itself 'like a rod of rippled jade' – less because he really thought that was how it looked, and more because he wanted to be provocative. Wilde's downfall in a homosexual scandal of 1895 almost took the world of Nineties decadence with him. A mob attacked the Vigo Street offices of John Lane, publisher of the decadent periodical *The Yellow Book*, and smashed the windows. Lane panicked and sacked Beardsley from the art editorship. Decadence was in retreat, but it bounced back in 1896 with a new periodical, *The Savoy* (named after the hotel where Wilde's offences were alleged to have taken place), published by Leonard Smithers from Royal Arcade.

A more prosaic threat to the status quo came from the trade union movement. An 1886 protest about unemployment led to fighting in Trafalgar Square, with mob disturbances and window smashing in the West End; the following year another Trafalgar Square demonstration was broken up by heavy-handed police violence (remembered as 'Bloody Sunday') followed by more window smashing. But this was the old way: the new way came in 1888, with the match factory girls.

Annie Besant wrote an article about conditions in the match factory at Bow, where young women worked fourteen-hour days for four shillings a week and risked 'phossy jaw' from phosphorus – a cancer causing brain damage and nightmarish disfigurement, with loss of the rotten lower jaw. Three women were sacked for talking to Besant, but the girls went on a well-organized strike, speaking to parliament and holding rallies, and won. Their success encouraged the less successful Great Dock Strike the following year.

The threat of 'aliens' also loomed large in *fin de siècle* London. There were justified fears of Fenian bombings (an 1867 bomb in Clerkenwell, intended to cause a jailbreak, killed twelve innocent people and injured many more, and there were further attacks in the 1880s, with targets including the Special Branch – originally the Special Irish Branch – and the Carlton Club), but these were joined by more imaginative anxieties about Continental extremists.

London had large European communities. Van Gogh spent an unusually happy year living in Brixton while working in Covent Garden, and Rimbaud and Verlaine lived together in Camden and Fitzrovia. When Verlaine writes in *Romances sans paroles* (Songs without Words, 1875) that it is raining on the city as it is raining in his heart, the rainy sky is quite possibly not over Paris but the Tottenham Court Road area.

The extremity and correspondingly extreme repression of Continental politics meant that large numbers of radicals came to London, particularly after the 1848 'Year of Revolutions' and the slaughter of the Paris Commune in 1871. Karl Marx lived in Soho and wrote in the British Library. Russian anarchist Prince Kropotkin lived in London, and international anarchists held meetings here, notably the 1881 Anarchist Congress in a pub behind Euston station. In 1907 the Russian Social Democrats held a congress in Hackney, including those well-known democrats Trotsky, Lenin and Stalin.

Extremism of a very un-English kind was vividly imagined by E. Douglas Fawcett in his 1892 novel *Hartmann the Anarchist*, where ruthless foreign genius Hartmann destroys Big Ben (already iconic) with his aerial warship. Anarchist fears gave extra resonance to the Greenwich explosion a couple of years later, when a French citizen named Martial Bourdin was accidentally killed by a bomb he was carrying towards Greenwich Observatory, inspiring Conrad's novel *The Secret Agent* (1907).

Anarchists came centre stage in public consciousness in the winter of 1910, when police disturbed three Russian-speaking men robbing a Houndsditch jewellers: without hesitation the anarchists shot five policemen, killing three. This aroused hatred against foreign extremists, and the authorities assured the public that most anarchists were peaceful and intended no harm. Britain, specifically London, had a tradition of tolerance, exemplified in a *Punch* cartoon of a Speakers' Corner-style orator calling for the downfall of Queen Victoria: 'It does 'er no 'arm,' says a watching policeman, 'and it does 'im good.'

The leader of the anarchists was said to be a man called Peter Piatkow, 'Peter the Painter'. A manhunt was on. A couple of weeks later, on 3 January 1911, police surrounded a house in Sidney Street and 'the Siege of Sidney Street' began, involving four hundred police, the Scots Guards and Home Secretary Winston Churchill. During a lengthy gun battle the men inside shot at everything that moved, including cats and dogs, until eventually the building caught fire. Two bodies were found, but not the Painter. Perhaps he had escaped – said a rumour of the time – by smashing his way through the floorboards and into the sewer system. It is more likely he was never there, but he joined London's legendary uncatchable characters like Spring-heeled Jack and Jack the Ripper.

There is an echo of his escape in the first of Sax Rohmer's best-selling Fu Manchu thrillers, *The Mystery of Fu Manchu* (1912), where fiendish Chinese mastermind Dr Fu Manchu seems to perish in a fire at his East End hideout – but his body is not found, and there are hints he might survive for a sequel. London's notably law-abiding and quiet Chinese community in Limehouse was popularly associated with cut-throat criminality and opium dens well into the 1920s. The idea of the East End opium den – in reality, so rare as to be almost non-existent – was launched with Dickens's *Mystery of Edwin Drood* (1870) and continued into Oscar Wilde's *Picture of Dorian Gray* (1891), and the Sherlock Holmes story 'The Man with The Twisted Lip' (1891).

Opium was smoked socially on Chinese premises, particularly by Chinese sailors, but when George Duckworth, a research assistant

The Siege of Sidney Street: a young Winston Churchill (first man in top hat) at this legendary 1911 shoot-out with cornered Russian anarchists in the East End.

of the indefatigable Charles Booth, finally tracked down a more or less commercial smoking establishment at 13 Jamaica Street, run by an unemployed Indian chef and his English wife (both smokers themselves), he found it was so far from being a den of iniquity that a tin served as an 'honesty box' for payment, with departing guests paying whatever they thought was fair.

Women still had no vote, despite over fifty years of agitation, and in 1903 this escalated with the 'Deeds not Words' policy of the Women's Social and Political Union, founded by Emmeline Pankhurst and her daughters. A Hyde Park rally attracted 300,000, and suffragettes became known for acts of disruption, such as chaining themselves to railings. The authorities responded with prison sentences, including force-feeding for women on hunger strike, and on 'Black Friday' in 1910 a women's deputation to parliament was met with what was later agreed to be excessive police force. But as time went on, the suffragettes made themselves increasingly resented, slashing Velázquez's *Rokeby Venus* in the National Gallery (the perpetrator, Mary Richardson, was later a prominent British Fascist), setting fire to pillar boxes and the Kew Gardens tea shop, and attempting to burn Lloyd George's house and the Royal Academy. They also attempted several bombings, including the church of St Martin-in-the-Fields and Westminster Abbey.

The mood turned in their favour in June 1913, after the death of Emily Davison. She had already trespassed in the House of Commons several times (a cupboard where she hid now has a plaque), served nine prison sentences and tried to throw herself down a metal staircase rather than be force-fed. She also wrote poetry, such as her sonnet 'London' ('Oh London! How I feel thy magic spell / . . . / The centre of the universe is here!'). And now, at the 1913 Derby, she was killed throwing herself under the king's horse, or so it was believed: it is now thought she only intended to grab the reins, and her death was a tragic accident. Her funeral procession from Victoria to King's Cross station (she was buried in Northumberland), with a service en route at the Hawksmoor church of St George's Bloomsbury, was attended by around 200,000 people. Despite that, with attitudes

THE SUCCESSFUL START FOR WESTMINSTER,
Which Ended in Failure to Reach Their Destination.

The 1909 suffragette balloon, in which Muriel Matters set out to bombard parliament with leaflets.

hardened by arson and bombs, in May 1914 the House of Lords rejected the Woman's Enfranchisement Bill.

The most extraordinary suffragette action was an attempt to bombard the Houses of Parliament with leaflets from a balloon. Muriel Matters, an Australian singer and elocution teacher, had interviewed Prince Kropotkin and given a musical recital at his house, after which he told her she should use her talents for something important: as she remembered it later, 'My entire mental outlook was changed.' She joined the Women's Freedom League, chained herself to the Women's Gallery in parliament and addressed crowds wearing a mackintosh to withstand being pelted with eggs. And in 1909, for the opening of parliament by King Edward, she chartered a balloon with 'Votes for Women' painted on the side, piloted by aeronaut Henry Spencer and carrying 25 kilograms (4 st.) of leaflets to shower on the proceedings below. She took off from Hendon Aerodrome and soon reached over 900 metres (3,000 ft), but they were blown off course and flew over Kensington and Tooting, finally coming down south of Croydon. As a publicity exercise it was still a success, and it was also the first powered flight from Hendon Aerodrome (already used for hot air balloons): her airship was a dirigible with a motor, like a mini-Zeppelin, and a portent of things to come.

When Muriel Matters found herself 1,000 metres over Cricklewood it was a new and modern experience in more ways than one. London had continued to grow, and the great development in the second half of the nineteenth century was the suburbs. They were spread by the new train lines (development tended to follow the trains, and not the other way around), and by 1911 around 2.7 million people lived in the outer suburbs, of whom around a quarter of a million commuted daily to the centre.

The spread of suburbs was caught in a music-hall song of the 1890s, 'The 'Ouses In Between':

Wiv a ladder and some glasses,
You could see to 'Ackney Marshes,

If it wasn't for the 'ouses in between.
. . .
And by climbing to the chimbley,
You could see across to Wimbley,
If it wasn't for the 'ouses in between.
. . .
If yer eye sight didn't fail yer,
You could see right to Australia,
If it wasn't for the 'ouses in between.

These developments varied from progressive garden suburbs such as Bedford Park to more industrial suburbs such as Becontree at Dagenham, but overall they offered a cleaner and more spacious life. At the same time, as they spread – and spread – they were resented, particularly by people attached to the often sylvan landscapes they were replacing. E. Nesbit, author of *The Railway Children* (1906), and a former member of the occult Order of the Golden Dawn – part of the strange cultural ferment of the 1880s and '90s – burned suburban houses in effigy, possibly for occult reasons, as they encroached towards her in Eltham.

Snobbery also played a large part in dislike of the 'suburban' (an attitude that lasted through the twentieth century, when comedians could get a laugh from places like Cricklewood, East Cheam or Neasden). It is epitomized by George and Weedon Grossmith's comic masterpiece *Diary of a Nobody* (1892), where the nobody in question is the carefully respectable and precariously genteel Charles Pooter, who lives with his wife in the recently built 'Brickfield Terrace, Holloway'. Despite the Grossmiths' mockery, poor Pooter comes out of it as a sympathetic figure.

There is a more epic treatment of white-collar suburban existence in John Davidson's poem 'Thirty Bob a Week' (1894), where the plight of the respectable working- or lower-middle-class man, trapped without quite enough to live on, is seen as an unsung daily heroism. The speaker is socially just a notch or two below Pooter, and

Like a mole I journey in the dark,
A-travelling along the underground
From my Pillar'd Halls and broad Suburban Park,
To come the daily dull official round;
. . .
They say it daily up and down the land
As easy as you take a drink, it's true;
. . . [that] the difficultest job a man can do,
Is to come it brave and meek with thirty bob a week,
And feel that that's the proper thing for you.

It's a naked child against a hungry wolf;
It's playing bowls upon a splitting wreck;
It's walking on a string across a gulf
With millstones fore-and-aft about your neck;
But the thing is daily done by many and many a one;
And we fall, face forward, fighting, on the deck.

As the wonders of Victorian modernity evolved into a more recognizably twentieth-century modernity, the London we know today largely fell into place. The first deep 'tube' was opened in 1890 (as opposed to the shallower 'cut and cover' method of the earlier underground), complete with escalators in 1898. Fleet Street became the centre of the newspaper industry, and the first tabloid, the *Daily Mail*, appeared in 1896. Well-known shops opened, including Marks & Spencer (1903), the present Knightsbridge Harrods (1907; it had traded more humbly for some years in the East End) and Selfridges (1909). The last great chunks of imperial architecture were built, including Aldwych, Kingsway and Admiralty Arch, finishing the Mall just by Trafalgar Square, and giant Bovril and Schweppes adverts appeared in Piccadilly Circus in 1910.

The worst of Victorian poverty was finally going, combined with a high standard of living for the middle classes. Restaurants and tea-rooms were appearing across the West End (Lyons Corner Houses arrived in 1894) and becoming popular with a more modest clientele. Further upmarket, hotels were a phenomenon of the era, with the

Ritz in 1906 and the Waldorf in 1908. This kind of plutocratic luxury went with the cigar-smoking, champagne-drinking figure of Prince Eddy, Prince of Wales, later Edward VII. The new era seemed to combine the best of nineteenth-century living with early twentieth-century progress, until it blundered into the First World War, as disastrously as hitting an iceberg.

The British and German royal families were closely connected: Wilhelm II ('Kaiser Bill') was Queen Victoria's grandson. Germany and Britain were old allies. Many Germans lived in London, often working in the catering industry or as barbers. German families came to Britain on holiday. And then suddenly war had been declared. A German band playing at Earl's Court had to put down their instruments mid-performance, and walk off stage.

The onset of the war was greeted with immense enthusiasm, as if it were a particularly exciting sporting event. A huge crowd gathered outside Buckingham Palace, spreading down the Mall towards Charing Cross. Taxis were caught in the crowd, and men and women climbed on their roofs to wave Union Jacks. They all sang 'Rule, Britannia!', 'Land of Hope and Glory' and the national anthem. But before long, the horrific death toll killed enthusiasm. Conscription had to be introduced in 1916, and 200,000 people demonstrated against it in Trafalgar Square.

For the first time London experienced bombing from the air, in night-time Zeppelin raids. The docks were bombed, the East End and finally the centre: the department store of Swan & Edgar on Piccadilly Circus was hit, and in the Dolphin Tavern, on Red Lion Street in Holborn, the clock is still stopped at 10.40 from a bomb on 9 September 1915.

Civilian casualties, including children (the first person killed was a three-year-old girl), increased hatred of the Germans, which was fanned by an efficient Fleet Street propaganda machine: by the end

Risen from the ashes: a plaque on a building at 61 Farringdon Road, Clerkenwell.

of the war, press barons Beaverbrook and Northcliffe were working closely with the Ministry of Information. Crowds smashed shops with German-sounding names, often Russian or Jewish, but the British monarchy kept their real name of Saxe-Coburg-Gotha until surprisingly late, 1917, when – particularly in view of the arrival of a German heavy bomber, the Gotha – they changed it to the altogether merrier and more English name of Windsor. Kaiser Bill, not known for his sense of humour, was moved to say he looked forward to seeing 'The Merry Wives of Saxe-Coburg-Gotha'.

6 Fit for Heroes: 1918–45

Finally Armistice arrived, and crowds celebrated on the streets again. The war had sealed and consolidated the mounting social changes of the late Victorian and Edwardian era, with the class system slightly dented and women doing men's jobs, working on buses and in factories. By now it had ceased to be tenable that they had no vote. In 1918 the vote was given to women over thirty, followed in 1919 by the first female MP taking her seat (Lady Astor, a wealthy American who had no connection with the suffragettes).

Greater employment opportunities and slightly less inequality meant society never returned to Victorian levels of domestic service (although even in 1921 around one-third of women were domestic servants of some sort, outnumbering women teachers nine to one). Three servants in a household – perhaps a cook and two maids – had been a minimum for securely middle-class respectability, but *The One Maid Book of Cookery* was hailed by the *Pall Mall Gazette* as a timely idea, 'now that so many people live in flats, and have only accommodation for one maid'. Apartment living – long normal in Paris – was still a relative novelty in London, but grew more common between the wars, and cartoonist Heath Robinson illustrated *How To Live in a Flat* (1936), full of jokes about ingenious space saving.

London's population continued to increase – by the late 1930s it reached almost nine million, one-fifth of the national total – and housing continued to be an issue. 'Homes fit for heroes' has entered the national memory (misquoting what Prime Minister Lloyd George actually said in 1918: 'a country fit for heroes to live in'), and this aspiration can be seen in the high quality of 1920s council flats, often with green space. This building initiative gave rise to London County Council leader Herbert Morrison's alleged boast to the Conservatives that he would 'build them out of London' by housing Labour voters. Council housing was spread throughout London, resulting in a surprisingly broad social mix in expensive areas.

The bulk of a growing population was housed in the suburbs as the city continued to spread outwards. This led to Morrison's initiative of saving a 'green belt' around London – recently under threat – to stop the endless sprawl identified in *England and the Octopus*, a 1928 book by Clough Williams-Ellis. There were vast council schemes to house former East Enders, notably at Becontree, where the sports facilities built into the plan bred a generation of 1960s footballers. Despite such plans, these developments were unloved, and felt to be sterile compared to the old East End community. Meanwhile the spread of formerly deprived inner-city Londoners into the Essex countryside gave the area a distinctive character.

Northwest London had the more definitively middle-class suburbs of 'Metroland', along the route of the Metropolitan line, where places like Harrow and Pinner were designed and marketed as semi-rural and idyllic. Half-timbered Tudorbethan architecture and leaded windows harked back to an ideal past, and allowed satisfying minor variations between houses. This leafy northern belt, clear of the problem areas beneath it, stretched as far east as Loughton and gave rise not only to poster adverts but songs and poems, only a few satirical. Metroland was celebrated by the poet John Betjeman, and formed an atmospheric backdrop for the 1960s television series *The Avengers*.

The London suburbs had a rich life of their own. They meant respectability and quiet aspiration, but their fertile privacy could suggest possibilities that ranged from sinister to erotic. Graham Greene praised Conan Doyle's 'sense of horror which hangs over the laurelled drive of Upper Norwood and behind the curtains of Lower Camberwell', and the suburbs have also been imagined as hotbeds of adultery. There was later great amusement and delight at the discovery of Cynthia Payne's very English brothel in suburban Streatham in the 1970s, which accepted luncheon vouchers.

There was a sense of release after the war. It was the jazz age, though not on the newly formed BBC (Radio 2LO, the BBC's early incarnation – the LO stood for London – began broadcasting in 1922, from Marconi House on the Strand). The BBC's director-general, Lord Reith, described jazz as 'this filthy product of modernity', but under his high-minded and puritanical leadership the station became an important institution in British consciousness. Early wireless announcers wore bow ties, and dinner jackets in the evening, 'because the listeners prefer it'.

Meanwhile Ciro's in Orange Street, located around the back of the National Gallery, led the way in syncopated dance music with its house band, the celebrated 'Ciro's Club Coon Orchestra'. Nightclubs became popular, two of the earliest being Oddenino's on Regent Street, which was also a restaurant, and Rectors on Tottenham Court Road, where clubbers danced around a block of ice to keep cool.

It was the era of the Bright Young Things, better known at the time as 'Bright Young People', as satirized in Evelyn Waugh's *Vile Bodies* (1930). They loved extravagant theme parties, along with elaborate practical jokes and hoaxes. Being a full-on Bright Young Thing (ideally upper middle class and recently arrived in London after a not too academic time at Oxford) was the preserve of the few, but the 'flapper', a jazzy girl in her twenties with a fast life (and, ideally, bobbed hair and a boyish figure), was everywhere. When the voting age for women was brought down to 21 in 1928, its opponents called it 'the flapper vote'.

The West End consolidated itself further as a leisure zone. The proletarian pub and upper-class club, both strongly male, were joined by a more democratic, metropolitan world of restaurants and theatres: couples or working women could go out for supper and 'a show', or to the cinema, travelling by public transport. The modern Piccadilly underground complex, completed in 1928, had murals showing London as the centre of the world. 'Life Begins at Oxford Circus' was an interwar hit for Jack Hylton and His Orchestra ('Life begins at Oxford Circus / When the busy day is done. / We don't care how much they work us, / Just as long as we have fun!'). It was almost belated when he recorded it in 1935, by which time the mood had darkened.

In 1926 came the General Strike: it began with a mining dispute, and a nationwide strike in solidarity was almost averted by negotiation, but when printworkers refused to print the *Daily Mail* and its anti-strike rhetoric the government refused to negotiate further. Dockers and rail workers stopped, and troops were deployed. Shapurji Saklatavla, Communist MP for Battersea, was jailed after urging the army and navy to strike with the workers, a Kronstadt-style escalation that might have felt like the beginning of civil war. Armoured cars escorted lorries through the dockers' blockade, and food was distributed from a militarized depot in Hyde Park.

The middle classes, including students, rallied against the strike in a way that would be unlikely even a decade later. Students unloaded ships, and private cars delivered milk and bread. Graham Greene became a special constable. In ten days the strike was over, and with hindsight it seems rather British in its moderation, but to many people at the time it was tantamount to revolution. It took some of the glitter off the 1920s, even before the Wall Street Crash of 1929 and the Depression.

Twenties optimism gave way to the generally more sombre and anxious Thirties, but there were upbeat aspects. There was a more general awareness of healthy living: sunshine, cod-liver oil, hiking and 'fresh air' were all in the public mind, though never reaching the heights of the interwar German craze for sunbathing and nudism. Public health met town planning in the swimming pools built in the 1930s by George Lansbury: 'Lansbury's lidos'. The first was built on the Serpentine in Hyde Park in 1930, and was followed by others including Victoria Park, Hackney, with the slogan 'Every East End child to be a swimmer'.

For less healthy leisure there was greyhound racing ('the dogs') and the movies, reaching new heights of popularity, together with cinema newsreels. There were magnificent Art Deco temples of cinema, often in unglamorous locations: the Elephant and Castle had the biggest cinema in Europe, the Trocadero ('a huge ferro-concrete refuge from the cares and troubles of modern life, complete

Diners at the London Casino, 1938.

with a marble fountain in the forecourt'). The Astoria in Seven
Sisters Road seated 4,000 and included a fountain with goldfish and
a 'Spanish village'; and the Granada in Tooting was (in the words of
architectural historian Ian Nairn)

> a cross between Strawberry Hill and the Soane Museum . . .
> Gothic arches are all around . . . when the lights go up there is
> an Aladdin's cave . . . the view may make you gasp. Pinnacle after
> gilded pinnacle, to the back of the gallery: one of the sights of
> London. Miss the Tower of London, if you have to, but don't
> miss this . . .

And it survives, as a bingo hall.

Other Art Deco masterpieces include the *Daily Express* building in Fleet Street, with its walls of chromium and black glass,

Piccadilly Circus, London's iconic central spot, with the Angel of Charity and period
advertising including Bovril, Gordon's, Schweppes and a cigarette-smoking Bonzo
the dog.

Broadcasting House on Portland Place, with something of the battleship about it, and Senate House in Bloomsbury. Senate House architect Frank Holden (who also designed some classic tube stations) said he was influenced by the rhythms of jazz, but the resulting building looks more Stalinist than jazzy, and George Orwell used it as his inspiration for the Ministry of Truth in *1984*.

Perhaps the most iconic building of the time is Battersea Power Station, completed in 1934, where Sir Giles Gilbert Scott drew on his experience of building churches to create a modernist cathedral of power. Long derelict, it is now being redeveloped, but its dramatic appearance – as on the cover of Pink Floyd's 1977 LP *Animals*, with flying pig balloon – is destroyed by high buildings around it.

Scott was also responsible for the classic red phone box that appeared between the wars: the K2 in 1924, ventilated by its royal crowns punctured under the roof, and the smaller K6 in 1935. Scott's boxes, or kiosks, are as British as Buckingham Palace guardsmen and the *Dr Who* Tardis, although the idea of the kiosk goes back to Turkey, as a small Kubla Khan-style pavilion or summer house. Scott's box has a closer inspiration in Sir John Soane's mausoleum, in St Pancras churchyard, with its distinctive squared-off dome – unlike a later generation of grey public callboxes with their functionalist flat roofs, useful for accumulating rainwater and fried-chicken cartons.

Even more iconic is the London tube map designed by Harry Beck in the early 1930s. Early editions show 'ghost stations' such as St Mary's and British Museum (some of them still lie untouched in darkness with their old advertising) but the central map remains similar today. Beck was an electrical engineer by training, and his map – topographically accurate, but distorted in positioning and distances – is essentially a circuit diagram.

More than just useful, the tube map is like the nervous system of London. It has an almost Platonic existence, like the Monopoly board, and seems to give a greater reality to places that appear on it. Journalist Julie Burchill dreamed of moving to London when living in Bristol as a teenager:

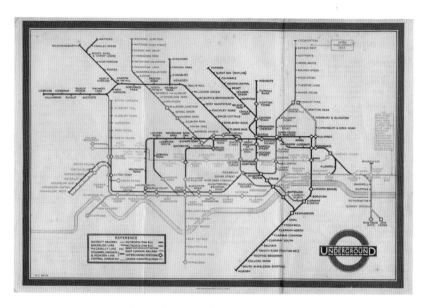

Harry Beck's ingeniously simplified tube map, 1933.

My friends had double-page *Jackie* posters of Cassidy and Stardust above their beds: I had a map of the London Underground. And I learned the names of the Tube stations – the stations of the cross! – with a speed and dedication I could not apply to more academic learning by rote. But what times table ever spoke such volumes or promised such riches as Angel, White City and Mansion House? To me that map – drawn by one Harry Beck in the 1930s, still to me the greatest artist in the history of the world – held all the promise of sex, fame, fun and money that my friends saw in Cassidy's appendix scar, Bowie's ill-matched eyes and Ferry's patent-leather sneer. London was the ultimate sex symbol, a map of dreams.

The economy worsened during the 1930s, bringing the Jarrow hunger marchers to London to protest; they arrived after a month's walking on 31 October 1936. There was a new fascination with the working classes and how they lived, as seen in the Mass-Observation movement's eavesdropping on ordinary British life from an anthropological, ethnographic perspective; Orwell's *Down and Out in*

Paris and London (1933) and *The Road to Wigan Pier* (1937); and a slew of more or less low-life books such as Hugh Massingham's *I Took off My Tie* (1936), Robert Westerby's *Wide Boys Never Work* (1937), Gerald Kersh's *Night and the City* (1938) and John Worby's *Spiv's Progress* (1939).

With poverty at home and fascism abroad, leftward sympathies increased among students and intellectuals. The Auden generation of poets and many Oxbridge students, including 'the Cambridge spies' Philby, Burgess, Maclean and Blunt, graduated and moved to London in the early 1930s, often taking jobs with the BBC or Foreign Office. Meanwhile more conservative spirits saw Hitler as a hope against the menace of Bolshevism: *Daily Mail* proprietor Rothermere believed 'the sturdy young Nazis are Europe's guardians against the Communist danger', and his flagship paper, the *Daily Mail*, cheered 'Hurrah for the Blackshirts'.

Home-grown fascism had a vigorous minority life, with the Blackshirts, or British Union of Fascists, led by the baronet, fencing champion and former Labour MP Sir Oswald Mosley, described by historian A.J.P. Taylor as the most intelligent politician Britain ever had. Mosley was an extraordinary demagogue, electrifying crowds not only in Bermondsey and Hackney but Hyde Park and Trafalgar Square.

Mosley overreached himself in October 1936 with an attempt to lead 2,000 Blackshirts on a march into Shadwell, just south of Whitechapel in the strongly Jewish East End, where they were outnumbered by around 100,000 anti-fascist demonstrators and had to be protected by the police and diverted; it is remembered as the 'Battle of Cable Street'. Public opinion was already turning against the Blackshirts after the savage way they dealt with hecklers at Mosley's 1934 Earl's Court Olympia rally. This lost them their more moderate sympathizers, caricatured by an MI5 man of the time as old ladies and clergymen. By the time Mosley addressed Olympia again in 1939 – with an audience of 30,000, said to be the world's largest indoor political meeting – his remaining supporters were more hardcore, and many of them would have supported Hitler.

More Jewish refugees were arriving. Sigmund Freud moved to Hampstead, and other arrivals included the art historians Ernst Gombrich and Aby Warburg, founder of the Warburg Institute, and the photographer Wolf Suschitzky, who documented the life of Charing Cross Road in the 1930s (and was later cinematographer on the Michael Caine film of 1971, *Get Carter*).

Unlike 1914, no one wanted war. People remembered the earlier carnage, and the large number of women from that generation – particularly noticed and remembered as schoolteachers – who were left single for life. Fear of bombing was a new factor: it was widely believed that modern aero technology could completely destroy London in the opening hours of a conflict, using not only explosives but poison gas, in a scenario of science-fiction-style horror.

Support for 'appeasement' – avoiding war by letting Hitler have his territorial claims in Europe – was not surprising, and was far more widespread than people liked to admit once war had begun. Cinema newsreel audiences saw Chamberlain return from a meeting with Hitler proclaiming 'peace for our time', but the era Auden remembered as a 'low, dishonest decade' drew to an end on the

The 1936 'Battle of Cable Street', when Oswald Mosley's fascists tried to march through the East End.

Sunday morning of 3 September 1939, when Germany refused an ultimatum to leave Poland. Families gathered round their wireless sets to hear Chamberlain say, as a result, 'this country is now at war with Germany.'

London settled into the anticlimactic months of the 'phoney war', as it was known. One of the more traumatic initiatives of the time was the well-meaning evacuation of children from big cities into the countryside, producing culture shocks for homesick children and host families alike; by January 1940 around 900,000 had returned home.

In August 1940 the Blitz began, continuing for 57 consecutive nights. Casualty calculations vary depending on the area counted as 'London', but there were around 30,000 people killed and over one million homes destroyed. People sheltered in tube stations, although this was initially discouraged, with notices saying 'During air-raids, passengers only admitted.' Even tube stations were not safe: six hundred people drowned at Balham when a water main burst, and over one hundred were killed at Bank when a bomb crashed down an escalator and exploded on the platform.

Falling more heavily on the industrial east, the early Blitz was socially divisive. Diarist Harold Nicolson wrote, 'Everybody is worried about the feeling in the East End, where there is much bitterness,' and recorded a rumour that the king and queen were booed. When Buckingham Palace was bombed, the queen said she felt at last she could 'look the East End in the face'. The royals refused to be evacuated to Canada, and the queen learned to use a revolver.

Morale during the Blitz was high: rates of suicide and depression declined, and the nation rallied behind Churchill and his defiant speeches. Churchill posed with a gangster-style tommy gun and led the war effort from the underground Cabinet War Rooms in Whitehall, a stone's throw from the ivy-covered Admiralty Citadel on the other side of Horse Guards parade, with its roof of 6-metre-thick (20 ft) concrete and fortress-like gun slits for last-ditch defence. St Paul's Cathedral remained undestroyed with the City in flames all around it, as recorded in iconic photos and newsreel

Blitz devastation in the West End's Duke Street.

footage, and there was a humbler boost to morale from the plant *Saxifraga × urbium*, which grew on bomb sites: by coincidence this was already known as 'London Pride', and Noel Coward wrote a song about it.

With America not yet in the war, and Russia in league with Germany after the Nazi–Soviet pact, Britain was standing alone against Nazism. The Blitz is widely celebrated as London's finest hour, although more cynical recent studies have emphasized the corruption, crime and looting. After the Café de Paris – an upmarket West End nightclub, with underground premises billed as the safest in London – received a direct hit through a ventilation shaft, looters removed jewellery from the well-heeled victims, cutting off fingers if need be. Many people continued to behave in character. Former Bright Young Thing Brian Howard, an inspiration for Evelyn Waugh's fictional Anthony Blanche and Ambrose Silk, was caught in a police raid on a louche Soho club and responded to questioning with 'My name is Brian Howard and I live in Mayfair. No doubt you, Inspector, come from some dreary suburb.'

Ordinary life went on. Along with the work of firemen and ambulance crews, postmen delivered letters, while the Blue Cross animal charity treated over 350,000 pets during the war. Dogs were frightened by bombing, and a morphine-based patent medicine called Calm Doggie was sold to help them endure the raids.

The devastation had a surreal aspect, and Elizabeth Bowen's short story 'Mysterious Kor' (1944) captures the way that 'Full moonlight drenched the city and searched it . . . The effect was remorseless: London looked like the moon's capital – shallow, cratered, extinct.' Rose Macaulay describes the greening of this lunar landscape:

> The maze of little streets threading through the wilderness, the broken walls, the great pits with their dense forests of bracken and bramble . . . all the wild rambling shrubs that spring from ruin, the vaults and cellars and deep caves, the wrecked guild halls that had belonged to saddlers, merchant tailors, haberdashers, waxhandlers, barbers, brewers, coopers and coachmakers, all the ancient city fraternities, the broken office stairways that spiralled steeply past empty doorways and rubbled closets into the sky, empty shells of churches with their towers still strangely spiring above the wilderness, their empty window arches where green boughs pushed in, their broken pavement floors . . . all this scarred and haunted green and stone and brambled wilderness lying under the august sun, a-hum with insects and astir with secret, darting, burrowing life, received the returned traveller into its dwellings with a wrecked, indifferent calm. Here, its cliffs and chasms and caves seemed to say, is your home; here you belong; you cannot get away, you do not wish to get away.

Macaulay was glad to have been in London during the Blitz. Many people felt unusually alive. Graham Greene felt working as an Air Raid Precautions (ARP) warden during the Blitz was the happiest time of his life. 'The nightly routine of sirens . . . the bomb-bursts moving nearer and then moving away, hold one like a love-charm.' The war, and the Blitz in particular, was also a time of legendary promiscuity, spurred by the threat of death. Venereal disease reached record levels, and prostitutes – already in a 'uniform' of furs and ankle chains – stood in dark doorways shining torches or bicycle lamps on their breasts.

American troops at the Rainbow Corner (an American serviceman's club in the former Del Monico's restaurant), corner of Shaftesbury Avenue and Denman Street, January 1945.

The United States joined the war in December 1941, and soon American troops came to Britain. The 'Yanks' were resented, particularly by British men, and subject to jibes of being 'over-paid, over-sexed and over here'. Americans had bubble gum, chocolate and silk stockings, and came from the glamorous Glenn Miller land of cars and fridges, or so British women imagined: in fact the American standard of living was not universally high, as many GI brides discovered.

Black American troops were a charming novelty to the British. In contrast to the racial enmity of the US, Britain had less prejudice, and many Londoners were appalled by American services' racism and segregation. This perceived racism was another justification for a larger and more complex resentment of Americans, which included seeming to have entered the war late. The dislike was mutual; talking to George Orwell, an American soldier confirmed anti-British feeling was widespread in the U.S. army, and said that when he arrived he had asked an American military policeman 'How's England?', only to receive the disgusted reply, 'The girls here walk out with niggers.'

It wasn't only Americans who had access to silk stockings: there was the 'spiv' or black-market wide boy, with a distinctively flash style – padded shoulders, showy tie, Ronald Colman moustache – that combined racecourse criminality with imagined transatlantic gangsterism. The transatlantic aspect had already appeared in pulp fiction with ersatz American-style crime writing of the sort pioneered by Peter Cheyney. Sometime head of Mosley's enforcers, the so-called 'Biff Boys', Cheyney was a prolific writer of books such as *Dames Don't Care* (1937) and *Dangerous Curves* (1939). This transatlantic tendency, and the cultural changes underlying it, was attacked by Orwell in his essays 'Decline of the English Murder' (1946), contrasting the meaningless Cleft Chin Murder of 1944 with the almost-cosiness of classic murders such as the Crippen case, and 'Raffles and Miss Blandish' (1944). The latter was directed against James Hadley Chase's sadistic 1939 novel *No Orchids for Miss Blandish*, but more generally against a mindset that found imaginary Chicago gangsterism more exciting than the real heroism of the French Resistance or the Blitz.

London's survival was so magnificent that even Germany wanted to share the glory. After early expectations that London would be completely destroyed, and any survivors reduced to panic, Germany now proclaimed that the British were a North European – virtually Germanic – race, and therefore at their best in adversity. When British bombing of Germany got seriously under way in 1943, propaganda minister Joseph Goebbels told his people to follow the example of the Londoners, but it did little good. German civilians suffered appallingly in the war, and morale was never comparable.

Already in 1943 the National Gallery held an exhibition entitled 'Rebuilding Britain', looking forward to post-war reconstruction. By the end, the war was less like a struggle between equals and more like an international operation against a rogue regime. Victory seemed a matter of time, but in 1944 the Blitz was followed by Germany's resort

The war ends: crowd near Piccadilly Circus, 8 May 1945.

to rocket weapons, with the v1 'doodlebug' falling on indiscriminate targets. The RAF had some success in intercepting doodlebugs and shooting them down, but they were succeeded by the v2, a full-on ballistic missile that was too fast to stop, and which is credited with 2,724 deaths and around 6,000 serious injuries.

Finally the war in Europe ended, on 8 May 1945. Damaged London erupted in celebrations of 've day', not only in Trafalgar Square and Piccadilly Circus but in the ordinary flags-and-tea street parties of east and south London. Along with relief, the expectation was that the post-war future would be better in every way.

7 Losing the Peace: 1945–77

'Nature makes her own garden in a blitzed site,' ran a 1945 photo feature: 'flowers now blooming in New Bond Street.' London was covered in bomb sites, stray cats and vegetation, and overgrown and moonlit ruins feature prominently in the dreamlike neo-Romantic art of the period.

Less romantically, it was a time of austerity and bureaucracy. Rationing was still in place. A seemingly ungrateful landslide vote against Churchill and for Labour ushered in the National Health Service, but the prolongation of wartime-style rules and regulations bred fears of a totalitarian future, as in George Orwell's *1984* – an anagram of 1948 – imagining a grey and shabby London a few decades into the future.

For sheer seediness Graham Greene had already matched it in 1936 with his 'Greeneland' London, and after the war it was worse: 'seediness has a very deep appeal . . . the sky-signs in Leicester Square, the "tarts" in Bond Street, the smell of cooking greens off Tottenham Court Road, the motor salesmen in Great Portland Street'. When he imagines showing London to a visitor, he slides from Trafalgar Square and Piccadilly Circus to 'the grim wastes of Queen Victoria Street and Tottenham Court Road . . . Great Portland Street because of the second-hand cars and the faded genial men with old school ties, Paddington for the vicious hotels . . . the Bloomsbury square with its inexpensive vice and its homesick Indians and its sense of rainy nostalgia'.

London needed cheering up, and in 1951 came the Festival of Britain. It was planned to revive the nation after post-war austerity,

Futuristic modernity at the 1951 Festival of Britain, showing the Skylon in the centre.

celebrate Britishness and develop the marshy South Bank area: 'to bring to the British way of life some enrichment that will endure for long after the Festival year is over', re-inhabiting 'this neglected and decayed area' ('so long abandoned by human enterprise') and consolidating the earlier development of County Hall and Waterloo train station south of the river. The Royal Festival Hall, from the original celebration, has become the nucleus of a culture site that now includes the National Theatre, the National Film Theatre and the Hayward Gallery.

The festival was the anniversary of the 1851 Great Exhibition, and it built on the tradition of Thames-side 'pleasure gardens' like Vauxhall Gardens, transforming Battersea Park with a tree walk and grotto. Visitors could see the Dome of Discovery, celebrating exploration and 'Outer Space', and celebrations of 'The Land' and 'The People' ('We are a people of mixed ancestry and now a blend of many different qualities'). A display themed on the royal Lion and Unicorn offered 'Clues to British character and tradition. The Lion symbolises action, the Unicorn imagination.' Combining education and 'highbrow' Henry Moore sculpture with a fairground atmosphere of candy floss and rides, the festival was a magnificent success, with over eight million visitors. Among them was the infant Ray Davies, of the Kinks: 'It made a lasting impression and made me believe there was a future.'

There was a Dan Dare futurity about the aluminium Dome of Discovery and the nearby Skylon, a cigar-shaped spire hovering on tensile wires. They are as modern as the Brussels Atomium, but more characteristic of London at the time was the steam railway that carried two million visitors through Battersea Park, designed by artist Rowland Emmett in a Heath Robinson style of retro-whimsy. Emmett's 'Far Tottering and Oyster Creek Branch Railway' featured three winsomely named locomotives with elements of steam train, paddle steamer and airship. Like much of Emmett's work – with its ornate birdcages, deckchairs, bowler hats and bathing huts, all existing in their own surreal space-age – it can be seen as a very English resistance to full-on transatlantic modernism, and perhaps a relief from the ruthless technology of the recent war and subsequent nuclear threat.

Variations on this can be seen in Ealing comedies, and the elaborate Edwardianism of Ronald Searle, along with several much-loved British films of the period featuring vintage cars (*Genevieve*, 1953), old railways (*The Titfield Thunderbolt*, 1953) and antique aviation (*Those Magnificent Men in Their Flying Machines*, 1965). It continues into the parodic gentlemanly style of John Steed in *The Avengers* (1961–9), with his umbrella and bowler hat, and Lady Penelope and her butler Parker in *Thunderbirds* (1965–6). London was becoming the capital of Retro.

Savile Row tailors tried to relaunch Edwardian style for men in the late 1940s, but with only limited success among the officer class it was aimed at. Instead it was taken up by working-class youth, the early 1950s Edwardian boys (later to be better known as Teddy boys). Early Edwardian boys could look remarkably respectable (eighteen-year-old Leonard Sims from Paddington, in a 1953 *Daily Mirror* article titled 'Why I Wear These Togs: A Teenage Edwardian Hits Back', wears an outfit that wouldn't be out of place on Gilbert and George). By the mid-1950s velvet collars and drape coats with Midwest accessories like the bootlace tie, originally thought of as 'Mississippi gambler' Ted style, became more ubiquitous, along with a taste for American rock 'n' roll, but almost from the start Teds – or 'cosh boys' as they were also known – were associated by the newspapers with violence. Writing to his friend Nancy Mitford, Evelyn Waugh's take on the situation moves from snobbish distaste to surreal deadpan at the expense of Cecil Beaton (society photographer, royal family favourite, and bona fide Savile Row dresser): 'Have you heard about "The Edwardians"? They are a gang of proletarian louts who dress like Beaton with braided trousers & velvet collars & murder one another in "Youth Centres" . . . Beaton is always being stopped now by the police and searched for knuckle-dusters.' The first great teenage style cult had arrived, complete with fears of 'juvenile delinquency'.

Thirty thousand people camped outside Buckingham Palace for the 1953 coronation of Elizabeth II, and the audience still stood for the national anthem at the end of cinema films, but times were changing. 'Sir,' said an angry letter in an early '50s issue of *Films and Filming*, 'Last night at my local Odeon, I stood at the end of the screening for the National Anthem. When I turned to leave, the cinema was empty, and I had been locked in!'

The standard of living was improving, and by 1957 Prime Minister Macmillan could say 'most of our people have never had it so good' (remembered as 'You've never had it so good'). Ordinary people owned washing machines, fridges, televisions and electric cookers – seen as clean and modern, compared to gas – in what would have seemed almost American luxury only a few years earlier. But more than just the wider availability of all mod cons, London was on the cusp of enormous transition, architecturally and demographically, in a period Roy Porter nicely calls 'old London's Indian summer', as he slides into something like a prose poem of the late '40s and early '50s:

> when the docks still thrived and the trams sailed majestically
> through pea-soupers; East Enders had their knees-up at the

The first great youth cult: Teddy boys.

pub and went hop-picking in August; contented commuters in Chessington tended their herbaceous borders; before it was finally killed by television, variety enjoyed its swansong at the Hackney and Deptford Empires, or Collins' at Islington. The coronation of Elizabeth II in 1953, when chummy neighbour-hood parties were staged in bunting-festooned streets, was the high spot of London as a prosperous, well-integrated, secure, safe city.

For the most part it was safe, and in 1954 Scotland Yard commander George Hatherill could reassure the public 'There are only about twenty murders a year in London and not all are serious – some are just husbands killing their wives.'

Foreign food was a rarity, pie-and-mash shops were popular, and a good deal of functional and even melancholy eating out was still done by single men who lived in 'digs' and lodgings, continuing the world of the cheap 'chop house'. Soho character Jeffrey Bernard remembered that when he left school in 1948, 'chicken was level with champagne in the luxury stakes':

> In most cafes then you could always spot the well off, the man who was doing well, because he was the one eating roast chicken. The rest of us were doomed to eat . . . mere steak and kidney pudding, roast lamb or fish and chips . . . A marvellous everyday meal you could get in workmen's cafes which you don't see any more was roast lamb, mashed potatoes and cabbage, all with proper gravy, for about two shillings and ninepence [about £4.50 today]. Now, you have to go to Simpson's for such food.

It was a city of heavily dressed white people, where navvies on building sites wore cheap suits as they swung pickaxes, and almost everyone smoked. The laureate of this post-war London is V. S. Pritchett, who captures it in his 1962 book *London Perceived*: an elegy, it now seems, for an already dated world of fish porters, bowler hats, grimy Victorian buildings and lower-middle-class respectability, all captured in a craftsman's prose that has dated like the monochrome photos. A flash of this world survives in Will Self's novel *Umbrella* (2012), where a character says, 'I'm old enough to remember when, in the waiting room of London suburban stations, you'd get a couple of oils of some civic dignitaries or other hung up on the wall and a stuffed bird or two in a glass case!'

It also lingers in the 1967 film *The London Nobody Knows*, based on one of Geoffrey Fletcher's classic London books. James Mason investigates a derelict theatre, and a public lavatory with goldfish, and strikes up a conversation with some painfully respectable homeless men in a Salvation Army hostel. The film's old-style wrecking ball, swung into buildings from a crane, represents the coming future, but there is no nostalgic animosity towards it. Change seemed positive and necessary.

Post-war social housing brought new towns such as Stevenage and Milton Keynes, and modernist council estates such as Roehampton and Thamesmead, where 17,000 homes were built in concrete. The feel of Thamesmead can be judged from the fact that it was used as a set for *A Clockwork Orange* (1971), the film of Anthony Burgess's futuristic 1962 novel about ultra-violent teenagers.

Modern architecture looked good in architects' models but brought problems when real people lived in it. With ground-level communities destroyed by modernization, women found themselves moved to high rises on distant estates where they saw no one all day. In tears by the time their husbands returned from work, they were diagnosed with 'depression' and prescribed pills. With pissed-in lifts routinely out of order, tower blocks bred loneliness, fear, crime and vandalism, and high rises that might have offered tremendous views for some were a disaster with a wider spread of population that included the vulnerable, the unhappy and the predatory. Novelist Jake Arnott describes a thinly disguised Broadwater Farm estate, scene of riot:

The Hardcastle estate seemed to have no other purpose than to stage endlessly repeated dramas of public disorder. It was what it was designed for. Its labyrinth of forecourts, low-rise walkways and access balconies, blind alleys of fear and danger. Its highrise vantage points a silhouette of menace. Its whole architecture was a solid fortress of deprivation.

London's high-rise housing has its great monument in Trellick Tower, by Erno Goldfinger, rising 31 storeys over Notting Hill. Ian Fleming disliked Goldfinger's early work in Hampstead so much he borrowed his name for a Bond villain, but he was spared Trellick: construction began in 1968, three years after his death.

Trellick has since been rehabilitated, but for a while it was hated, and the reputation of high rises – made worse by the tragic collapse of Ronan Point in 1968 – was tainted with failed social policy. The negative connotations were exploited by J. G. Ballard in his 1975 novel *High Rise*, where the inhabitants of a tower block – more middle-class this time, like the Barbican – descend into savagery.

High residential blocks were built particularly in deprived boroughs (Newham and Tower Hamlets had over a hundred each), but high-rise building was all over central London after a period of speculative office building that wrecked whole swathes of the city. Architect Richard Seifert built over four hundred blocks: it has since become clear that his real genius was not architecture, but getting around planning regulations. His most celebrated building, the 34-storey Centre Point, was completed in 1966 for developer

Erno Goldfinger's Brutalist landmark, Trellick Tower (1972), looming over the Golborne Road, west London.

Harry Hyams, who left it standing empty – in a city with a major homelessness problem – to watch its value increase. Built on the old St Giles Circus, it is striking from a distance but awkward at pavement level.

The 1960s were a period of architectural devastation across London, and the loss of Euston Arch in 1962 was a landmark for conservation fears. Two attractive gatehouse or lodge structures survive – currently as bars – but the arch itself, a classical portico with monumental pillars, was demolished to make what was for years an exceptionally bleak concrete piazza in a Seifert development. Its fountain-ish water feature, now removed, was about as far from a fountain on the life-loving Continental model as you could get; it looked more like a machine for the industrial dissemination of cholera. There has recently been a visionary campaign to restore the arch, but it is fighting against the odds.

Goodbye London (1973) is a key book of the time. Even Covent Garden was almost razed. Quiet and deserted after the vegetable market moved to Nine Elms in the early '70s, the area is atmospherically remembered by Michael Bracewell as 'mostly derelict; violin menders and esoteric bookshops kept their air of the 1930s'. Scheduled for replacement by high-rise building and a dual carriageway, it was saved by a public campaign and the intervention of central government, who thwarted the demolition-happy London council of the day by giving the buildings 'listed' (protected) status.

More than architecture, migration changed the London landscape for ever. Back in 1939 Orwell wrote: 'What we always forget is that the overwhelming bulk of the British proletariat does not live in Britain, but in Asia and Africa.' But Britain granted citizenship to those living in the Commonwealth in the 1948 Nationality Act, and soon large numbers of this formerly invisible group did live in Britain. The *Empire Windrush* arrived from Jamaica in 1948, carrying around five hundred passengers: among them was calypso artist Lord Kitchener, with his new song 'London is the Place for Me'.

Black people were not new in London. There had been 'Moors' in Elizabethan times, and unemployed black men congregated around St Giles in the eighteenth and nineteenth centuries. There were so many following the American War of Independence, after the British freed American slaves, that the government attempted to settle around four hundred of 'the Black Poor of London' in Sierra Leone. Black people lived in London as domestic servants in the eighteenth century, with their own clubs and drinking venues, but they were largely single. Now, in the 1940s, Caribbean men and women were coming to stay and have families: by 1961 around 177,000 had arrived, 100,000 of those in London. Anxieties about immigration led to the 1962 Commonwealth Immigration Act, causing an increase in immigration as Commonwealth citizens rushed to get in before the gate closed. In 1959 there were around 3,000 arrivals from India and Pakistan, and 16,000 from the Caribbean; in 1961 this jumped to 48,000 and 66,000 respectively.

Many Caribbeans settled in the Brixton area after being housed in a former air-raid shelter at Clapham South, with Brixton as its closest labour exchange, while others became tenants of the notorious slum landlord Peter Rachman in Notting Hill. Notting Hill (or

Regulars at the Portobello Road pub the Piss House (or the Colville, now the Distillery), 1969.

'Rotting Hill') was by now a deeply run-down area, reaching its psychic nadir at 10 Rillington Place, now demolished, where the seedily respectable-looking Reginald Christie murdered at least seven women, and his unfortunate lodger Timothy Evans was hanged in error; Christie himself was hanged in 1953. Notting Hill flared into so-called 'race riots' in 1958 when Teddy boys attacked the black population; sporadic trouble continued over three days, followed by the fatal stabbing of Kelso Cochrane, from Antigua, on the Golborne Road in May the following year. Community initiatives after the murder, for which no one was ever arrested, led to the foundation of the now famous Notting Hill Carnival.

Cosmopolitanism in the '50s was concentrated in Soho. The old Continental district, with French and Italian restaurants and delicatessens, was tinged with vice by the 1930s, and a clutch of high-profile murders sealed the area's rackety reputation. This grew stronger, with the spivs and mobsters of the '40s giving the area a popular reputation for transatlantic-style gangsterism and pimping, and the rise of 'clip joints' fleecing punters who hoped to meet prostitutes. Meanwhile Soho and Fitzrovia had a Bohemian scene of artists and writers, with the poet Tambimuttu warning Julian Maclaren-Ross that if he spent time drinking in Soho he would catch 'Soho-itis' and get nothing done. It was concentrated on clubs like the Gargoyle and Mandrake, the French House pub (still there) and the Colony Room (or 'Muriel's'), a famously bitchy drinking club – a necessity for drinkers, when pubs were legally shut in the afternoons – behind a green door up a flight of stairs on Dean Street, frequented by Francis Bacon. Soho was a playground for the rest of London, and its French, Italian, Polish and Greek restaurants were joined in the '50s by a new Chinatown, moved from the bombed-out district of Limehouse.

With black clubs like the Big Apple on Gerrard Street – before it became Chinatown – Soho was already associated with jazz and music venues. The 100 Club on Oxford Street, originally the Feldman Swing Club, had been a venue for jitterbugging during the war, and Ronnie Scott's and the Marquee arrived in the late '50s. There was a particularly happening scene in the early '60s at the Flamingo Club on Wardour Street, associated with Mods and rhythm and blues, and where Georgie Fame and the Blue Flames played as house band. Johnny Gunnell, involved in running it, remembered their 'Do the Dog' had a sensuality whereby 'even the most coolly suburban members of the audience could not fail to be moved to an almost jungle-like frenzy'. Not everyone liked the idea of jungle frenzy, including the home secretary, Henry Brooke, and in 1964 he commissioned a report into what was going on: council infiltrators reported 'traffic in "pep pills" and . . . a great deal of "necking" especially with coloured people. In this atmosphere any young person is obviously in serious moral danger.'

Something was starting to bend: deference to authority and hierarchy was weakening. The spies Burgess and Maclean fled to Russia in 1955, and a journalist's article in the *Spectator* suddenly popularized the idea of 'what I call The Establishment': a network of conservative power and privilege soon understood to mean senior civil servants, the Foreign Office, MI5, the BBC, old Etonians and the rest. Suddenly it was possible to be 'anti-Establishment'. When John Osborne's play *Look Back in Anger* (1956) premiered at Sloane Square's Royal Court Theatre it caused shock waves – from the squalor of putting an ironing board on stage, as much as anything else – and launched the media idea of the Angry Young Men (a disparate bunch of writers from Kingsley Amis to Doris Lessing, shunted together in a publicity exercise).

There was an early '60s satire boom, and in 1961 Peter Cook founded the Establishment Club – a satirical comedy club, with jazz – on Soho's Greek Street. The other Establishment took some hard knocks in the period, with the 1955 spy scandal followed by the Suez crisis and the Profumo affair. But still the Establishment seemed to be surviving: when Macmillan's Tory government was returned to power in 1959 he announced that 'the class war is obsolete' before forming the most upper-class government in memory, including three earls, a marquess and a duke who also happened to be his nephew.

The possibility of nuclear annihilation was not so funny. The Campaign for Nuclear Disarmament (CND), launched in 1958 with

The 2i's Coffee Bar in Soho, *c.* 1959.

a rally in Trafalgar Square, followed by a march to Aldermaston, became another anti-Establishment force. It attracted all ages, overlapping at the younger end with an art college world of existentialism, jazz and duffel coats. The seriousness of the cause was confirmed by the Cuban Missile Crisis of 1962, and the real threat of nuclear war, attended with paranoia about a sinister infrastructure involving underground bunkers and secret government plans, made life feel interim and precarious.

As authority was slipping, youth was rising, with the celebrated appearance of 'teenagers' as a post-war group with money to spend and their own identity. Youth had a new coffee bar culture, just as their elders had pubs: the first cafe to have a real Italian espresso machine, the Moka Bar on Frith Street, had been opened in 1953 by Gina Lollobrigida. By 1958 the teenage coffee and music scene was parodied in the movie *Expresso Bongo*, with Cliff Richard as the charmingly named pop star Bongo Herbert.

After the Teds, London Mods and Rockers fed newspaper scare stories with their Brighton day-trip fighting around 1964. Mods – the label came originally from hip 'modern' jazz fans, as opposed to traditional jazz fans – were at the forefront of youth consumerism, with their close attention to sharp and often Italianate dressing, record-buying and customized scooters. Mod band the Who released their first LP, *My Generation*, in 1965, and Pete Townshend – who described their music as 'anti-middle-age, anti-boss-class and anti-young-marrieds' – told numerous outlets of the music press that 'the big social revolution' of the last five years was that youth was now more important than age.

British music seemed to be changing the world after the Beatles conquered America in 1964. Along with the Beatles and their supposedly more dangerous counterparts, the Rolling Stones, came other world-class bands including the Kinks and the Yardbirds. Music and Mod fashion, particularly the style of the more foppish 'smooth Mods', came together with the so-called 'permissive society', and before long it was the Swinging Sixties. Originally a pejorative term to suggest things were going too far, by the time of Frank Habicht's 1967 photography book *Swinging London: Permissive Paradise*, the word 'permissive' had taken on a voyeuristic promise, and a central connotation of sexual freedom. Censorship had been defeated at the *Lady Chatterley* trial of 1960 (remembered for the judge's thoroughly Establishment question to the jury, 'Is this a book you would like your wife or servants to read?'); the contraceptive pill arrived in 1961 (at first it could only be prescribed to married women); and miniskirts were pioneered by King's Road fashion designer Mary Quant from around 1962. In the flippantly melancholic lines of Philip Larkin's poem 'Annus Mirabilis', 'Sexual intercourse began / In nineteen sixty-three' between the *Chatterley* ban and the Beatles' first LP ('which was rather late for me').

Vogue editor Diana Vreeland pronounced London 'the most swinging city in the world' in 1965, but there was something more radical to come: excited by more than just records and fashion, the so-called 'underground' scene was both druggier and more political. There was an early gathering of the tribe with the International

Poetry Incarnation, at the Albert Hall in June 1965, when Allen Ginsberg and others read to an audience of 7,000 – many of them young men still in jackets and ties. The London Free School was established in Notting Hill the following year; not much was taught, but it led to the founding of the *International Times* newspaper, central – with *Oz* magazine – to the underground press. Underground papers had a distinctive graphic style, often highly sexualized, so a political article might be illustrated with topless women or porno-graphic cartoons. The papers increased their readership with personal contact ads: 'FORTY PLUS GUY, very square, wants way out dolly to make life interesting, own flat and Jag'; 'Is there any female who wants a place to live for free, if so she can share a bed with me'; 'Beautiful coloured swinger needed to occupy spare seat Ravi Shankar recital.'

Having started with jazz musicians, 'spades' smoking 'reefers', and a few merchant seamen, cannabis was now more popular. Indica, the cool bookshop and gallery in Mason's Yard, near Jermyn Street, where John Lennon met Yoko Ono, took its name from *Cannabis indica*, and by the time that *Time* magazine's 1966 cover article on LONDON – THE SWINGING CITY ('every decade has its city') said London had so much green space 'you can walk across it on the grass', grass had a sniggery double-meaning. *Time* went on to say 'In a decade dominated by youth, London has burst into bloom. It swings, it is the scene.'

There were weirder scenes on offer, and LSD offered a potentially life-changing experience. The Beatles first took it in 1965, leading to the LP *Revolver* (1966) and on to *Sgt Pepper's Lonely Hearts Club Band* (1967), and it was associated with the UFO club on Tottenham Court Road – the name standing for 'unidentified flying objects', which were part of a quasi-mystical zeitgeist, and 'unlimited freak out'. UFO music was provided by Soft Machine and Pink Floyd, with stroboscopic and oil-pattern light shows. There was a magnificent culture clash when Pink Floyd were given a hostile BBC interview by musicologist Hans Keller (Syd Barrett responds earnestly and politely, while Roger Waters is cockier): currently available on YouTube, it is an extraordinary moment from a bygone broadcasting

Carnaby Street, mid-Swinging Sixties.

culture, like Huw Wheldon's avuncular 1957 interview with a young Jimmy Page and his skiffle group.

The summer of 1967 was the Summer of Love. London blossomed further with the American-style hippy culture of long hair and 'flower power'. Scantily clad, sometimes body-painted chicks with heavy eye make-up could be seen grooving at outdoor concerts and rallies in those grassy parks. Eastern religion, joss sticks and the *I Ching* were in the air, along with 'ley lines' in the sacred English landscape (in the words of Barry Miles, 'The King's Road led straight to Glastonbury in those days').

London was the grooviest city in the world, and a quiet street behind Liberty's department store – Carnaby Street, formerly associated with the second-hand motor trade – was soon known to tourists as a fashion centre. London boutiques included Granny Takes a Trip (on the King's Road) and I Was Lord Kitchener's Valet (on Portobello Road) with the more elaborate end of army surplus, where Jimi Hendrix bought his hussar jacket.

The work of Peter Blake, designer of the *Sgt Pepper* cover collage, shows Swinging London's retro element. Art Nouveau, old advertising and Lord Kitchener pointing his finger were all popular, and Victoriana – totally unfashionable, outside of a little cult, for much of the twentieth century, with the Albert Memorial regarded as laugh-out-loud kitsch well into the 1950s – was all the rage, with chaises longues and Aubrey Beardsley (subject of a major V&A exhibition in 1966). Tourist London was a kaleidoscopic whirl of old and new, with Union Jacks and Carnaby Street, guardsmen and hippies, miniskirts and Tower Bridge. London was simultaneously embarked on 'apeing its past' (in the words of London writer Benny Green) and there was a canny take on this in Agatha Christie's *At Bertram's Hotel* (1965). Set in a quiet backwater of the West End, both the hotel (with its Edwardiana and kippers and marmalade and afternoon teas) and even most of the clientele (old dowagers and clergymen and retired officers) seem almost too old-fashioned and parodic to be true. And they are, because the whole thing is a gigantic criminal front.

The full-blown, high '60s, Granny Takes a Trip world was for a relatively elite few. Most people only glimpsed it in newspaper stories like the Redlands drug bust, when Mick Jagger and Keith Richards were arrested in the company of a half-undressed Marianne Faithfull and Etonian art dealer Robert 'Groovy Bob' Fraser, and the image of Jagger and Fraser handcuffed together became a print by Pop artist Richard Hamilton, *Swingeing London* (1968–9). Fewer people hung out at Indica, Gandalf's Garden (a King's Road tea shop) and the rest than we now imagine, and ordinary life went on in a world of privet hedges and overdone beef. Robert Irwin, who was 'there', remembers you still had to go a long way to find a sitar or a *Dr Strange* comic, and in the words of David Widgery, an East End GP involved with the underground press, 'All you need is love, but a private income and the sort of parents who would have a Chinese smoking jacket in the attic help.'

Ordinary life might not have been so groovy, but the standard of living continued to rise. Central heating, fitted carpets and foreign holidays became widespread, along with hire purchase ('the never-never') and telephones – although less than half of homes had them, and telephone boxes were widely used. 'Serving hatches' started to appear. Unmodernized homes (before the 'through lounge' was knocked through) would usually have two small rooms downstairs: a front room with a black and white television, and a dining room with a table. On top of the TV might be a budgerigar or canary, and in the kitchen, behind the back room, a kettle might be whistling on the gas hob. Tea, rather than coffee, would be drunk by older people; younger people might drink instant coffee. Cheap roasts were routine, prawn cocktail was sophisticated, and avocado pears were becoming better known, but people were not sure how to eat them, perhaps confused by the word 'pear' (back in the '50s James Bond had one for dessert). Olive oil was hardly known in cooking, but you could buy it at the chemist's to soften ear wax. Indian restaurants were not common, and dried Vesta packets offered much-loved approximations of foreign food including chow mein (with crispy noodles to be fried separately) and beef curry with sultanas.

Katharine Whitehorn's best-seller *Cooking in a Bedsitter* began life in 1961 as *Kitchen in the Corner*, but was reprinted with the more zeitgeisty Bedsitter title from 1965 to 1970. The single girl in London was becoming a new type, with secretaries in bedsitters and flat shares catered for by books like Jane Reed's 1965 *Girl about Town* ('How to live in London – and love it!'). They could shop at the boutique Biba, where fashions with a nod to the 1920s and Deco eras were reaching a wider audience, just as quality design was becoming more mass market with Terence Conran's Habitat.

The class system was weakening (but in a way that was still class-obsessed: the main angle in any profile of a working-class lad 'made good' was his working-class origins). Grammar schools encouraged social mobility, Mods saw themselves as working-class aristocrats by virtue of their consumer tastes, and Prime Minister Harold Wilson said he preferred tinned salmon to smoked salmon (and 'with vinegar').

East End boys were dating West End girls, and certain 'classless' professions were rising, such as actor, model and hairdresser (only a decade earlier, Vidal Sassoon had had to change his accent: 'In those days, you couldn't get hired in the more fashionable West End with an Artful Dodger accent like mine'; 'I went to the theatre week after week to hear English the way it was meant to be spoken'). Photographers were particularly fashionable, with Terence Donovan (Cockney, born in Stepney), Lord Litchfield (Eton and Guards), David Bailey (born in Leytonstone) and the sports-car-driving, modern-jazz-listening photographer in Antonioni's 1966 *Blow-up*. Espionage seemed like another 'lifestyle' career: Michael Caine (born Maurice Micklewhite in Southwark, his mother a char-lady) brought his charisma to Len Deighton's innovatively prosaic spy, Harry Palmer. Palmer is emphatically not Bond – that is the point of him – but he likes real coffee (freshly ground at home, even) and he shops in Soho for Continental food, leading to the classic line 'You're quite a gourmet, aren't you, Palmer?'

The class shake-up extended to blurring the boundaries of criminality, the Establishment and celebrity. The photos in David Bailey's 1965 portfolio *A Box of Pin-ups* feature not only Michael Caine, Jean

Michael Caine at home with his mother Ellen Micklewhite and brother Stanley, 1964.

Shrimpton and Mick Jagger, but the Kray twins, Reggie and Ronnie (who also had an entrée, via Ronnie's homosexuality, to the world of Lord Boothby and Tom Driberg, totally alien to older-style London gangsters like Jack Spot and Billy Hill). Sharp dressers, the Krays were in many ways conservative figures, and Ron – the more unstable one – would psyche himself up by swinging an axe and glugging gin from the bottle while listening to a gramophone record of Churchill's speeches.

Along with peace and love, violence was in the air: anyone indiscriminately nostalgic for pubs of the 1960s and '70s – then much more numerous, including endless bad pubs in bad areas – should remember the words 'Who are you looking at?' The first generation of skinheads, a wilfully proletarian youth cult related to 'hard' Mods, inspired real fear in the streets, stoked up by rumours and friend-of-a-friend stories of their atrocities. 'Aggro' and 'bovver' (as in 'bovver boots', usually ox-blood Doc Martens) were major words of the time, from the oddly genteel gangland euphemisms 'aggravation' and 'a bit of bother'. Skinheads particularly loathed hippies – soft, middle-class, long-haired, studenty and left-wing – and immigrants, despite their own love of Jamaican ska and reggae. 'Paki-bashing' was another phrase of the '70s that no one could be nostalgic for.

'Race relations' were at an all-time low. 'Mugging', a nineteenth-century British word, had come back from America to mean black street robbery. Enoch Powell, a former professor of classics with his memorably odd Old Testament name, was a popular figure with sections of the working class after his 1968 'rivers of blood' speech predicting racial violence, and 1,000 Powellite dock workers marched from the East End to parliament.

The economy was in trouble, with unemployment, high inflation, militant trade unionism – the docks, in particular, were having their death throes hastened by strikes – and a decline in manufacturing. The Northern Ireland troubles hit the mainland with IRA bombs going off – including one at the Post Office Tower in 1971, after which its high-tech revolving restaurant was closed – and there was more intellectually driven trouble from the Angry Brigade, who bombed the house of the home secretary. Ted Heath's government was hit by the oil crisis, a miners' strike, the three-day week and television technicians' strikes. With no television and no electricity, families played board games by candlelight.

The underground had evolved into an 'alternative' scene – as in the seminal paperback guide *Alternative London*, which first appeared in 1970 – associated with the squatting movement, but embracing everything from civil liberties to macrobiotics. The listings magazine *Time Out* began as part of the same scene, featuring music, cinema and a political 'agitprop' section of demonstrations: anti-apartheid, gay and women's issues, and 'Troops Out of Ireland'.

There was a sense of late blooming and going to seed. Biba had expanded from a small boutique to a larger boutique (bombed by the Angry Brigade) and then to a seven-storey Art Deco department store in the old Derry & Toms building – famous for its roof gardens – selling its own glamorously branded baked beans. Glam rock was in the air. As well as the latest news of small Trotskyite factions you might want to join, *Time Out* carried ads for water beds; the height of luxury. Along with patches for denim and 'executive toys' such as chrome Newton's cradles, Carnaby Street and Kensington Market were selling cocaine-themed jewellery, with spoons and silver razor blades popular as pendants. Cowboy boots were popular, and Mexican moustaches. By the time the Eagles' 'Hotel California' was being played in every jeans shop and tourist restaurant, around 1977, serious changes were on the cards. The era of punk and Mrs Thatcher was coming.

The Sex Pistols posing in a skip, 1977.

8 Jack the Hipster

Punk confirmed London as a world driver of subculture. Punks were depicted by the tabloids as the violent dregs of society, but the average punk was more likely to be an art student. It was spearheaded by the Sex Pistols, who grouped around the King's Road clothes shop Sex (1974–6; Seditionaries from 1976–80; since 1980 World's End, with its backward-spinning clock). Sex was run by Vivienne Westwood, who still owns World's End, and Malcolm McLaren, the Sex Pistols' manager. McLaren channelled the enduring London influence of Dickens into his Oliver Twist-style accounts of what he was up to, describing himself as Fagin, with Johnny Rotten and the band as the Artful Dodger and the urchins.

The Pistols' single 'God Save the Queen' (1977) kicked against the Queen's Silver Jubilee of that year, in which the monarchy showed itself still capable of inspiring street parties with tea and bunting, like something from the 1940s. By 1977 the monarchy was looking like the icing on an increasingly rotten cake, and the run-down state of London can be seen in *Uninhabited London*, Jon Savage's photos of derelict North Kensington.

Industrial relations and 'race relations' – a phrase of the day – seemed to be reaching an all-time low, and in 1977 the Clash recorded 'White Riot', inspired by trouble at the Notting Hill Carnival. Extreme times provoked extreme reaction: in 1979 Margaret Thatcher was elected, beginning a decade in which she defeated the unions and massively expanded the policy of selling off social council housing (which had already been begun by the Greater London Council).

The Thatcher years were marked by greed (parodied in comedian Harry Enfield's character 'Loadsamoney', a flash, ignorant builder); the rise of 'Yuppies' (straight, affluent, upbeat 'young urban professionals'); and a new excitement about the City financial district, ignited by the 1986 deregulation of the stock exchange (the 'Big Bang'). City-style striped shirts became popular casual wear. The regenerated City put new energy into east London, as the centre of the city seemed to shift eastwards, and the Thatcher decade has a physical monument in Canary Wharf and the new Docklands area (the bleakness of the old Docklands in its last years can be seen in the 1980 gangster film *The Long Good Friday*).

All this was accompanied by a more niche interest in the old East End, which seemed like an exotically unmodernized district existing in a time warp. In the words of Patrick Wright on Dalston, 'you can drop in on previous decades with no more effort than it takes to open a shop door. Pizzey's High Class Florist is still trading out of the Fifties, and the Star Bakery (a little further down the road) offers immediate access to the decade before that.'

There was particular interest in the Spitalfields area, old Ripper territory with semi-derelict Georgian houses and a Hawksmoor church. Near the church was the thoroughly unmodernized Market Cafe, the haunt of artists Gilbert and George, where asking if there was anything vegetarian would bring the reply 'Prunes and custard.'

Spitalfields was a centre of the 1980s New Georgian movement, related to the 'Young Fogeys' and deeply conservative in style (though not necessarily in politics). The New Georgians would 'follow the architecture' into run-down areas, and had an effect on gentrification. Their worldview was distilled into the 1985 *New Georgian Handbook*, modelled on the immensely popular *Official Sloane Ranger Handbook* from a couple of years earlier: a handy aspirational manual of upper-class lifestyle, disguised as satire. Even the *New Georgian Handbook* had the very '80s strapline 'Conservation keeps you moving swiftly (upwards).'

Meanwhile in the world of modernity, design was all the rage, with a temple in Paul Smith's clothing and accessories shop in Covent Garden. Deyan Sudjic's *Cult Objects* (1985) was a book of the moment, celebrating Anglepoise lamps, Barbour jackets and the Mont Blanc fountain pen, a 1980s fetish object. There was further attention to hip detail in the 'style culture'-themed new breed of men's magazines: as well as music and current affairs, both *The Face* (from 1980) and the more mainstream *Arena* (from 1986) thrived on a new male consumerism that had a strong continuity with Mod.

The more alternative style magazine *i-D* had closer links to the burgeoning post-punk club scene. The New Romantic movement was born at the Blitz club in Covent Garden, the Batcave in Soho's Meard Street was the centre of London Goth, and there was a more outré, polysexual scene at Leigh Bowery's Taboo club. Coolest of all was probably the Wag club in Soho, where David Bowie and even Robert De Niro might show up.

The hardcore partying of the 1980s was dancing on a narrow ledge. AIDS was a constant fear, and many of the key players lived in squats or 'hard to let' council flats (a policy of the time) in what

Homelessness in Spitalfields, with Christ Church in the background.

still seemed like distant, grim areas of east and south London. The world was troubled; Britain was locked in the miners' strike during 1984–5, and there was ongoing fear of America's cruise missile programme (bringing CND centre stage again), combined with larger anti-Americanism. Ronald Reagan was seen as a joke figure, and there was youth and student sympathy for Russia: Cyrillic writing was suddenly cool enough to appear on clothing in Camden Market and Soho, and 'Support the Miners' posters were designed in Russian Constructivist style.

Highly visible homelessness and begging came back during the Thatcher era, accompanying her declared return to 'Victorian values'. It is easy to forget street poverty had meanwhile almost disappeared. I found an elderly woman sleeping in the doorway of my building on Tavistock Place one morning, and a shanty town of cardboard boxes, 'Cardboard City', sprang up near Waterloo in 1983 (lasting into the late '90s). Lincoln's Inn Fields became another homeless encampment.

A 1986 Church of England report, *Faith in the City*, noted the decay of London's social fabric. Some estates were becoming 'areas which have a quite different social and economic system . . . the degeneration of many such areas has now gone so far that they are in effect "separate territories" outside the mainstream of our social and economic life.' As social historian Roy Porter pointed out, the concerns of *Faith in the City* echoed the Victorian 'darkest England' reports in books like the Reverend Mearns's *Bitter Cry of Outcast London* (1883).

Racism was exacerbated by the migrant influx of the 1970s, and Asians on run-down estates had burning paper pushed through their letterboxes. Many black people felt aggressed by heavy-handed policing (caricatured in the offence of 'wearing a loud tie in a built-up area'). Black youth suffered from 'stop and search' or 'sus' (suspicion) tactics, but at the same time there was predatory behaviour and street crime, and some streets in Brixton became virtual no-go zones.

Brixton went up in flames in April 1981 during the Brixton Riots: a hundred vehicles were set alight and 280 policemen injured. There were more riots in Tottenham in 1985, centred on the Broadwater Farm Estate, in which a policeman, Colin Blakelock, was killed. Three young men – from three different ethnic groups – who were arrested and convicted were widely thought to have been framed, to play down a 'race' aspect to the disturbance, and their convictions were eventually overturned.

In 1989 Mrs Thatcher introduced the poll tax, or 'community charge', disregarding the principle of taxation according to income, and in 1990 around 200,000 people attended a rally in Kennington Park before marching on Trafalgar Square. Fighting with the police broke out and the West End was trashed, including the burning of Covent Garden 'yuppie' wine bars. King Mob was back, and it was one of his better efforts, helping to bring down Mrs Thatcher, who resigned that year. Mixed feelings towards the event – far from wholly negative – can be seen in John Bartlett's 3.7 metre (12 ft) *History Painting* in the Museum of London, which gives an idealized picture of a battle in Trafalgar Square with nods towards Renaissance painters like Pierro della Francesca and Uccello.

Mrs Thatcher was succeeded by John Major and his more anodyne brand of Conservatism, which accompanied an unexpected mutation in popular culture. Ecstasy (MDMA), acid house and the rave scene came in at the very end of the '80s, spelling the death of 'style culture'. The more elitist scene of clubs like the Wag gave way to house music venues like Ministry of Sound in Elephant and Castle, which arrived in 1991. The Ecstasy scene was more proletarian than previous student or hippy drug cultures, overlapping with the world of the soccer terraces. MDMA-fuelled raves, often at semi-secret, last-minute gathering places in warehouses or the countryside, offered thousands a communal, empathetic experience of oneness with each other in an unselective solidarity. The clubbing subculture also spawned a fantastically inventive art form in its flyers, which became almost as much a part of the landscape as the 'tart cards' that filled London phone boxes in the '80s and '90s.

'Britpop', led by bands such as Pulp and Blur, arrived together with the Young British Artists (YBA) scene associated with Damien Hirst, Tracy Emin and art dealer Jay Jopling. Britpop was steeped in a jokey Britishness and London experience: 1995 saw Jarvis Cocker sing about going to Saint Martin's art college ('Common People'), living in a horrible block in Mile End ('Mile End') and getting rave tickets from 'some fucked-up bloke in Camden Town' ('Sorted for E's & Wizz'). Meanwhile Blur were accused of speaking 'mockney', as faux-cockney public schoolboys. London was once again 'the coolest city on the planet' (according to a 1996 cover story in the American magazine *Newsweek*, 'London Rules: Inside the World's Coolest City'). This was the era of 'Cool Britannia', and it had something of the '60s about it, including the rehabilitation of the Union Jack – tainted by extremist politics – into a fun fashion item, Carnaby Street-style.

As Britpop lost impetus, the comparatively inane Spice Girls (one of whom described Mrs Thatcher as 'the first Spice Girl'[4]) moved centre stage, complete with Geri Halliwell's iconic Union

Poll tax demonstration, 1990.

Jack dress. Modernity, populism and so-called 'dumbing-down' were hallmarks of the later '90s, and this populist momentum continued into the millennium, when some of London's most famous retailers rebranded themselves with more demotic advertising, massively expanding a trend that was arguably there already in the 1980s with V&A advertising ('An ace caff with quite a nice museum attached'). Shops trying to shift their market appeal included a royal jewellers (with 'bling bling' and 'rock hard') and a venerable gentleman's outfitters (with 'Are you looking at me?' – a question appropriate to dandyism, but more commonly associated with starting fights). Lillywhites sport shop was a pioneer, having revived its fortunes by going downmarket and shifting the emphasis from tennis to training shoes.

Tony Blair and 'New Labour' came to power in 1997, ruling in the name of 'the People'. Almost apolitical compared with the class war of 'Old Labour', New Labour continued Mrs Thatcher's rejection of the unions, and New Labour politician Peter Mandelson was famously quoted assuring American businessmen that New Labour were 'intensely relaxed about people getting filthy rich' (to be fair, the full statement was '. . . as long as they pay their taxes'). The public grief that followed the death of Princess Diana in 1997, with over a million bouquets laid at Kensington Palace, gave Tony Blair a chance to describe her as 'the People's Princess'.

New Labour-style modernity involved the erasure of a supposedly irrelevant past, but meanwhile the writer Iain Sinclair became the leading name in London writing with an opposing project of 'not forgetting' – and remembering, in particular, the history and associations of place. Sinclair's work helped put 'psychogeography' on the map. He had been writing quietly since the 1970s, and his book *Lud Heat* (1975) had inspired Peter Ackroyd's best-selling *Hawksmoor* (1985), launching a cult around the supposedly arcane and occult aspects of Hawksmoor's early eighteenth-century churches.

Sinclair and Ackroyd were at the fore of London writing, as Ackroyd picked up resonances of a supposedly eternal past and Sinclair explored a mixture of the esoteric, the low-life and the disappearing, like old-style London 'caffs'. Psychogeography was a reaction against a new blandness and placelessness spreading across the city, with redevelopment and plate glass everywhere. Dennis Severs's recreated time-capsule house became a cult destination, celebrated by Ackroyd in his foreword to Severs's book *18 Folgate Street: A House in Spitalfields*. The magic of London seemed to be endangered, crystallized for me by the disappearance of an extraordinary conjuring shop opposite the British Museum: it is now a branch of Starbucks.

For better or worse, London was modernizing: the impressive new British Library in King's Cross replaced the much-loved but increasingly impractical British Museum Reading Room, with its blue dome ceiling. Less popular was the Millennium Dome. It has since redeemed itself as the O2 Arena, but its origin in the ill-conceived Millennium celebrations looked like a symptom of a society that had lost its way. Compared with the pride and clear mission of the 1851 Great Exhibition and the 1951 Festival of Britain, the human achievements celebrated by the Dome seemed chosen so as not to offend anyone: they included Shakespeare, Easter Island, Florence Nightingale, television, the fall of the Berlin Wall and the sandwich. The sandwich came in for particular ridicule.

Also in 2000 but a world away from millennial sandwiches, on an estate in Peckham, a studious ten-year-old named Damilola Taylor bled to death after being jabbed with glass by bullying youths. Damilola was from Nigeria – his family had come to London in search of a better life – while his attackers were Peckham-born black youth, and his death exposed lethal rifts in the supposed black 'community'. The Damilola case also launched the phrase 'feral youth', and a couple of years later Jonathan Miller could talk about 'gangs of feral children' in Camden: 'Call it middle-class timidity, but at night there are these gangs wearing their hoods and you really do need to avoid making eye contact with them.' London was becoming afraid of its youth, with so-called 'hoodie' culture, and if anyone failed to get the point there was a book entitled *Our Kids Are Going to Hell* (2009), with a text by Iain Sinclair and photos of drug raids in Hackney.

Multicultural London spawned music genres such as jungle (associated with the Blue Note club in Hoxton), dubstep and grime, but at the same time 'gangsta' values turned some estates into something like open-plan prisons. For many kids a gang seemed the only route to status, identity and not being a victim, as the young male peer group became the decisive social unit: it went with the all-importance of wearing the right brands and speaking the right speak, and an epidemic of youth-on-youth knife crime.

Race and ethnicity were now as central as the former grip of social class had been, and the all-purpose respectful address of 'guv' gave way to 'bruv' (replacing the social deference of 'guv'nor' with the black-to-black 'brother'). A touch of pidgin English became widespread with 'innit?' at the end of statements, as in 'I like chips, innit?' or (the title of a 1998 play) *Don't Look At My Sister, Innit!*

Multiculturalism started to get a critical press around the millennium. In 2001 a boy's torso was found floating in the Thames, with the head and limbs removed; he was believed to be Nigerian and was named 'Adam' by the police. The case drew attention to ritual and 'muti' murders, and newspapers ran sensational multiculturalism stories that ranged from illegal trafficking in 'bush meat' (giant snail, or monkey) to children killed in exorcisms. Multiculturalism – now largely superseded by 'diversity' – was no longer the uncritically positive buzzword it had been in the earlier '90s, and by the second decade of the new century, female genital mutilation (FGM) became a major issue where cultural relativism ceased to be any excuse.

London's paranoid edge was hardwired into the landscape: London is the world capital of closed circuit television (CCTV) surveillance (where are all these cameras monitored? who watches them?). More than street crime, terrorism provoked a new paranoia, with the '7/7' July 2005 attack on tubes and buses killing 56 and injuring over 780: it was noticeable how international the victims were, with the dead coming from at least eighteen countries. Individuals claiming to act in the name of Islam became a new feature of London life, and in 2017 a man drove a car along the pavement on Westminster Bridge, killing and injuring people from at least a dozen countries, including French schoolchildren and an American celebrating a wedding anniversary. Again, the international nature of the victims was characteristic, together with the disgusted and cohesive response of Londoners from all backgrounds. A couple of years earlier in 2015, an Islamist stabbing attempt at Leytonstone tube, by a man having a psychotic episode, was met with the words 'You ain't no Muslim, bruv.'

Twenty-first-century London suffers from a bursting population, a growing gulf between rich and poor, and a desperate housing situation. Aerial footage of east London shows dormitory sleeping sheds in back gardens and behind shops, with a ruthless Third World economy exploiting migrant workers. House prices outstripped other forms of inflation to a grotesque degree, and in 2010 the housing charity Shelter showed that if groceries had risen at the same rate, a chicken would cost £47.51; the point is only underlined by the fact that the figures were almost immediately obsolete, and so that chicken might now cost £75 or more. People have started living further and further out of the centre (with endless upbeat articles announcing ever more distant area Y as 'the new' area X) or moving right out to Hastings or St Albans, and a whole generation – 'Generation Rent' – has little prospect of ever owning London property.

If younger people weren't buying, overseas investors were. Britain's political stability made London a good investment, like gold, in times of international turbulence. At night some of London's classier districts feel like ghost towns, because so few people live there: as Laura Thompson writes in her book on Lord Lucan, 'rows of stucco houses stand like so many bank-vaulted Picassos, the uninhabited acquisitions of foreign money.'

With London increasingly split between rich and poor, the middle classes are squeezed out. Many areas are not good places to bring up children, leading to what has been variously seen as 'white flight' on the American model, or as the familiar tendency of Londoners to move out to a better quality of life when they can afford it, the classic instance being from the East End to Essex.

Former mayor Boris Johnson said in 2015 that London is 'to the billionaire as the jungles of Sumatra are to the orang-utan' (London had outstripped New York in billionaires by around seventy to forty). The former Naval and Military Club on Piccadilly was offered as a private house at £250 million, while on the Jubilee tube line, for the eight stops running eastwards from Westminster to Canning Town, local life expectancy decreases by a year for every stop.

Social unrest flared up again in 2011 after a minor criminal, going equipped to kill after buying a gun from an informer, was shot by the police: rioting broke out in Tottenham, spreading to Hackney. Youths blamed tension with 'the Feds' – a tellingly transatlantic word for the police – but unlike the Brixton Riots, sparked by injustice and leading to the Scarman Report on police racism, these were some of London's most meaningless disturbances, as people from neighbouring areas piled in for leisure rioting, setting cars and businesses alight and looting trainers.

The most memorable episode involved a black Hackney woman, Pauline Pearce, who heroically saved a youth from serious assault and shouted 'You lot piss me the fuck off! I'm ashamed to be a Hackney person because we're not all gathering together and fighting for a cause, we're running down Foot Locker [a trainer store] and TV shops!' The fact that she brandished a walking stick amid smoke and flames gave journalists the gift of a 'battling granny' aspect, like a 'London Can Take It' story from the Blitz, although she turned out – in contrast to grainy stills from CCTV – to be a woman of 45.

Riots, overcrowding and poverty are perennial, but bad architecture is a more recent curse. Post-war redevelopment was widely described as more damaging than the Blitz, and in the 1970s architectural writer Theo Crosby noted the psychological aspect of a great city as a mental space, and said we couldn't afford to have any more 'brain surgery' with hated architect Richard Seifert 'wielding the axe'. But since the millennium, redevelopment has increasingly been throwing up glass-and-concrete accommodation boxes, without making much of a dent on the housing shortage, and the deliberate use of 'brownfield' sites – as in Westminster's 'clever development' programme – means that every last atmospheric low-rise corner is getting demolished and replaced, leading towards a nowhere landscape with a few designated heritage sites.

The character of London is being erased. After the popularity of the word 'secret' in London book and magazine writing – roughly equivalent to 'unspoilt', but sounding more exciting – the newer word is 'lost'. Time was up for the Routemaster bus and the Protein Man of Oxford Street, but small shops, pubs, old-style cafes and second-hand booksellers have also been disappearing at a disastrous rate, like pie-and-mash shops and the hedgehog (which still survives, just, in Regent's Park). It is sad to find that a perfect lane-cum-alley, typical of deep Kensington (whitewashed walls, old streetlamp, grapevine hanging over wall), now has a multi-storey plate-glass development on it. It is not unusual to hear that London is 'over', it's finished, as if changing demographics and architecture make it a different city with the same name. Iain Sinclair's *London: City of Disappearances* (2006) was a landmark publication here. It's easy to exaggerate (or on the other hand to be cynical about nostalgia for cockney sing-songs and jellied eels), but something is being lost, whether we frame it in terms of landscape, authentic memory or sense of community.

Even counterculture is over, as Peter York sees it. In his analysis, Shoreditch-style 'hipster' culture – a style almost unrelated, or only ironically, to the word's cooler origins in 1940s America – is what happens when the fight goes out of subculture and leaves only consumer choice, organic chocolate and designer gin. For York, the solvent and conformist hipster represents the end of Bohemia, because Bohemians were 'hedgerow creatures' – they needed cheap, socially marginal areas to live in – but modern life (industrial farming, in York's metaphor) 'ploughs up the hedgerows' with property prices and redevelopment. Artists move into run-down areas – like yesterday's Hoxton – those areas 'come up', property prices rocket, bankers move in, and then no one else can live there; certainly not artists. This relentless dynamic, also visible in America, is sometimes known as 'art-washing'.

As the reality of London becomes eroded, so the idea of it is having an extraordinary renaissance. There is a boom in publications about London, filling whole walls of gallery bookshops. Something similar happened with the Amazon rainforest: it was once the 'green hell' of the Mato Grosso, but suddenly – as it started to vanish – it was one of the world's most fascinating and valuable treasures.

London is not just modernizing, but modernizing its past. There are attempts to rebrand zones with a transatlantic readability, giving them estate-agent-style labels such as 'Noho' (Fitzrovia, or 'North Soho'), 'Midtown' (Holborn) and 'Royal Quarter'. London recycles itself endlessly, with designer clothes shop A Child of the Jago taking its name from an 1896 novel about London's most notorious slum. Its Gothic heritage echoes and bounces around, with hairdressers called Jack the Clipper and the Demon Barber of Carnaby Street, and newspaper stories about 'Jack the Hipster' prowling the new Whitechapel. 'Ghost' shop signage has been a feature of heritage excavation, with old gilt lettering laid bare over modern premises, like a sausage shop over a jewellers or the mysterious E. Mono ('For Value') over an excellent kebab shop on Kentish Town Road. Ghost fronts are so attractive there are even fakes, like a bar pretending to occupy the premises of a pork butcher that never was.

It is not easy to say what London is 'like', but it's certainly different from the rest of the UK. Planet London, as it has been called, is almost a city-state. The standard of education – in terms of qualified adults, not schools – is higher than in the rest of the country, and it is far more multi-ethnic, with around three hundred languages spoken. The majority of children – around 60 per cent, rising to around 80 per cent in some boroughs – are born to mothers from outside the UK. People in Paris or Venice have long been used to hearing foreign languages on the street, and now this has become normal in central London. The French contingent alone would make London the sixth French city: it has more French people than Marseilles or Strasbourg. London is also incomparably richer than the rest of the UK, and the reasons for the Brexit vote in 2017 – with the 'leave' vote strongest in poorer and less educated areas of Britain – included provincial resentment against prosperous and international London.

London is now the world's number one tourist city, with towards twenty million visitors a year. Along with the obvious attractions – major museums and galleries, West End shopping, royal London, curry houses and old pubs – there are old street lamps, garden squares, mews; the West End arcades and Cecil Court; Brick Lane; giant greenhouses and Hindu temples; the river and the green spaces; half-hidden areas like Kinnerton Street; and jewel-box museums like the Soane and the Wallace.

London is not the world's biggest city, nor the most important, but it is the greatest on a balance of past and present. It is neither a major city with little history, nor a museum city preserved. Many cities are dynamic or charming, but London manages to be both. Visitors often say they love 'all the history' – a phrase that used to strike me as odd, but I have come to see their point (what did I expect them to say? they love the accretion of narratives?). And it is also – in the unlikely words of Conservative Party minister Michael Gove – 'a fantastic city with great opportunities to be successful, enjoy a great culture, have a good time and loads of hot sex'.

Razed but resurgent, London is a city of tradition and transience ('Come back tomorrow,' writes the ubiquitous Iain Sinclair, 'and the British Museum will be an ice rink, a boutique hotel, a fashion hub'). Future visions include Richard Jefferies's 1885 *After London*, with London as a swamp inhabited by dwarves, William Morris's *News from Nowhere*, with Parliament Square an enormous fertilizer market, and Benjamin Fontane's vision of a city of minarets for the Prophet. More soberly, it is likely that the population will continue to increase, London will continue to spread, and the recent tendency to push out the non-rich will cause exclusion and social problems at the edges, like the Paris *banlieues* (until recently, one of London's strengths was a relaxed mix of richer and poorer even in the centre). More futuristic predictions include a rising water level and the increased importance of roof gardens.

Major commentators have been full of gloom: Roy Porter saw post-Thatcher London as a free market nightmare, an unregulated international zone; Iain Sinclair has made an industry out of recording decline and loss with a baroque black humour; and Peter Ackroyd, despite his extraordinary detail, ultimately takes refuge in a dubious 'mystorical' vision of London enduring with a supernatural continuity. We have to hope the great things will survive: the architecture, the green spaces, the immense variety, the cultural memory and the creative energy.

Even as the material quality of the place is eroded by property prices, high shop rents and bad building, some idea of London rises above it, and some peculiar London spirit – nothing supernatural – can manifest even at the smallest and most unexpected moments. A few years ago a friend of a friend was burying his dead cat one evening in a royal park – please do not try this – when he saw a uniformed keeper coming towards him. He naturally thought he was in trouble, but to his surprise, before escorting him off the premises, the man not only helped him dig but then – with his cap on his chest in a gesture of respect – stood back discreetly with the words 'I understand if you'd like a few moments to yourself, sir.'

London, in the words of the great German-born photographer E. O. Hoppé, is like a gem with a thousand facets. City of Handel and Hendrix and Sherlock Holmes, it is a place of infinite coexistence, with genius enough and people enough to contain endless visions and possibilities. Or in the words of William Blake:

There is a Grain of Sand in Lambeth that Satan cannot find
Nor can his Watch Fiends find it: 'tis translucent & has many
    Angles
But he who finds it will find Oothoon's palace, for within
Opening into Beulah every angle is a lovely heaven.

THE CITY TODAY

SEE HOCKNEY AT TATE BRITAIN 9 FEB – 29 MAY

The Shard from ground level.

Towers of Babel

Urban explorer and 'place hacker' Bradley Garrett became famous in 2012 when he confessed that he had trespassed and climbed the Shard, Britain's tallest building (and he had the photos to prove it). But there are easier ways of going up. You can just pay (currently about £50 for two) and take a lift to the top of what is currently Europe's highest skyscraper, initially named London Bridge Tower, offering spectacular views from its 360-degree observation deck.

I'm with Nancy, a friend from America, and we have a few minutes to kill before our timed entry, so we wander around the formerly run-down London Bridge area. Walking past the London Tombs and London Bridge Experience ('The World's Top Horror Attraction,' says the flyer, offering 'Horrifyingly Educational Fun' from 'London's Spooky History'), we look at Covent Garden-ized side streets and go into the sprawling foodopolis of Borough Market, one of London's most successful revamps. There are ostrich eggs, caviar and screwtop jars for truffle-sniffing, but there is only time for a quick crocodile burger before we go back and join the queue for the Shard's airport-style security.

Designed by Italian architect Renzo Piano, the 95-storey Shard has a distinctively 'fractured' sculptural structure at the top, and it tapers like a massively elongated pyramid: the way it both narrows and leans away from the viewer at ground level gives an exaggerated perspective from close up, like a skyscraper in a Marvel comic ('Holy f***!', I heard someone say on a train leaving London from Charing Cross, 'What's that?'). The viewing platform gives little

The Shard viewing platform.

An almost aerial view from the Shard.

sense of the building's idiosyncrasy, although it is noticeably smaller than the ground area.

And the view is, indeed, spectacular. The organic sprawl of London lies all around, with a view that goes beyond it to distant bluish hills. Tiny moving people are visible, and the buildings look like precision cardboard models, while the trains, in particular, look like a model railway layout. There are trees growing throughout, and to one side we can see the municipal housing estates of south London. Here we see the Tower of London (dwarfed), Tower Bridge and Wren's now insignificant-looking Monument, and there we see a building with three propellers inset into its top (the Strata building, near Elephant and Castle, with its rarely working wind turbines). Battersea Power Station is surrounded by cranes, and a cluster of sculpturally designed mega-buildings rises out of the City financial district. Elsewhere there are some grungy flat roofs, the occasional roof garden, and here, beside a railway line, what looks as if it might be an old-style pub with 'Take Courage' advertising painted on the

A city ruined? A view over contemporary London.

side (matching it up at ground level later, this is Redcross Street, and Take Courage is a 'ghost' sign on an ordinary house).

John Lanchester's Hong Kong novel *Fragrant Harbour* (2002) features a high-rise hotel with the gents' urinal against a high window: the effect is one of plutocratic pissing down on the city and its ordinary life. It is worth saying that the Shard is not like that, at least on the face of it. Visiting the viewing deck is a cheerful, friendly, inclusive affair: there is even a prominently featured LGBTQ rainbow arch of paper flowers. There are a couple of serious restaurants on slightly lower floors, but up here there is chocolate, champagne and ice cream, and you can have your photo taken (they are processed with remarkable speed into a personalized album, on the off-chance you might want to buy it). It all tends towards an upmarket, futuristic, 'seaside pier'-style experience, and there have been numerous wedding proposals.

Less romantically, the Shard created the world's most unequal neighbourhood for property prices, with its ten flats rising over a deprived area at around £35 million each. The Shard itself cost around £1.5 billion to build, and it was the scheme of the late Irvine Sellar, former market trader and Carnaby Street clothing retailer, with 80 per cent of funding from the government of Qatar: a delegation of Qatar royals came to see their project when it was completed. Ironically the flats have been very slow to sell. They were all unsold as of 2018, after five years, and have been taken off the market; this has been attributed to the unfashionability of the unloved land south of the river, which the Shard is (just). It is a snobbery which – if this explanation is true – even affects foreign money.

But the biggest problem with the Shard, splendid though it might be in itself, is that it is not alone up there. Another famous building, Norman Foster's well-liked 41-floor 'Gherkin' (described by cartoonist Martin Rowson as the 'Dalek's dildo', but more prosaically titled '30 St Mary Axe'), is now barely visible from the Shard because it has already been obscured by the 'Cheesegrater', the 52-floor Chinese-owned Leadenhall Building at 122 Leadenhall Street. There is now a highly visible clump of these City buildings, all with their nicknames, a particularly distinctive and much maligned one being the 38-storey, Hong Kong-owned 'Walkie-Talkie' at 20 Fenchurch Street. Despite the friendly gesture of a roof garden, in practice the building is rather disappointing. It was awarded *Building Design* magazine's annual 'Carbuncle Cup' for the worst building of the previous twelve months, and it has become notorious (as the Death Ray, and the 'Fryscraper') for the unforeseen way it initially focused reflected sunlight intensely enough to damage parked cars, melting the bodywork. To emphasize the point, a journalist fried an egg in a frying pan on the pavement. New York-based architect Rafael Vinoly blames global warming: 'When I first came to London years ago, it wasn't like this . . . Now you have all these sunny days.'

Renzo Piano has another vast building on the cards, with the controversial Paddington Cube going ahead despite opposition. This fourteen-storey, mirrored-glass cuboid on stilts, with a design no one could call imaginative or subtle, replaces his previous plan

Undeveloped east London as seen in 1984, in this view from Canary Wharf.

for a 72-storey 'Paddington Pole' on the same site, again for Irvine Sellar, which was successfully resisted by local people and heritage groups. In the City, meanwhile, the 73-storey Trellis is currently rising for Singaporean developers at 1 Undershaft – where it will look down on the Gherkin and Cheesegrater – and the 300-metre (1,000 ft) Tulip (also known as the Phallus, the Cottonbud or the Sperm) has been approved.

A large proportion of high-rise buildings are residential, despite the unhappy history of high-rise social housing. Europe's tallest residential tower, the 67-storey Spire, is under construction near

The Wapping area at night, with the white pyramid at the top of One Canada Square, Canary Wharf.

Canary Wharf, with more municipal projects nearby on the Isle of Dogs (South Quay Plaza) and around fifty towers planned or delivered in Tower Hamlets. The Vauxhall, Nine Elms and Battersea area has been transfigured by a particularly discordant spread of unco-ordinated residential towers and boxes in various designs, and yet all this building seems to make little difference to London's housing crisis. Absentee investment buying is a commonly cited reason for this, with property privately let at top rates or even left empty. When Peter Rees – former chief planning officer for the City, and now a professor of Places and City Planning at University College London – tried to make contact with his neighbours to form a residents' group at Heron Tower on Bishopsgate, he discovered that after a year, a quarter of owners hadn't even picked up the keys.

Rees has warned of the skyline being trashed by the pepper-potting of barely regulated building: standing by the quality of buildings like the Shard, he contrasts it with the 'inferior designs of the wave of residential "investment" towers which is disfiguring the London skyline', which 'should engender a deep sense of shame in those who created and approved them . . . From Vauxhall to Whitechapel, the cranes are raising the dumbed-down "product" into offensive heaps.'

When it comes to high-rise building, London is currently one of the least protected cities in Europe. Not only the museum city of Venice, or central Paris (with its one tower in Montparnasse, and the rest of its skyscrapers confined out in La Defense), but Stockholm, Amsterdam and Barcelona are staying far more intact. London's current development is more comparable with Asia. Much of London's skyline is due to ruthlessly ambitious former mayor Boris Johnson, who reduced the controls on high buildings. They were fine, according to Johnson, as long as they didn't have 'an unacceptably harmful effect on their surroundings': a nebulous statement which raises the question of what constitutes acceptably harmful.

There are less socially damaging alternatives to high-rise residential building, notably mansion blocks, and also terraces, as advocated by the impressive research group Create Streets. At first glance the deceptively simple logic of multi-storey buildings, with their multiplication of floor space, seems as clear as the logic of shelving or filing cabinets, but the economics are less obvious and often surprising. Aside from the social and aesthetic cost, the developers of skyscrapers have been known to lose money, and historically the second owners have done better. Not only are they expensive to build, but the internal use of space is less efficient than in low-rise buildings, with the need for lifts and other building systems.

Whatever the finer points of the problem, there is no doubt about the scale of it: on top of its three hundred languages, hubristic towers are making London the new Babel. There were over 540 approved in the pipeline as of March 2019, despite the fact that few people without a vested interest actually like them; the rest of us, whether we have to see them, have to raise children in them, or miss what was there before, are generally less enthusiastic about London becoming 'Dubai on Thames'. Alexander Jan of architectural consultancy Arup has said it would be disastrous to 'fall into the post-war trap of allowing poorly designed buildings to sprout up. To do so would risk damaging not only London's economy, but its heritage and aesthetic qualities.'

And while speculative investment blocks spring up seemingly unchecked, the often poor quality of London's social housing remains a festering issue. In June 2017 over seventy people died in the Grenfell House tower-block fire in North Kensington (a relatively deprived enclave in Kensington and Chelsea, one of London's wealthiest boroughs), and the use of materials that were known to be flammable drew tragic attention to cost-cutting and inadequate commitment to safety.

Skyline pollution has become a major issue in London, and UNESCO has noted that the World Heritage status of the Tower of London and Big Ben is being compromised by the jarring buildings in the same view. There are similar concerns about St Paul's. William Blake's grave at Bunhill Fields (a Grade I listed graveyard park that also houses Daniel Defoe, and around 120,000 other Londoners) now looks set to be towered over by looming high-rise office development. Worse than just a bad backdrop, the once classic sight of Battersea Power Station is already obscured by the buildings springing up in front of it. Tall buildings are in your face whether you like it or not, destroying atmosphere even at a distance.

Close up, the plate-glass security lobbies of London's high-rise buildings are often dead at ground level, without the period features and retailing of Manhattan. They are even more dead when they block out the light in permanent canyons of shadow, a particular issue with the 62-storey building at 22 Bishopsgate.

More than darkness, the effect of unchecked modern building is an erasure of character, leading to the wastelands along Euston

Road and Victoria Street which could be almost anywhere. There is a peculiar dystopian effect caused by high-rise modernism over traditionally scaled vernacular building, when concrete and glass rising over tiles and chimneys make the older buildings look decrepit and ready for demolition, despite the fact that in their own right people tend to prefer them. Among the most symptomatic sights in London is the much-loved LASSCO building at Brunswick House, an eighteenth-century villa overlooking Vauxhall station and roundabout (its business, aptly enough, is architectural salvage, and it is filled with architectural antiques along with a bar and restaurant). It is hanging on, dwarfed by the buildings around it, and there is a similar effect on Victoria Street with the Albert pub.

Churches are disproportionately preserved – you can't help wondering if the City, with its often wonderful alleys, lanes and old pubs still surviving in the Bank and Cornhill area, will eventually be nothing but high rises with a few churches – but the loss of vernacular two- and three-storey Victorian building is hardly less important and it continues. Ordinary streets with no high-concept unique selling point or claim to fame are crucial to a city, like the indefinably charming low-level area around Hogarth Place, near Earl's Court tube station, with its mini Filipino-town. And after another block or street has gone, replaced with steel and glass, you can hardly even remember what was there, but the character continues to leach away out of London, like a Victorian painting oversprayed with great patches of silver-grey.

Green Spaces

Britain was once covered in woodland – Julius Caesar thought the entire island was 'one horrible forest' – and it is sometimes said that a squirrel could cross the whole country, from the River Severn to the Wash, without coming down from the trees. The idea of this epic squirrel is already several hundred years old, and I think of this very hypothetical animal when I hear of routes across London keeping to the green spaces. A friend with a central office job who used to live in run-down North Kensington ('flyover territory') recaps the daily cycling commute for me:

> ten minutes of dodging Chelsea tractors [meaning sport-utility vehicles, or SUVs] in Notting Hill and then the ride: Ken Gardens . . . Hyde Park . . . Green Park . . . St James's . . . ending 100 yards [90 m] from my office. Imagine that twice a day. Amazing. And transformative – that was the year I really started to love London, rather than it just being the city I work in.

Another friend had a similarly green route down through Hampstead Heath, Primrose Hill and Regent's Park.

Today I'm walking across central London grasslands with two visitors: they want to see the central parks, and I want to see what it feels like to stitch them together in one journey. We're walking west from St James's Park, coming into it from the Horse Guards Parade edge, and before we go in I want to show Nancy and her friend the dragon cannon that sits quietly overlooked on the parade ground. The once-famous 'Regent's Bomb' (or Cadiz Memorial, as it is more properly known) is a French mortar from the Napoleonic War, used to bombard Cadiz until the Duke of Wellington defeated the French at Salamanca, after which the Spanish nation presented it to the Prince Regent in gratitude. The sheer excess of it, and the fact that Bomb was then pronounced Bum, caused great amusement in Regency London, captured in the caricature prints of the time. And now, if you forget for a second that the extraordinary dragon was only applied later to a soberly technological and lethal piece of machinery, the whole thing is a fantasy cannon, or as Nancy's friend puts it, 'a Harry Potter cannon'.

Crossing the road into parkland, we are in St James's, the oldest of London's eight Royal Parks, all bound up with monarchy and hunting. Even the word park reflects the reigning Norman and colonized Saxon split in the English language, as much as pig and pork (*porc*) or cow and beef (*boeuf*): the Saxons had no concept of a *parc*, as an enclosed and cultivated space for deer and game, let alone for flowery leisure. Once a marshy field attached to a leper hospital, where the lepers kept pigs, it was drained by Henry VIII, who adapted it for jousting and made it part of a wooded chase for hunting, going up to Marylebone, Islington and beyond. Elizabeth hunted in this park, James kept a menagerie in it with crocodiles, and Charles I walked across it to his execution on Whitehall, followed by his loyal dog. As the centuries went on it declined, with prostitution and violence, including duelling, and by Victorian times its character was also marked by the close proximity of the notorious Westminster slums such as Devil's Acre. Henry James wrote in 1888:

Much of its character comes from the nearness to the Westminster slums. It is a park of intimacy, and perhaps the most democratic corner of London, in spite of its being in the royal and military quarter and close to all kinds of stateliness. There are few hours in the day when a thousand smutty children are not sprawling over it, and the unemployed lie thick on the grass and cover the benches with a brotherhood of greasy corduroys. In the London parks are the drawing rooms and clubs of the poor . . . these particular grass-plots and alleys may be said to constitute the very salon of the slums.

More useful than a salon, the lake would also have provided somewhere to wash. The idea of parks as an amenity for everyone received a great boost in mid-Victorian times, re-envisaging a more civic identity for older parks and creating new ones. The first purpose-built modern park was Victoria Park in Hackney, out in the notorious 'East End', which opened in 1845: the name and the location already tell a story.

As for St James's, it feels good to be off-road and into greenery, like Andrew Marvell's 'green thought in a green shade' (as a seventeenth-century Member of Parliament, as well as poet, he probably knew this park). Along with plants it contains a great variety of bird life, including various exotic ducks, and pelicans (the park's first pelicans, in the seventeenth century, were a diplomatic gift from Russia). It also houses what might well be London's most picturesque building, Duck Island Cottage (Charles I had created the sinecure post of governor of Duck Island), built in early Victorian times as a

The Cadiz
Memorial mortar
cannon, or
'Regent's Bomb'.

lodge for the Ornithological Society. The lodge's vaguely Swiss or 'Mitteleuropean' style gives it a fairy-tale, Hansel and Gretel quality – very different from the imperial might standing all around it.

Walking towards Buckingham Palace, at the other end of the park, we watch the coots and moorhens (one with a red head and one white; like an open-air aviary, there are boards to help you identify the birds). Crossing the bridge, we look back at the post-card view of Whitehall's ornate skyline; it is like a capriccio city, a dream of rooftops, that doesn't quite suggest the reality at street level. This famous view was altered by the London Eye appearing in front, rising up like London's answer to the Eiffel Tower, and is now more unequivocally marred by high-rise buildings on the South Bank looming discordantly behind it.

Different parks have different inhabitants, at least in my head – I associate Regent's Park, for example, with rollerbladers and Muslim families picnicking – and the St James's Park of my mind should be full of tourists and Whitehall workers on their break. This afternoon, despite its being a weekday lunchtime, workers with sandwiches are thin on the ground, but overseas visitors are clearly enjoying the place and we run into an increasing density of them as we come

Duck Island Cottage, St James's Park.

The Whitehall capriccio skyline from the bridge in St James's Park.

out of the park outside Buckingham Palace: a large undistinguished building that seems to bring great joy.

On the left, in the final bowl-like curve of the park, is the tree-covered West Island: it is the sort of place you'd have fantasized about getting out to and exploring as a child. It was more than fantasy for a deranged American, Robert James Moore, whose skeleton, with a bottle of vodka attached by a string, was found in 2011. It is thought he set himself up on the island, Crusoe-style, sometime around 2007, because it was the perfect place for him to keep an eye on the palace and maintain his stalker-like obsession with the queen, to whom he sent hundreds of intercepted letters and packages. Like those Japanese soldiers who hid out in the jungle for years, unaware the war was over, Moore's desperate vigil could be seen to have a kind of misguided heroism about it. Less debatably, I and thousands of other people walked past it a few times a week but had no idea he was there: that's big cities.

Crossing, we jump off-road again into Green Park, a surprisingly tranquil sloping space just south of Piccadilly's main road,

Rotten Row (from *route du roi*, the king's route) in Hyde Park.

with a history that includes duelling and balloon ascents. I've seen sheep grazing here, but there are none today. Passing the palace, we come to the Commonwealth war memorials, dignified and monolithic blocks embellished by a less than breathtaking sentiment from Booker Prize-winning Nigerian novelist Ben Okri, 'Our future is greater than our past.' Crossing the road again, at Hyde Park Corner, we go through the gates for the main leg of the journey. Hyde Park/ Kensington Gardens is central London's largest park, our equivalent of Central Park, and was once a royal hunting ground inhabited not only by deer but boar and wild bulls. It was plagued by highwaymen through the seventeenth and eighteenth centuries, and its long horse-riding path, Rotten Row (a corruption of 'king's route': *route du roi*), was the first road in England to be lit at night, after William III put three hundred lamps on it to deter crime.

Leaving Speaker's Corner behind us – once a famous spectacle and political safety valve, it is psychically squalid, and probably always was – Hyde Park is magnificent. Walking by the Serpentine lake and the Serpentine Gallery, we cross the bridge, so that we are now strictly speaking in 'Kensington Gardens'. There is a famous

Peter Pan statue in here somewhere, which we don't bother to look for, but we do see the obelisk memorial to the explorer Speke, and the Albert Memorial in the distance.

If a park can be monumental, then Hyde Park/Kensington Gardens is. It is something to do with the vistas. It feels excellently Victorian (in a more than literal sense, and in a way that Regent's Park doesn't). Carriages and frock coats would not be out of place. On a less sensitively atmospheric note, I have a great and probably antisocial urge to ride a bike in here and to fly a drone, but a quick look at the noticeboard leaves the degraded urbanite in no doubt whatever that this is expressly forbidden.

Meanwhile some horses and riders go by. The sheer size of the park shouldn't be a revelation, but somehow it is, and some of us are not willing to walk any further. There are mutinous noises about hailing a black cab: we saw a few driving past us on the main road through the park, but fortunately they were already occupied. As a compromise I at least want to see the dog cemetery, one of those described by George Orwell as 'perhaps the most horrible spectacles in Britain' (he was thinking about sentimentality and wasted money), so we head north towards Victoria Gate and Victoria Gate

Summer in Hyde Park.

The Japanese garden in Holland Park.

Lodge, with the cemetery – not open to the public – behind it. Peering through the railings on the main road we can see a glade of small headstones, with bluebells. Thanks to the Internet I know this includes monuments to Little Tippo, Dear Old Ponto, Our Faithful Friend Wobbles and Emma, 'faithful and sole companion of my rootless and desolate life'. (It is open by appointment only, on Thursdays and for groups of up to six, and it costs £60 to have it specially opened for you.)

The popular vote is that we should have a break, so we leave the park and find a street across the road, Bathurst Street. London is like a book that always has a page you've never seen before, and I've never been to Bathurst Street; for a moment it makes me think of streets out this way (Paddington–Marylebone) like the Middle East-tinged Connaught Street or Crawford Place, but it is far smaller, little more than an atmospheric corner, with the unmodernized facade of an Indian restaurant, a riding stables down a mews, and a French bar-restaurant in a former pub.

Emerging from the bar, we short cut to Queensway with a one-stop tube journey and catch up with the northwest corner of the park again, north of Kensington Palace, before walking down the wealth-and-surveillance row of Kensington Palace Gardens, with its embassies, and continuing by street across to Holland Park. This has a very different ambience. Its woodland, ponds and sloping lanes have a countryside feel, contrasting both with the deliberately exquisite Japanese garden, and the house with its orangery. It is a gem of a park, and seems more extensive when you're in it than it looks on the map.

The consensus, excluding me, is that we are now parked out, but we are agreed it has been magnificent. If I'd been on my own I'd have continued the walk by turning northwards, but we have already crossed London almost from – in terms of longitude – the British Museum to Kensal Green, or from Whitehall to Wormwood Scrubs (not in this case a disastrous career, but a doable walk), keeping for the most part to parkland.

We are also struck by how varied the green spaces were, each one with a distinctive air of its own. London might even – to coin an unlovely new word – be the parkiest of the world's major cities, with its great and very individual green spaces. There is Kew Gardens, with its greenhouses; Richmond Park at the top of Richmond Hill, with its deer bellowing in the rutting season and Isabella Plantation enclosed inside it; Wimbledon Common, where I've watched bats skimming the ponds; Hampstead Heath, where a friend and his

The Palm House, Kew Gardens.

partner were followed by a peculiar man in a silver jumpsuit; Battersea Park, with its pagoda and Buddha; Crystal Palace with its dinosaurs; Woolwich's Maryon Park, as in the Antonioni film *Blow-up* (1966); Meanwhile Gardens in Notting Hill, a community space salvaged from redevelopment; the more recent Dalston Curve, similarly salvaged in the inner city; and many, many others, down to the allotments, useful and sometimes eccentric places, with Union Jacks and pirate flags flying from little sheds. And somewhere, perhaps out near Ham House or Syon House, is a park I've half-forgotten with water and a strange towering plant growing beside it, like giant prehistoric rhubarb.

Plant life and green space is deeply integrated into London, like the 'garden squares' of the prosperous Victorian west, with railings and grand Victorian terraces around them: local residents have keys, but they are open to the rest of us during the annual Open Gardens event. London streets have London plane trees, with their trademark mottled and peeling bark: since the eighteenth century or before, they have been found to be the only tree that can withstand London grime and pollution, because they slough it off with the bark. There is a much-loved giant specimen down in Barnes, dating from the 1660s and now named Barney, and they are the main tree in St James's Park, although they seem most themselves when planted in a pavement.

London's green spaces are loved and vital, but they have had to be fought for and are perennially under threat. The unobtrusive army of people that keep them all going needs to be paid, and although parks were revitalized in the 1990s with Heritage Lottery funding, they now face council budget cuts. There is a further threat to every kind of quality space from London's overpopulation and accommodation crisis, which now threatens the Green Belt. It was decided in the 1930s that London should remain surrounded by largely agricultural and recreational space, and that this space should be protected to prevent an endless subtopian spread encroaching outwards, but there have recently been calls to start 'rethinking' the Green Belt and building on it. It is a highly emotive debate on both sides.

Happier future projections include more vertical gardening on the sides of buildings, and more roof gardens on top of them. London's most famous roof garden, subdivided into Tudor, Woodland and Moorish-style Spanish gardens, is the Kensington Roof Gardens on top of what was once Derry & Toms department store on High Street Kensington (then briefly the glam boutique Biba). More recently they have been a nightclub, although, as I write this, they are currently closed. Home to flamingos, and site of a Vietnam-satire helicopter napalm attack in Michael Moorcock's 1971 novel *A Cure for Cancer*, they are redolent of 1930s Deco, the gentility of the '50s and decadent '80s nostalgia, and they will flourish again. They look set to be joined by other roof gardens, several in the City district, which include plans for aerial beekeeping. Other lush projections have included a garden bridge across the Thames – a plan cancelled after much controversy and expense – and a pedestrianized, traffic-free Fleet Street with extensive planting and hanging gardens. London could do with some hanging gardens, catching up with 'the hanging gardens of Marylebone' in *Finnegans Wake* (1939).

From Holland Park we have drifted back to Queensway, been to a downstairs tiki bar, and gone on to a Chinese restaurant. I'm seized with an urge to see the moonlit pet cemetery through the railings once more, but it turns out to be an unspectacular sight in the gloom (I'm now resolved to get a party of six together and see it properly). The park is still just open (it shuts at midnight, and is 'open' mainly for traffic to drive through), but although London parks are largely safe, like all parks it's not a good place to hang out after dark. Barnes Common and Epping Forest are wonderful, particularly Epping, but – in very rare incidents – women have been murdered in them. And more generally, parks can be equivocal places. In the sinister words of undeservedly forgotten novelist William Sansom (1912–76), put into the mouth of a fictional park-keeper, 'parks has a shady side nor do I mean the shade beneath a leafy tree, there's a darker shade than that in parks'. But for now it's more than shady – it's midnight – and time to get the night tube home.

DEAD: the self-designed grave of artist Patrick Caulfield, at Highgate.

Highgate Gothic

There's nothing like a good day out with the dead, and few places better for having one than the decayed magnificence of Highgate Cemetery, 'Victorian Valhalla'. Climbing out of Highgate tube station with Nancy, we wander around the lower reaches of Highgate for a while, admiring a shop window with a tea towel of a tattooed hamster, before trekking up the hill to Highgate village proper, in this famously leafy and pleasant part of north London, and then descending down the steep wooded slope of Swain's Lane on the other side.

Dating as a whole from 1839, the cemetery falls into two halves, and our first call is the slightly newer (1857) eastern side, on the left as you go down. This has relatively open access, and we pay our money to go in and wander around. It is still a working cemetery, and more recent graves include Sex Pistols impresario Malcolm McLaren, the MM of his initials styled in imitation of the Warner Brothers WB (as if to say 'That's showbiz'). Not far away is the imposing monument of pop artist Patrick Caulfield, with the letters D E A D cut through the stone in descending steps. More of a surprise is the grave of a man I knew slightly – I knew he was dead, but not that he was here – lying under the more modest and generous monument of a bird bath. Elsewhere a group of young people, perhaps from a school, are gathered around a grave with candles in daylight.

The most famous and physically imposing grave is that of Karl Marx, his massive bronze head sculpted by Laurence Bradshaw, but it is uncharacteristic of the larger ambience of the place, dominated

The Circle of Lebanon catacombs.

by angels, crosses, urns and obelisks, and traversed by paths through trees. As ever, the forest of Victorian inscriptions offers almost endless pathos and novelty, and today I'm particularly struck by the grandiosity of Issachar Zacharie, 'First Grand Supreme Ruler of the Masonic Order of the Secret Monitor within the British Empire'.

The West Side or 'Old Ground' is open for guided tours only, and after going to the Prince of Wales pub and poking through the charity shops, we return to join a group with a guide from the Friends of Highgate Cemetery. Founded in 1970, following a public petition to save the cemetery – when its condition had become so grim there were plans to close it, move the bodies and sell the land – the Friends are one of the great volunteer success stories. In 1981 they took the cemetery over completely, and they have since restored it extensively: the ruination before the Friends' era had an undeniably powerful spell of its own, but could have resulted in the loss of the cemetery altogether.

Our group seems to have a fairly even balance of British and overseas visitors, including a Scandinavian girl with a black faux-leather coat so long it risks getting caught under her boots on sloping ground. The west side is also a working cemetery, and we stop at the grave of Alexander Litvinenko, the former Russian security agent who was assassinated with polonium in 2006 after finding asylum in London. But we've really come to see the necromantic heart of the place in the form of the Egyptian Avenue, with its Pharaonic arch and rusting metal doors, leading to more Egyptiana in the vaults of the Circle of Lebanon. Behind it come the Terrace Catacombs, where we see the coffins as we all walk around – part-wary, part-avid – inside its dark interior.

Inmates of the western cemetery include Radclyffe Hall the novelist, George Wombwell the Victorian animal dealer, who became a rich man with his travelling menagerie of wondrous animals, such as the tiger and the elephant (biblical animals to the Victorians, our guide points out), and Tom Sayers the once-famous bare-knuckle boxer, whose 1865 funeral drew a crowd of 100,000. Better remembered today is the story of Lizzie Siddall and Dante Gabriel Rossetti, hinging on the Rossetti family tomb. Siddall was the model and later wife of the Pre-Raphaelite painter and poet, but, suffering from consumption, died two years after their marriage from an overdose of laudanum, the great Victorian opiate. As she lay in an open casket, Rossetti had the impulse to bury with her a manuscript book of poems that he had written for her. It was a beautiful gesture, but as the years went by he began to regret it. Finally, seven years later, he arranged to have the grave discreetly exhumed one winter night, with men working by lantern light and the warmth of a bonfire. Rossetti wasn't proud of what he had done, and wrote to his brother that 'I fear the truth must ooze out in time.' He couldn't bear to be present at the uncovering, but a man who was there reported that Lizzie's celebrated red-gold hair was as luxuriant and bright as ever, and had even – he thought – grown longer in death.

Another grave on this side belongs to the cemetery's architect, Stephen Geary, a versatile entrepreneur who also designed London's first gin palace. He died aged 56, before his scheme to extend to the eastern side of the road had come to fruition. Our guide reminds us that the average age of death in Whitechapel in 1839, the year the cemetery opened, was 26 (an average dragged down by infant mortality), although it is unlikely that many Whitechapel inhabitants were able to pay their way in. Highgate was expensive and fashionable from the start. Originally it wasn't dense with trees, like today, but a lawn park, popular for Victorian picnics; the popularity of the new cemetery parks as leisure spaces helped to inspire the spread of London's more normal parks.

As the twentieth century wore on, Highgate Cemetery went from park to wood to ruined funereal forest, and by the 1970s the place had reached its nadir (or peak, depending on taste) of decay, during the dog-end of the popular occult and satanic revival of the late 1960s. Graves were being regularly vandalized and desecrated, with reports of occult ceremonies, and even of a tall dark apparition haunting the cemetery and Swain's Lane area: the 'Highgate Vampire'. Vigilantes and self-appointed vampire hunters took up the

The grave of Victorian prizefighter Tom Sayers, with his dog Lion.

case, and a series of sensational events followed: in the 1974 'nude rituals trial', as recorded in *The Times*, Old Bailey jurors were 'shown photographs of a desecrated coffin, hieroglyptic [*sic*] symbols and a naked woman dancing inside a cemetery vault. Evidence was also given about the discovery of a headless corpse in a car.'

Pockets of ruin and whispers of post-Victorian gloom still remain within the necropolitan grandeur of the now admirably maintained cemetery, and there is little doubt it is the ambience of Highgate that most people visit it for, rather than individually notable graves. Marx aside, the likes of William Foyle the bookseller, Leslie 'Hutch' Hutchinson the pianist, Dickens's wife Catherine, and Leslie Stephen, the father of Virginia Woolf, hardly compare with Chopin and Proust in Paris's Père Lachaise (the London equivalent, for eminence, would be Westminster Abbey: a very different experience). Our guide's talk, in tune with this ambience, has its share of the enjoyably doomy and gloomy, including the story of Enon Chapel (discussed earlier in this book) and the fact that churches seem to sink, with graveyard overcrowding, because the land around them rises. The Highgate Cemetery experience is essentially Gothic, in the popular sense of the word.

Leaving the cemetery while the light lasts we continue down the hill, until we come to another version of Gothic on the left-hand side, 'Holly Village'. It is not open to the public – in fact it is a prototypical 'gated community' – but the gate is unlocked and we trespass quietly into a hauntingly atmospheric space of eight so-called 'cottages' (really more like eccentric miniature mansions) around a lawn space with lamp posts, built in 1865. 'Picturesque and fanciful', in the words of the *London Encyclopaedia*, each one is different and their ornate and almost rambling design belies their small scale.

In spite of the fact that not one of these slightly crazed mini-mansions would be out of place in a Hammer film, Holly Village brings us to the more high-minded sense of Gothic in the Victorian Gothic revival, with its aspirations towards an idealized version of the Middle Ages. This is the Christian–medieval–High Church strand in Victorianism, expressed in brick and stone with its faux-ecclesiastical spires and carved leaves, as in the work of Augustus

Pugin, notably in the Palace of Westminster (popularly the Houses of Parliament), designed by Charles Barry with ornamental detailing by Pugin (who felt the resulting building was still too classical, and not Gothic enough). Pugin notoriously became insane in the course of the work and was committed to Bedlam. Gothic is a distinctly obsessional style, and Gilbert Scott, designer of the magnificent (now magnificently restored) St Pancras Hotel, had a characteristically obsessive dream one night that he had found the real botanical plant-prototype of leafy Gothic ornament.

With a few notable exceptions – such as the British Museum, in pillared classical style, or the Foreign Office – Gothic is perhaps the definitive Victorian public style. When an Act of Parliament was passed in 1885 to authorize the building of Tower Bridge – a miracle of modern Victorian engineering, with its hydraulically lifting 'bascule' structure – one of the stipulations was that it must be Gothic, just as the government had earlier specified for its own home in the new Palace of Westminster.

London is deeply Gothic in every sense of this widely mutated word, and its various meanings unpack at different sites. The funereal sensibility of Highgate Cemetery, and its later decay, have a strong Gothic appeal in the popular modern sense – something dark, deathly and psychologically extreme, with antiquarian tendencies – as do the other great cemeteries such as Abney Park, Brompton and Kensal Green. This same popular appeal extends to Dracula locations (such as Piccadilly, where Jonathan and Mina Harker see the count for the first time by the real-life jewellers Giuliano's); locations of modern Goth subculture, such as the former Batcave club; and Goth retailing, which seems to have its world capital in Camden.

The roots of popular Gothic go back beyond the High Victorian to the Gothic novels of the late eighteenth century, such as Walpole's now almost unreadable *Castle of Otranto* (1764), and his 'Gothic Revival' mansion in southwest London at Strawberry Hill, its castle-style crenellated top edge trying to suggest a world of dungeons, bygone barbarism and all the antique transgressions that make Gothic 'the shock of the old'.

Karl Marx, Highgate's most famous inhabitant: the totalitarian-looking bust was funded by the Communist Party in 1956.

Earlier still came the Baroque architect Nicholas Hawksmoor's 'English Gothick': Iain Sinclair has suggested a distinctly un-Christian, pagan feel to his churches and presented them as a dark style in their day, a suggestion famously developed by Peter Ackroyd in his novel *Hawksmoor* (1985). Ackroyd has gone on to see this sense of a dark side lingering even in the Victorian High Gothic, and suggested that the Victorian passion for historical reassurance ('the consolation of supposed antiquity') paradoxically laid them open to the Gothic as 'the pagan or the barbaric' – very un-reassuring, as in his satanic version of Hawksmoor. He further suggests that Gothic can combine horror and comedy, and sees this as natural to London: it is certainly true of Sweeney Todd, 'the Demon Barber of Fleet Street'.

This sense of camp Gothic comedy feeds into the way that London's dark past becomes fun at a safe distance, like the 'plague-rat glove puppet' I saw in the Museum of London gift shop a couple of years ago. It is a large part of what people seem to want from London: the Tower of London advertising itself as a place of beheadings; Sweeney Todd; Jack the Ripper; gaslit 1880s mysteries; the Necro Bus of the Ghost Bus Tour company, with destinations such as Trafalgar Scare, Earls Corpse, Notting Hell and Ladbroke Grave; and the London Dungeon, a major tourist attraction that trades on plague, torture, martyrdom and murder in a knockabout, black-humoured, affably downmarket form. It all taps into the appeal of what was previously the most celebrated and *guignol* part of Madame Tussaud's waxworks, the Chamber of Horrors, featuring real-life murderers such as Christie of Rillington Place, and Dr Crippen.

It is hard to think of another capital that would support all this so naturally and centrally; the Paris catacombs are magnificent, but they are slightly marginal to Paris in a way that the Tower and the Ripper are not to London. If Paris was as Gothic as London then 'the Guillotine Experience' and suchlike would be major attractions, but they are not. I once noticed a book, *Murder! Horror! London: The Handbook Guide* (1998), announcing itself as a guide to the 'other' London. Useful compendium though it is, I couldn't help feeling it wasn't very 'other': this gory and doomy side is a celebrated part of the mainstream heritage, from the gallows to Gin Lane to the Krays. Altogether and in every sense, the dark spirit of place is as hauntingly present as it was when the topographical writer and artist James Bone – author of *The London Perambulator* (1925), in the sense of walker – identified 'a Gothic genius loci of London'.

At the foot of Swain's Lane is a small gem of a charity shop (possibly London's smallest; less like a room, even, and more like the start of a hallway) belonging to St Anne's Church, but I rarely find it open, and even if it kept normal hours we'd have pretty much missed it, so we turn back up the hill towards Highgate. On the left we pass the quietly extraordinary Holly Lodge Estate, 'London's loveliest garden colony', with the dreamlike sight of what looks like an estate of half-timbered high-rises: they are multi-storeyed,

'Tudor cliffs': The Holly Lodge Estate, Highgate.

and although their four or five floors are barely high-rise by current standards, their appearance as 'Tudor cliffs', as they have been called, is helped by the slope of the hill. Initially built for single women by Lady Workers' Homes Limited in the 1920s, the estate is part of a pervasively retro vibe in London architecture: in this case the same period wave that gave rise to Liberty's half-timbered department store – the current premises date from 1925, part-salvaged from two timber warships, HMS *Hindustan* and HMS *Impregnable* – and the formerly reviled 'Tudorbethan' suburbs, but here on Swain's Lane it has intensified into an almost visionary landscape.

Highgate is as charming as ever – and (slightly) less obviously plutocratic and exclusive than its neighbour Hampstead – and we cross the enviable, forgivably self-contented landscape of Pond Square towards the pub the Red Lion and Sun. My friend works with dogs, and she strikes up an acquaintance with a white Jack Russell terrier sitting next to us; he is possibly the yappiest dog in north London, though it is excitability and not aggression. Conversation with the dog soon leads us into conversation with his owner, a middle-aged man who seems to be distinctly unexcited by the subject of the cemetery, in fact almost disapproving. He is clearly immune to the charms of the Gothic, and I wonder if we're talking to the last person in London who still finds Victorian cemeteries unbearably depressing. It occurs to me later that he might have recent family or friends in there, but at the time I wonder if my own friend's American accent is causing him to put on this po-faced, deeply underwhelmed act especially for tourists.

Nancy's being American leads to a more general conversation about things to see, and she mentions wanting to go on a Jack the Ripper walk. The extraordinary popularity of these is a mystery in itself (following the thread of a truly hideous series of atrocities visited on prostitutes, most of them middle-aged, alcoholic and homeless, in what was then one of the most deprived and squalid places not just in London but the world). Our lugubrious dog owner knows of these walks, although he's never been on one, but he suddenly brightens and seems almost enthusiastic: 'The Ripper,' he says warmly: 'Bit more cheerful at any rate.'

Whitechapel Traces

You have to be careful if you go on a Jack the Ripper walk. Careful, for one thing, that you're on the walk you booked, because there are so many of them. On a darkening Monday evening thirty or forty of us gather outside Aldgate East tube station, make ourselves known to the tour guide's assistant, school-register style, and cross Whitechapel High Street to slip beside the White Hart pub into Gunthorpe Street, with its alley-like entrance. Having left a couple of other tours congregating behind us at the station, we pass no fewer than two other Ripper walks in the alley, one of them led by a woman in a top hat. We make our first stop towards the end of Gunthorpe Street, and I look around to notice that the man next to me, with his young daughter, has a tourist leaflet about 'The Clink' prison. Meanwhile our guide warns us to be wary of newcomers sidling up to the back of the group: the problem is not that they want to hear about the Ripper for nothing, but that they might pick our pockets.

The landscape around Gunthorpe and Wentworth Street has been extensively rebuilt since the Blitz. It couldn't be described as charming but it's paradise compared with the 1880s, when the police would only venture into Wentworth Street in groups of at least three. After a mention of the first two 'Whitechapel Murders' – Martha Tabram, stabbed 37 times and found in Gunthorpe Street, and Emma Smith, sexually assaulted by a gang, but neither of them now thought to be victims of the Ripper himself – we come to the first true Ripper victim, Mary Ann Nichols. She was in a pub (now a halal-certified restaurant, the Shaad Grill) until 1.20 a.m., and at

3.40 her body was found in Thrawl Street. Our guide fills in the role of the anti-Semitic gutter newspaper *The Star* in whipping up Ripper hysteria, and the local conditions of the time, when the infant mortality rate was 50 per cent and there might be ten or twelve families to a house. Like Nichols, most of the Ripper's victims were not only prostitutes but homeless, paying to sleep in a line with other homeless people leaning on a rope stretched across a room – the rope was let down sharp in the morning, when it was time to wake up and get out – and they would have worn several dresses at once, less for warmth than because they had nowhere else to keep them.

As the walk continues we hear of other victims: Annie Chapman in Hanbury Street, and Liz Stride in Goulston Street, found outside what is now the Happy Days fish-and-chip shop. It was after Annie Chapman that the police received the 'Dear Boss' letter, source of the name Jack the Ripper but now widely believed to be a hoax: there were around 1,400 hoax letters. The Ripper might have been

Not just any squalid alley but Gunthorpe Street, a Ripper location.

The warmth of decay, in Princelet Street.

caught after attacking Liz Stride – there was even a possible sighting – but the man who first saw a woman's body assumed it was just his own wife, sleeping on the pavement drunk, and he didn't bother to look any closer. In the ensuing delay the Ripper escaped to murder a fourth victim, Catherine Eddowes, 45 minutes later.

In Princelet Street we admire a decayed period house with shutters, number 4, now popular as a film location – something about the state of the exterior makes me think of spaghetti westerns as much as Victorian London – and pass Brick Lane mosque, before Fournier Street brings us to Commercial Street and the Ten Bells pub, where at least two of the Ripper's victims are known to have drunk (and allegedly all of them), and where the great-great-grandfather of TV chef Jamie Oliver was the landlord in the 1880s. At this point we are under the magnificence of Hawksmoor's Christ Church Spitalfields, looking particularly sublime lit at night and from this close low angle, as our guide details the particularly vile final murder of Mary Kelly, where the killer was alone indoors with the corpse for long enough to adorn the room with body parts as if they were Christmas decorations. A police photograph is passed around the group, face down for the benefit of anyone reluctant to see it. No one is.

Christ Church, Spitalfields, by Nicholas Hawksmoor, 1714–29.

Our guide also does a convincing demolition of the famous theory that the murders were a conspiracy involving Prince Albert Victor, Duke of Clarence ('Prince Eddy'), the artist Sickert and the royal physician Sir William Withey Gull – a fiction from the 1970s that became the basis of a film starring Michael Caine as Inspector Abberlyne. It is one of many theories, ranging from plausible suspects such as Montague Druitt and Francis Tumblety to lunatic scenarios featuring the poet Ernest Dowson, Dr Barnardo and Lewis Carroll. All that most of these theories prove is the fascination of the case, which may have changed over the years. It began with media-led public hysteria, but for our guide, Barry, the main fascination now is simply the fact that the Ripper was never caught, and the mystery: 'we'll never know.' If it were ever solved, thinks Barry, this fascination would be dented: people would be disappointed to know 'it was the local greengrocer'.

I wonder. I wonder how much this popular fascination has to do with violence against women. And more than that, I wonder if there would be anything like the same mystique to a series of five unsolved and gruesome prostitute murders if they had happened in, let's say, Cardiff in the 1950s. My own feeling is that by now the vague popular image of the Ripper crimes (a man in a top hat and cloak, carrying a small Gladstone bag, flitting through a shadowy landscape of gaslight and fog – despite the fact that not one of these details is accurate) has come to seem like a quintessence, a part-for-the-whole crystallization, of Victorian horror and Victorian London itself.

And, more than the Ripper narrative or even the aura of Victorianness that clings to it, I also wonder about the extraordinary popularity of the whole walking-tour phenomenon – of which Ripper walks are perhaps a definitive example – over the last couple of decades. There are now any number of special interest walks and trails, from the Thames Path and classic pubs to LGBT Soho and stained glass. Many of them are in books, such as the espionage trails in *A Spy's London* (1994) by Roy Berkeley, or the genteel crime-writing world of the *Mystery Reader's Walking Guide: London* (1988), by Alzina Sloan Dale and Barbara Sloan Hendershott, but the really mushrooming phenomenon has been guided walks, which seem to go back – at least – to a regular Ripper walk in the 1960s; in pre-Internet days walks could be found advertised at the back of listings magazine *Time Out*. The same firm who conducted our Ripper walk also offers the more current interest of a street art walk, but the overwhelming majority of guided walks are broadly in the field of 'heritage'. There are Sherlock Holmes walks; Dickens walks; a pub-oriented 'London by Gaslight' walk; Old Jewish Quarter walks; King's Road pop culture walks; Soho walks offering 'Roots of the Swinging Sixties', Soho vice ('Tasty Tales from London's Red Light District') and Soho borders ('On the Edges', taking in the musical associations of Denmark Street or 'Tin Pan Alley', and up into formerly Bohemian Fitzrovia); occult walks; literary Bloomsbury walks; and the perennially popular ghost walks.

In fact most of these walks are ghost walks in a larger sense of the word, and if commercial walking tours go back at least to the 1960s, then the sense of trails, traces and presences can already be seen in books such as E. Beresford Chancellor's non-supernatural *Literary Ghosts of London* (1933), detailing Dr Johnson et al., and Walter Thornbury's popular *Haunted London* (1865), which, as

Thornbury says, 'deals not so much with the London of the ghost stories as with the London consecrated by manifold traditions'. His book was a response to what he already saw as the widespread desecration of London, with his sense of hauntedness resisting it.

Like the celebrated work of Iain Sinclair, exploring London on foot as a city of memories and associations – a project, to borrow his description of Rachel Lichtenstein's work in Whitechapel, of 'not forgetting' – these are early instances of what became known as 'psychogeography', a word which reached epidemic popularity in the 2000s and had several overlapping meanings, the most relevant here being a particularly resonant form of what might more prosaically be called local history. Its popularity has gone hand in hand with a sense that London, like many of the world's big cities, is losing its character to corporate blandness and sterile development.

The East End's ever-changing street art: Brick Lane, with a work by Dale Grimshaw.

London is a city of change – far more than, say, central Paris – and this is particularly clear in the history and diversity of the Spitalfields and Brick Lane area, where the dancing twin forces of migration and 'heritage' are unusually vivid. Taking its name from hospital fields, the area was once the medieval site of St Mary Spital hospital for the poor, run by monks, but by the time of Daniel Defoe it had become built up and even crowded. Already associated with nonconformists and foreigners, such as French weavers, the area had its glory days after the influx of Huguenot refugees from France, fleeing religious persecution after the Revocation of the Edict of Nantes in 1685, who established Spitalfields as a world centre of silk weaving. The more prosperous of them lived and worked in Fournier Street, a still intact and now much restored Georgian street contemporary with Christ Church, Spitalfields, the Anglican church next door. Sloping into slummy territory by the turn of the nineteenth century, the area had a further influx of East European Jews who gradually assimilated and moved away to more salubrious areas, to be replaced in the later twentieth century by Bangladeshis. The process is reflected in the changing fortunes of the French Protestant church, built in the 1740s, used by Huguenots and then Methodists before becoming a synagogue, and now a mosque, within an area – 'Banglatown', with bilingual street signs, already part of the area's sense of heritage – recently associated with curry houses, but now diversified into design and media businesses and 'hipster' retailing and leisure.

Meanwhile there are larger, less enjoyable, hyper-capitalized modifications to the area that look less like a constant round of change and more like a permanent erasure. Early on the walk Barry apologized for the fact that much of the landscape had been destroyed by the Blitz, and for stretches of it there is little continuity with any past landscape. Development is as much to blame as bombing. Walking down Wentworth Street we admired *Blade Runner*-style tower blocks with lights on them, rising over the end of the road, and finished the walk in a high-rise financial district at the unwelcoming base of One Creechurch Place, a 17-storey development with 270,000 square feet of office space.

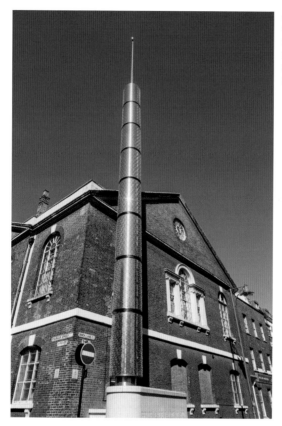

Jamme Masjid – Great Mosque and minaret-like silver tower sculpture – on the corner of Fournier Street and Brick Lane.

As for the Spitalfields market area, a large bland featureless development offering office space and retail units has been built opposite the Hawksmoor church on Commercial Street, on to the old 'Fruit and Wool Exchange', keeping some of the old facade but replacing virtually a whole block as far as Crispin Street, where the old frontage of Donovan Bros Paper Bags survives. A handful of these old frontages – often shops become restaurants – survive here, where the writer Jeanette Winterson until recently kept a small delicatessen going at 40 Gun Street, formerly the site of 'Verde and Company Fruit Importers'. These ghost signages are a feature of the area, with 'A. Gold, French Milliner' at 42, while back on Fournier Street an upmarket barber still has the signage of David Kira, banana importer, and the Town House (antique shop, gallery and kitchen) two doors down has fainter signage of the Market Cafe. At the Liverpool Street end of the market, in contrast, plate-glass modernization has created something less like the modern Covent Garden and more like the retail units inside a major train station.

Walking on towards Liverpool Street (after a drink in a pleasantly hipsterized pub run by the Weird Beard Brewing Company, served by a bartender from Oregon), we go through the Artillery Lane area. Artillery Passage and part of Artillery Lane still keep some character, but much of it has been redeveloped so thoroughly that it could be anywhere. Everywhere you can see this widely noticed erasure, the same across London and across the world (to quote a typical recent fiction, in this case by William Boyd, 'one of those smoked-glass eight-storey blocks just off Park Lane . . . you left London and could have been in Singapore or Dubai, Tokyo or Acapulco').

London's changes – transient and characterful, or characterless and seemingly terminal – are accompanied by an almost unique degree of echoing and reverberation, with the bouncing around of (often tongue-in-cheek) 'heritage' references. A newspaper article about the new East End lifestyle is headed 'Jack the Hipster', and Brick Lane now boasts a 'Jack the Clipper' barber shop, while

Bananas and tomatoes here: old 'ghost' signage in Fournier Street.

elsewhere there is the Demon Barber of Carnaby Street, and 'Hawksmoor' is now a reliably upmarket group of steak restaurants. Heritage recycles itself faster and faster, and a 267-room hotel near Liverpool Street, the Andaz, now has pinstriped carpets to echo the City and the old-style city gent, and tattoo-style embossed graphics on the headboards to echo the new hipster culture of Shoreditch.

Like these bounces of heritage, and the enormous number of recent books about London, walking tours seem to be everywhere. As corporate blandness threatens to consume the reality of the streets, then ghosts, traces, echoes and footsteps of meaning become more attractive. The dream of London, as a mythologized spirit of place, survives to superimpose itself on concrete and plate glass; it is as if the song is over, but the melody lingers on.

Cabinets of Curiosity

Not so long ago Hackney, Hoxton and Shoreditch were famously bleak and run-down, but over the last few years they have started to overflow with organic coffee, beard oil and hipster enterprises of one sort or another: tattooists, a cat cafe, charcoal croissants and what-have-you. Not everyone likes this mutant gentrification, and in September 2015 a mob of around two hundred people attacked Shoreditch's Cereal Killer Cafe – a '90s-nostalgia-themed eatery with branches in Camden and Kuwait – which was allegedly serving up bowls of Rice Krispies at ridiculous, restaurant-style prices.

Notorious until recently for a sign on the door that said 'No Poor People', Viktor Wynd's Museum of Curiosities, Fine Art and Natural History is the strangest jewel in the treasure chest of this new East End. It is at 11 Mare Street, roughly midway between Bethnal Green tube station and the strip of Vietnamese restaurants that played a vanguard role in regenerating the area. Formerly the Empire cafe, by the time Wynd took it over it was an abandoned call centre. I used to walk to it from Bethnal Green tube, past the window of a second-hand office-furniture shop in which there was a 1950s boxing poster for the young Kray twins; local lads. Now I've discovered the best way to get there is via Cambridge Heath overground station, much closer to Wynd and just two stops from Liverpool Street. So it's goodbye to the Krays, but suddenly it seems less of a trek.

I know Wynd a little – he collects an artist I wrote a book on – so we're having a drink in the salon area of his emporium before I join one of his personal tours for the public. As I admire the stuffed crocodile hanging from the ceiling, he tells me his great collecting heroes are the Tradescants, seventeenth-century 'curious gardeners', and that his original vision was to create a cabinet of curiosities, 'a twenty-first-century *Wunderkabinett* in the spirit of the Tradescants, as they would do it today – with wonders of the natural world and other things'. He started up in 2006 as Viktor Wynd's Little Shop of Horrors, thinking it might last a few months, but it has gone from strength to strength. Wynd is modest about it, and says he collects to stop himself becoming depressed. He has done this so successfully that film director John Waters has described him as 'a cheerfully obsessive eccentric hoarder . . . Viktor Wynd is a sick orchid who seems like the perfect man to me.'

Wynd may be a sick orchid when he is in town, but he has a house in the country where he leads a more normal existence, raising newts and children. I also know that in a previous incarnation he was the artist Robert Wyndham Bucknell, whose one-man shows included 'Why I Think I'm So Fucking Special' (2004). As he admits, he now has the world's largest collection of work by Bucknell, and his artistic ambitions have gone into his museum instead. The original shop was an artwork in itself, and the entrance to the museum area was formerly through a wardrobe full of fur coats, 'in homage to Narnia'.

It is 6.30 p.m., time for the tour, and about fifteen of us are now sitting in the Spare Room at the back of the gallery. This room shows work by the artist and occultist Austin Osman Spare, along with tribal art, particularly African masks (other odds and ends include an articulated mouse skeleton and a death mask of Napoleon). Wynd likes masks, he tells us: 'when you put them on you're a less inhibited, different person'. As a preamble to the tour he tells us a longish fairy tale, possibly of his own invention, about a man who makes a bargain with the Devil. The audience look captivated and restive by turns: some of them clearly wonder where the evening is going.

After a few remarks about modern galleries – dull white cubes with ten pictures you'll never return to see, unlike here, where you can have a drink and talk beside the pictures, and just take them in out of the corner of your eye – it is time to see the museum proper and its 'dead things in bottles'. Going down a spiral staircase, we encounter some Regency erotica, a hideous 'feejee' fake mermaid, and a spread of works by the aesthete Stephen Tennant, valued by Wynd as a really magnificent failure: 'far more difficult', in Wynd's opinion, 'than to actually do anything'. This is next to a red-sequinned suit worn by another of Wynd's heroes, the late Sebastian Horsley, artist and dandy. A tray of gin and tonic follows us downstairs, courtesy of Wynd's sponsors, as we look at some of the cover art Tennant designed for books he never actually got around to writing.

Moving on, we meet Gilbert, Wynd's deceased pet hedgehog – the museum is rich in taxidermy. Much of it is anthropomorphic, including some toads having a beer and a clairvoyant mole, the great Moltar, who inhabits a little Gipsy tent with a turban and a crystal ball. Further on comes a motorized piece with a moth knitting a jumper, 'making its supper'.

Passing a tongue-eating louse ('the most disgusting thing I've got'), we also puzzle over an artificial foreskin and admire an empty Viagra packet from a Rolling Stone's hotel room, complete with a letter of authenticity from the chambermaid ('I, Maria de Silva . . .'). Nearby is a gold-plated hippopotamus skull, which once sat on the desk of cocaine billionaire Pablo Escobar. Among the world's most dangerous creatures, hippopotami cause more deaths in Africa than any other animal, and Escobar kept them in his moat (which didn't stop him being shot dead in 1993).

Ahead is the Gnostic Temple of Agape, with its windows and a table. Its miniature-room quality, in a downstairs installation, makes me think of the Monk's Parlour in Sir John Soane's Museum. A frog clings to the window, and we're told the members of the Temple still meet down here. Further on is a jar of moles, an oddly satisfying object with a surreal beauty all its own. Wynd expatiates on the occult significance of moles, and their use in magic, but confides that he has found modern occultists disappointing. They dress badly, they often have personal hygiene problems, and moreover 'they are not really in touch with any of the great powers of the universe that I'm in touch with.'

A nearby case contains the mummified erection of a man hanged in the eighteenth century, said to have once belonged to Oscar Wilde.

Skulls, dolls, crucifixes and shrunken heads: a cabinet in Viktor Wynd's museum.

The museum is not suitable for children: Wynd thought twice about displaying the vaginas of Glasgow prostitutes, pickled in bottles, but then concluded they weren't private in their lifetimes anyway. Other human remains include bottled babies, a small foot and the shrunken, mummified head of a Chilean boy, along with three shrunken heads under a glass dome. You can't go wrong with shrunken heads – the American impresario Ripley, of *Ripley's Believe It or Not*, promised his public that all his museums would have a shrunken head – and Wynd also has some magnificent skulls, including a Tibetan skull carved with a sacred calendar, and headhunter's trophies from the Asmat and Dayak peoples.

There is a book about cannibalism on display, entitled *Eat Thy Neighbour*, and books are scattered about the museum like light relief: *Fish Who Answer the Telephone*, *How to Poo on a Date* and *Sex Instructions for Irish Farmers* all find a place, together with *Group Sex: A How to Guide*, bits of period sleaze from the 1960s and '70s, and *Let's Play Nurse and Doctor* (a bona fide children's book) next to *The Passions and Lechery of Catherine the Great*. We've now seen hundreds of items, and we dutifully pay attention to an early work by Tracey Emin, then perk up for a giant woodlouse-like creature from a mile under the sea and some ominously mutated seashells from Fukushima. Our tour is reaching the end, but the wonders keep coming, with some simple but beautiful *coco de mers*; a sixteenth-century print of a witch out gathering babies, *The Witches' Rout* (*c*. 1520) by Agostino Veneziano; and a box purporting to contain some of the original darkness Moses called down upon the Earth.

At first the museum was open only by appointment ('in those days,' Wynd observes mildly, 'Hackney was very different from how it is now'), and one day someone made an appointment and unexpectedly brought David Bowie along. Bowie was very friendly and proceeded to ring occasionally, but – somewhat to Wynd's disappointment as a dealer – although he admired Wynd's bezoar stones the only thing he bought was a copy of the *Cunt Colouring Book*. Other well-known visitors have included Peter Blake, who donated a print, Richard Attenborough, who admired a book on *The History and Social Influence of the Potato*, and the Duke of Edinburgh, who was charming but didn't stay as long as Wynd might have liked.

The final room is a jokey homage to Sir John Soane's Museum, with a skeleton sunk in a window-topped table as a gesture towards Soane's Egyptian sarcophagus. Around the table are more artworks: Hogarth, Hans Bellmer, Mervyn Peake and erotica from around the world including Japan, Austria (seemingly 'the land of the pervert') and 'then I'm afraid we come to England, and it's just unmitigated filth.' Wynd bids us goodnight, telling us that we're welcome to stay down here to talk among ourselves, and if we want to have an orgy he'll be watching on the CCTV.

Wynd's enthusiasm for the Tradescants makes me want to know more, and I find John Tradescant the Elder (*c*. 1570–1638) was Keeper of Gardens, Vines and Silkworms at Oatlands Palace on the Thames, and royal gardener to King James. He sailed to arctic Russia and North Africa in search of plants and specimens, but he was interested in more than botany, and later asked other travellers and explorers to bring back items such as the heads of a sea cow (a manatee), an elephant and a hippopotamus, tribal objects from West Africa, and in short 'Any thing that is strang [*sic*]'.

In 1629 Tradescant settled in Lambeth, which was then outside London, where he planted a botanical garden and displayed his 'Ark',

The Enlightenment Gallery in the British Museum.

a collection of natural history and ethnographic objects. This was the first museum in Britain to be open to the public, and was thought to be the greatest museum in the world. It followed in the tradition of Continental *Wunderkabinetts* and more particularly *Wunderkammers* (wonder cabinets and wonder chambers) such as that of Rudolf II of Prague, but with a newer and more scientific spirit, and closer to home it was probably inspired by Sir Walter Cope's collection in London of 'queer foreign objects', including a rhinoceros horn, an embalmed child, a petrified thunderbolt and an Indian canoe.

Along with exotic fruits – figs, pomegranates and the 'curious peach' (to quote Andrew Marvell's 'The Garden') – Tradescant's collection included a fragment of the True Cross; the Native American mantle of Powhatan, the father of the Red Indian woman Pocahontas; 'a natural dragon, above two inches long'; some blood that had fallen from the sky; and a dodo. His son John succeeded him as royal gardener to Charles I and continued the Ark, cataloguing it in his *Musaeum Tradescantium*, the first printed catalogue of an English collection. Unfortunately, in 1650 he met Elias Ashmole, antiquary, alchemist and unscrupulous collector, who ended up getting his hands on the collection by legalistic means. He took it from Tradescant's widow, who drowned herself, and carried it off to Oxford where Tradescant's 'Clossitt of rarityes' was incorporated into the Ashmolean collection, but ended up decayed and dispersed. The Tradescants are remembered in Lambeth's Museum of Garden History, at St Mary's church, Lambeth. It is a fine museum but lacking in the 'curiosity' element. The strangest object at present is Tradescant's curious tomb, in the churchyard, showing apocalyptic scenes and a seven-headed hydra rearing over a skull.

Unlike the earlier royal origins of the Louvre, or the later plutocratic collections of America, this aspect of the scholarly or amateur cabinet of curiosities is a feature of London. Even the British Museum has its origins in the private collection of the physician Sir Hans Sloane, who died in 1753 after offering his collection of art, antiquities and natural history to the nation for £20,000 (less than they had cost, and a posthumous bargain). At first it was simply divided into 'natural and artificial rarities', and the ground-floor Enlightenment gallery now recreates the feel of the amateur scholar's collection,

Collection mania at Sir John Soane's Museum, looking across the central dome area.

evolving from the world of the seventeenth- and eighteenth-century antiquaries. Its backdrop of leather-bound books sets off a spread of Asian gods, bronzes, Greek vases, ethnographic weapons and musical instruments – a miniature gamelan orchestra, no less – Babylonian demons such as Pazuzu, hieroglyphic steles from ancient Egypt, and much more. One case displays the obsidian mirror supposedly used by Dr John Dee and his rascally assistant Edward Kelley to talk with angels. In fact the Dee link to this mirror is inconclusive, but it is an impressive pre-Columbian object and a prize item in an amateur's collection of antiquarian curiosities, in this case that of Horace Walpole, the Gothic revivalist, who loved its supposed connection with Dee and pre-Enlightenment magic.

Wynd's inspiration might be the Tradescants, but the underground profusion of his collection makes me think of Sir John Soane, an architect of genius whose house – now the museum that bears his name – at 13 Lincoln's Inn Fields is one of London's great troves. Soane's stripped-down Neoclassicism plays with space, recesses and particularly light, so even the lower level of his house has a subterranean natural glow, and its three-storey dome, stacked with ancient fragments, reaches up to a skylight. He was a professor of architecture, and the original function of his collection of fragments and details was to be a vast, labyrinthine work of reference, a memory palace. The centrepiece of this eccentric space is the massive sarcophagus of Pharaoh Seti I, in the Sepulchral Chamber below the dome, and rising around it are stone leaves, busts, capital column tops, urns and a multi-breasted goddess Diana. The seriousness of Soane's collection is at the opposite end of the scale from the frivolous or dilettantish, but it has still given rise to a dreamlike interior.

Soane's main allegiances – at least intentionally – are classical rather than romantic or Gothic, and his house-cum-museum-cum-mind is full of Greek and Roman fragments, but he wasn't immune to the *Castle of Otranto*-style medievalism of his time: there is a Monk's Cell and a Monk's Parlour, the underground fantasy den of a Gothic revival monk who seems to have lived pretty well by monastic standards. A few flashes of pure collecting also creep in at the Soane, with Napoleon's pistol, Christopher Wren's watch, a 'scold's bridle' for nagging wives, slavery shackles ('to the honour of humanity no longer in use') and a natural wonder in the form of a stony Neptune's Cup Sponge, described as 'a large fungus from the rocks of the Island of Sumatra'. Other notable items include *The Rake's Progress* by Hogarth, and works by Canaletto and Piranesi. Some of Piranesi's work, like his *Carceri* or Prisons, almost prefigures Soane's dome in the way his classicism flips over into its opposite by sheer excess, becoming romantic and almost delirious.

For many years the Soane was relatively little known, and something of a hidden gem. Looking at the the door of this grey, narrow building gave little clue to the sublime spaces opening up within, and this Tardis-like quality was part of the fascination. More recently it has had so much recognition – particularly after Soane was rediscovered in the 1980s by postmodern architects such as Arata Isozaki – that it has been able to re-expand into the houses on either side at 12 and 14, which were built by Soane and now contain a shop, exhibition gallery and project space; as I write this, upcoming events include 'architectural yoga'.

The Wallace Collection is another gem that has become better known. For years it stood in a backwater square, in what was then the genteel time warp of Marylebone, and it had such a quiet air of culture and refinement that walking round it was enough to make you feel like a character in an Anita Brookner novel. Long before I knew what culture was I visited the Wallace, not because I wanted to see any paintings but because – along with a childish interest in dinosaurs and First World War aeroplanes – I liked knights in armour, and a library book by a man with the memorable name of Ewart Oakeshott told me there were suits of armour at the Wallace, horses and all.

No longer feeling so hidden, the Wallace has been tactfully refurbished to include education areas and a restaurant, but it still shows the personal touch of the Wallaces: the first to fourth Marquesses of Hertford and the fourth marquess's illegitimate son Richard (a philanthropist, who donated the green Wallace drinking fountains to Paris). Contrasting it with the Frick collection in New York, built by the industrial tycoon Henry Frick, Viktor Wynd mentions this aspect of personal taste as opposed to just being 'what the world's richest man was sold as the best of everything'.

To say it has armour, painting and French porcelain doesn't convey the understated idiosyncrasy of the place. The porcelain includes the rococo lunacy of Sèvres vases with cherubs on the sides and elephant's heads – albino skin and pink eyelids, with ears like fungi – that also hold candles with their trunks. Even Madame de Pompadour seems to have felt these vases were over the top – she 'chose not to display them', says the accompanying text – but there's a quality of hyper-civilized kitsch about them that might have pleased Salvador Dalí. Elsewhere there is a beautiful German jousting shield in black with gilt foliage, from around 1500, and an Asanti ritual sword with one blade and four handles, perhaps used to affirm brotherhood. And then there are the paintings, including Jean-Honoré Fragonard's discreetly salacious *The Swing* (1767), with its fantasy French parkland ramping up to jungle density, and Nicolas

Nicolas Poussin, *A Dance to the Music of Time*, c. 1635, oil on canvas. Time plays a lyre, while a cherub blows ephemeral bubbles.

The back State Room at The Wallace Collection.

Poussin's *A Dance to the Music of Time* (1634–6), the inspiration for the novel series by Anthony Powell, about the patterns time makes in a life. Standing in front of it now, decades after I first saw it, it has come to mean more to me.

Perhaps the simplest fact about the Wallace is just how good it is. Praising this totally blue-chip, five-star quality, art critic Matthew Collings has written, 'I don't know if a cult of the Wallace Collection even exists, but if not I'd like to start one, and make myself the Green Dragon or High Wizard.' If it ever happens, I'll join.

The King Lud on Ludgate Circus, in the 1920s.

Pubs and Bars

London is over: it's finished, it's gone. It's all lost, or so people tell you; it's just a city with the same name on the same site, or at least a city in transition. For Iain Sinclair, we're in a 'limbo between cities', and this is 'the last of a certain kind of London and the new has not emerged or defined itself exactly yet'. If you walk around, you'll find rumours of London's demise are – like the man said when he read his own obituary – greatly exaggerated, but some things *are* definitely going, and one of them is the pub. The whole country is affected: despite the growing population, there are around 25 per cent fewer British pubs than in the 1980s, and nearly 1,000 closed in 2018 alone.

When I think of lost pubs I remember one in particular, and I'm not even sure if it was where I think it was. Set among the floorboards was a thick pane of glass, and through it you could see a river below (one of London's 'lost rivers', unless it was just a sewer). But where was this pub? I think it was probably at the St Paul's end of Fleet Street: past Mr Punch's Tavern and keep going over the crossroads of Ludgate Circus.

Ludgate Circus is supposedly named after King Lud, mythical builder of London (at least according to Geoffrey of Monmouth, the less-than-reliable chronicler – Geoffrey also has King Bladud, apocryphal father of King Lear, crashing in the Ludgate Hill area after an attempt to fly, which a later source confabulates further into a Druid flying machine). Less romantic etymologies have been suggested, notably 'flood gate' and 'hlid geat', a gate on a hinge or pivot, but Lud might be the man for the missing pub. There was a well-known Victorian pub on the corner called the King Lud, which was lost when the whole block was totally redeveloped. In a symptomatic change, the former Victorian pub is now a branch of Leon (a chain selling coffee and relatively healthy fast food).

That seems the most likely candidate, though I've looked in endless old pub guides and there's no mention of the lost river in the floor. It's one of those lost memories in a city that become a personal symbol of something, like the opium chemist on Oxford Street that Thomas De Quincey claimed he could never find again, or the vague place or venue called The American Dream that Hunter S. Thompson gets directions for in *Fear and Loathing in Las Vegas* (1971). Other possibilities include a more touristy pub further up the Hill towards a branch of All Bar One (more about All Bar One in a moment) called The Olde City of London, and a New King Lud that was just round the corner. There was no shortage of pubs in the area, or any other (in Victorian times the Strand had around thirty, Soho 150 and Hammersmith 140, and in *The Night Side of London* J. Ewing Ritchie gives a total, for the year 1853, of 5,279). But in recent years the concern has shifted from too many pubs, and pubs as a social problem, to pubs as a vanishing social amenity.

Quiet pubs, which some of us like best, were the first to go. There was a beautiful pub with a large open fireplace deep in Knightsbridge, near Brompton Oratory, through a gate in a brick wall and on to a quieter road. One day I went to find it, and it had become a featureless private house with a flash car parked outside. Much the same thing happened with another quiet traditional pub in a Mayfair yard near the Myanmar Embassy, the Red Lion. Suddenly the Victorian building had been given a modernistic facelift, greywashed with emphatically plain double-glazed windows: it was another multi-million-pound house. Everybody can remember pubs that have gone – there's at least one website commemorating them – including a few curiosities. I was just too late to catch a workingclass pub in Kennington called the George and Dragon that still had a frontage boasting it was 'The Only Pub With A Pool!'. Drinking and swimming don't mix, but perhaps it was aiming for a Spanish holiday poolside vibe, or parents had poolside drinks while the kids sploshed about. I'll never know.

Not that it's all nostalgia. Some pubs could be menacing (I was reminded of this when reading a reminiscence of Ward's Irish House, a vast drinking station under Piccadilly Circus that was before my time, and the writer 'trying not to catch anyone's eye'). Others were safe enough, but badly run. I was in one a few years ago where a middle-aged drunk was being sick. He turned out to be the landlord. But that was okay, as an affable regular told me: 'It's his birthday.' Miraculously – and happily, because at least it was unpretentious and friendly – it's still there (I won't name it).

It was common not to be able to see inside pubs, a hangover from the era of not-quite-respectable drinking, or even of wives looking for their husbands. With partly frosted glass, curtains and a card-board advert or two in the window, you had to push the door open to find out what you were getting into. And sometimes everything would then suddenly stop, as everyone turned around to look at you.

Many pubs were not comfortable for women. The rise of the All Bar One wine bar chain, in the mid-'90s, was built on the idea of giving female drinkers safe, friendly, open places where two or three women could split a bottle of wine, with large plate-glass windows addressing the old problem of off-putting and sinister non-visibility. Around the same time a new breed of pubs rejoicing in novelty names – the Frog and Firkin, or Slug and Lettuce – appeared, again aimed at women and also students. Pubs were changing, but not all for the worse. For a while, bar staff all seemed to come from New Zealand – hired not because they were cheaper and undercut the locals, or any other reason than simply that they were friendlier. The New Zealanders have now become less ubiquitous, but London bar staff are still often foreign; you could easily be served by a Spanish postgraduate student. London is a place where everyone seems to be from somewhere else, and the fact that so many people are here because they want to be – very different from the kind of town where I grew up – gives it a distinctive energy.

But it will take more than women, students and friendly foreign staff to revive the overall fortunes of the British pub. Shifting demo-graphics and the rise in the non-drinking Muslim population have also tilted the balance against pubs in areas like Newham, and drinking habits have changed. The taste for 'bitter' and various old-style beers – which didn't keep well at home and were best had from pumps in pubs – has diminished, and more people now drink wine, or canned or bottled beer, at home. Pubs were once so cheap and widespread that you could nip out to one (across the road, or to the corner) for an inexpensive drink or two at the end of the night without having to trek to an off-licence, but now supermarkets – almost as widespread as pubs used to be, and now open until late – cater for the customer who just wants a drink.

Drinking in pubs has become relatively more expensive, partly because of health-conscious taxes on alcohol and much higher overheads. Business rents and rates in London are racking, and insane property prices mean that it is more profitable to sell a pub as a townhouse or convert it into three or four flats, suddenly making millions instead of paying staff to pour drinks through slow evenings.

The first time I really noticed this – those quiet pubs in Knightsbridge and Mayfair just seemed like two bits of bad luck, though perhaps the word quiet should have been a giveaway – was with a pub in a backwater near the King's Road, the oddly named Phene Arms (once associated with George Best and Bob Marley, situated just by the atmospheric residential street of Margaretta Terrace). The

The Carpenter's Arms, a former Kray twins pub on Cheshire Street, Bethnal Green.

owner, a property developer, planned to close the pub and turn it into a £15 million house, but was stopped from doing so because it was a local amenity with a value in something more than money.

A local amenity. I had not seen it spelled out like that before, but of course good pubs are good for communities: estate agents know this, and a pub with enough community to run a pub quiz is one of the indicators of a good area. Increasingly communities and enthusiasts have been fighting to save their pubs, and often succeeding. The Pineapple in Kentish Town was sold in 2001 with a promise that it would stay a pub, but this was immediately broken and it was set for redevelopment. Locals (some famous, thanks to the gentrification of the area) fought back and obtained English Heritage listing for the building, with its magnificent Victorian bar area, and now it has not only a conservatory and Thai food but a tongue-in-cheek plaque commemorating 'The Pineapple War, 2001–2002'.

The Greenwich Pensioner, in Poplar, is doubly a survivor: first it was the only building left standing in its street after the Blitz – the exterior, in this charmless area of post-war architecture, makes you realize how much good ordinary building London has lost – and now its chequered fortunes as a pub have been revived by the community art-spaces charity SET, who now own it. The 1930s pub the Ivy House in Nunhead was once a gig venue for the likes of Dr Feelgood and Ian Dury (although the main thing likely to take non-locals there now is Nunhead Cemetery, one of the 'Magnificent Seven'), but in 2012 it was put up for sale. Local people formed a collective, bought it, and it now has hundreds of shareholders; it is London's first co-operative pub, and along with pints of beer it has jazz, a chess club, a knitting group and even mother-and-baby classes.

The Elephant and Castle, a basic 1960s building on Newington Causeway, is another notable survivor: associated with rave and garage music, it closed in 2015 and almost became a branch of Foxton's estate agents, until squatters moved in and covered it in 'F*** Foxton's' graffiti. The fight was on, and after being classified as a community asset the pub was saved. The Chesham Arms in Hackney is a much more traditional pub, boarded up in 2012 to be turned into offices and luxury flats, but again the locals fought a two-year legal battle to have it recognized as a community asset and protected. It is now a perfect example of a traditional pub, discreetly modernized only by being made 'better' – the wine magazine *Noble Rot* helped with the wine list, and in 2016 it was a Campaign for Real Ale (CAMRA) 'Pub of the Year'. The Wenlock in Hoxton is another classic pub saved from being turned into luxury flats, now safe within the extended Regent's Canal conservation area, and in the words of one of the people who saved it, Tessa Norton, 'I love this pub with all my stupid heart.'

Back west, and into central London, the decline in pubs is less obvious: Westminster (not the district but the whole borough, including Soho, Covent Garden and the West End generally) is one of the few areas not losing pubs, thanks to the tourist trade, commuting workers and the fact that it is still a playground for the rest of London. With all due respect to the many wonderful pubs that have gone, there is a more positive aspect to the fact that those that survive now often have something extra: some 'added value' over and above alcohol.

At the most desperately downmarket level this might be strippers. Some years ago a friend had a 'hard to let' council flat in south London, and the three or four competing pubs serving his block were clearly in a bad way. When things got really Darwinian, it was the one that went for the blacked-out windows and 'dirty birds' that survived, finally killing off the others. And a pretty grim experience it was too, as I remember it (all male and virtually no conversation, with rapt staring; it's strange how people's facial expressions, when they're not engaging socially, can look absolutely murderous). It was miles away from more cheerful pubs that offer drag acts and suchlike. Theatre is a more upmarket draw; the play I've enjoyed most in my life was Marlowe's *Dr Faustus* above a pub on Fulham Road, but the theatre space wasn't enough to save the pub.

Food is the most obvious thing pubs now like to offer, with the rise of the 'gastro-pub', halfway (sometimes more than half) to a restaurant, and inseparable from gentrification. Times have changed when a pub on Hackney Road, the Marksman, becomes Michelin Pub of the Year. The very pleasant Carpenter's Arms in Bethnal

Green, at one time owned by the Kray twins (bought as a present for their old mum, Violet, nicely misprinted more than once as Mrs Violent Kray), is now a charming place with a French guv'nor (Eric, who runs it with partner Nigel) serving not just great Sunday roasts but pies and charcuterie. There is a picture of the twins; and a long-standing local rumour, going back to the good old bad old days, has it that the bar top is (or was – depending who you talk to) made from coffin lids.

London has become Heritage Babylon, a city where 'heritage' is running berserk – a couple of council blocks in Sidney Street have been named Peter House and Painter House, despite the fact that the semi-apocryphal Peter the Painter, or his comrades, murdered three policemen – and surviving pubs are one of its better aspects. A good old-style pub is one of the places where heritage works, and the 'added value' in many traditional pubs consists in soaking up the atmosphere.

Happily there are still too many to name, but along with the pubs in the listings sections I'd recommend the Churchill Arms on Kensington Church Street, the Hare in Hackney, the Golden Heart in Spitalfields, the Rising Sun on Carter Lane, near St Paul's, the Grosvenor in Pimlico, the Hour Glass on Old Brompton Road, the Anglesea Arms on Selwood Terrace, the Seven Stars on Carey Street, and the Elephant and Castle in the quiet foothills above Kensington High Street. The Elephant and Castle is run by Nicholson's, and despite being notionally a 'chain' their pubs seem to be in safe hands (the Swan at Hammersmith and even the celebrated Black Friar are also traditional Nicholson's pubs). The same is true of Samuel Smith's, a brewery chain with reasonably priced drinks who look after trad-itional interiors; claiming to be influenced by George Orwell's idea of the ideal pub, their pubs include such classics as the Angel on St Giles High Street, at the edge of Covent Garden, the Princess Louise, the Cittie of Yorke and even the famous Cheshire Cheese.

London is a city hell-bent on having a good time; if anyone ever gives it a new coat of arms, the motto should really be 'Just for Jolly' (it is a phrase from the Ripper letters, and you can't get much more heritagey than that . . .). I'm told nothing is manufactured within the

The Churchill Arms, on Kensington Church Street.

City area anymore (except handcrafted gin, significantly enough, from the City of London Distillery). Instead London is becoming a giant service industry, the restaurant and leisure capital of the world. Few major cities are as geared up to unqualified pleasure and leisure at all levels. Paris has a particular cultural appeal for the discerning consumer, and New York has attractions but gets on with its own massive business, whereas London is a fun-for-all-the-family, two-for-the-price-of-one, heritage-day-out, eat-the-world sort of place, a city that positively rolls over on its back to have its tummy tickled if you have a few pounds in your pocket.

Given the giant funhouse London has become, it would be odd if licensed premises weren't doing well in some form. A few years ago a tycoon fell to his death from a Marylebone rooftop, and there was a lot of media interest because it seemed to be one of a series of falls happening to people with Russian oligarch connections. It was a tragic and possibly sinister story, but the detail that really struck me was that he and his wife were said to have been spending £1 million a year in London restaurants: a ridiculous feat only possible with a nightly bashing of stratospheric wine lists. But no doubt it could be done. And a while before that (still back at 2002 prices . . .) five investment bankers were disgraced after it was revealed they'd had a £44,000 dinner at Gordon Ramsay's Petrus restaurant in Belgravia (the restaurant was so impressed by their wine spend it threw in the food for free).

Even with all the money sploshing around, it's a long time since I've seen any new pubs opening (there was a time when former banks were changing into large pubs, but that seems to have stopped) – but I can't keep up with the spread of new bars. There is a shift in London's drinking habits from pubs to bars, now proliferating like mushrooms, and it will be a long time before they need saving with campaigns, cooperatives or Grade II listing.

It's not always easy to define the difference, and there is some overlap, but you generally know it when you see it. If it's house-sized with several bars, beer on draught, and a slower, 'whole evening' pace, and if it resembles either a giant country cottage or a Victorian gin palace, then it's probably a pub. If it's one room, especially downstairs, one serving area, tends more to bottled beers, spirits and cocktails, and it's either dark, glitzy or neon-lit, then it's probably a bar. Old English says pub; transatlantic or New York-style says bar.

There have long been a handful of excellent bars – Gordon's wine bar on Villiers Street, underground and crowded, may be the first of them, dating from around 1890, and El Vino's on Fleet Street is as traditional as any pub, but definitely a wine bar. Hotel bars, slightly different again, are a long-established and expensive world of their own, and now there are some excellent cinema and theatre bars (including the Coronet theatre in Notting Hill, and especially the Regent Street Cinema). Modern 'wine bars', female-friendly and often Continentally themed, became popular in the 1980s as a more middle-class alternative to the pub (and were resented for that very reason, going with the 1980s words 'trendy' and 'yuppy'). The best of the modern yet traditional wine bars may be Noble Rot on Lamb's Conduit Street, home of the wine magazine of the same name.

But the new wave of bars is about something different. Freed from any obligation to be like a 'public house', the game is novelty and strong identity. Bars attract a younger crowd, and the game has been raised from social drinking to actively having a good time with drink. The Four Quarters on Peckham Rye is a bar full of arcade games (Pac-Man, Asteroids and the rest), while the Doodle Bar in Bermondsey encourages drawing on the walls (only in chalk, sadly) and the Beer Shop (that is, bar) in Nunhead had a collage group called the Glue Club (recently in abeyance – but if it starts again, I'll go). God's Own Junkyard, in an industrial estate at Walthamstow, is crammed with neon signs (for sale), with weekend cafe, brewery and gin, and Untitled on Kingsland Road has an Andy Warhol theme (for more serious art, but not quite a bar, the Don restaurant and

Gordon's wine bar in Villiers Street.

bistro is filled with original John Hoylands). There are truly state-of-the-art designer cocktails engineered at the classy, vaguely noir-style Bar With No Name (69 Colebrooke Row), and punch for a select crowd (book in advance) at the clubby Punch Room, inside the London Edition, on Berners Street. Reservations or membership are also needed at the Prohibition-speakeasy-style Milk and Honey, on Poland Street, and the speakeasy theme is taken further, in a more jokey fashion, at Evans & Peel Detective Agency, in a basement on Earls Court Road, where you book, give details of your 'case' to get in, and are ushered into a bar hidden behind a moving bookcase.

Licensing hours – which came in with the First World War, and have gone only recently – were the nearest Britain came to Prohibition, and after-hours bars and clubs had a necessary role when pubs had legally restricted opening times. The intimate but loud Arts Theatre Bar in Dean Street (Soho) still has the feel of a downstairs after-hours club, as does the much larger but similarly theatrical Phoenix Artists Club on Charing Cross Road (members, Equity cards, and/or open entry before a certain time; I've never quite understood their admissions policy). Also in Soho and after-hours style are the excellently seedy New Evaristo ('Trisha's', nominally for members) and heavy-metal hangout Crobar on Manette Street.

Far from Soho, newer bars in formerly godforsaken parts of town include Ruby's in Dalston, with disco-glitz inside and a cinema-style lettering display outside (often changing, not with what's showing but with the message of the moment); and Satan's Whiskers in Bethnal Green, with a discreet neon sign on its semi-derelict frontage and serious cocktails within. The same owners run the 'Hunter S' in Dalston (as in Hunter S. Thompson), a gonzo-themed pub – this time as over-the-top as any bar – stuffed with taxidermy. Then there are quality cocktail bars Original Sin and Happiness Forgets (sister establishments in Stoke Newington High Street and Hoxton Square respectively), and another very deliberate push for quality at Black Rock, a downstairs whisky bar on the City edge of Shoreditch which boasts over 250 whiskies and the 5.5-metre (18 ft) trunk of an oak tree – split in half, hollowed-out and glass topped – as both table area and reservoir for the house whisky, with taps at the end, against a soundtrack of '90s hip-hop. It was wasted on me since I'm not serious about whisky, and I just had a glass of house whisky with umami vermouth in it, but I was still impressed by the set-up. And that barely scratches the surface of London's bar scene. It would be a temptation to wind up a piece on drinking in London with something about last orders, but no; the night is young.

LISTINGS

Sites

Dennis Severs's House
18 Folgate Street, E1 6BX
Time-travelling in Spitalfields: the life of a family of Huguenot silk-weavers imaginatively recreated in a series of atmospheric interiors. Severs's motto: 'Aut visum aut non!' – you either get it or you don't.

Royal Botanic Gardens, Kew
Kew, TW9 3AB
Acres of green parkland around the largest Victorian glasshouse in the world, with an upper gallery, together with orchids, orangery, eighteenth-century pagoda and treetop walk.

Leadenhall Market
Gracechurch Street, EC3V 1LT
Eating, drinking and retail in magnificent multicoloured Victorian ironwork, used as a film set for *Harry Potter and the Philosopher's Stone*. The market dates to the fourteenth century and the present building to 1881, now juxtaposed with unusual success against Richard Rogers's inside-out masterpiece, the Lloyds Building.

Brixton Market
Electric Avenue, SW9 BJX
Two main markets, Brixton Village and Market Row, off the surreal curve of Electric Avenue. Dried fish, vegetables, African and Chinese groceries, good cafes. Smells like an indoor market should. No photography in the Voodoo Shop.

Zoological Society of London: London Zoo
Regent's Park, NW1 4RY
One of the world's great zoos. The lemurs, the venomous but lovable slow loris and the rest, with Rainforest Life and Nightlife.

Chelsea Physic Garden

66 Royal Hospital Road, SW3 4HS
Dreamlike secret garden with small greenhouses, between the King's
Road and the river, founded in 1673 for growing medicinal plants.
Currently under threat of modernization.

Hampton Court Palace

East Molesey, KT8 9AU
Lived in by Henry VIII and all six wives. English Renaissance
grandeur, with tapestries and the extraordinary Chapel Royal
ceiling, together with Charles I's Mantegnas, the famous maze
and the 'Great Vine' – the largest grapevine in the world, bearing
grapes since 1673.

The Tower of London

St Katharine's Dock, EC3N 4AB
The ravens and the armoury, not forgetting the Crown jewels,
with over 25,000 gemstones. So popular you have to slowly slide
past them on a sort of conveyor belt.

Swaminarayan Hindu Temple

Brentfield Road, NW10 8LD
Popularly 'the Neasden Temple', this only dates to the 1990s but
it is the real thing: over 25,000 pieces of marble were carved in
Gujarat, shipped to England, and assembled without using steel,
which was thought to impair meditative energies. Open to all,
this is one of the wonders of the world.

St Paul's Cathedral

St Paul's Churchyard, EC4M 8AD
Wren's iconic masterpiece, with its dome, Whispering Gallery and
monumental black basalt tomb of Nelson in the crypt, topped with
a coronet. The cathedral is accompanied by Temple Bar, also by
Wren, which once stood at the end of Fleet Street, spent years of
exile in Hertfordshire and now stands close by.

Museums

Victoria and Albert Museum
Cromwell Road, SW7 2RL
One of the world's most beautiful museums, with art and design from netsuke and Dale Chihuly to Tipu Sultan's tiger. The cast courts (giant Victorian replicas of Michelangelo's *David* and the like) are a memorable space. Open late on Friday nights, with a bar.

Sir John Soane's Museum
13 Lincoln's Inn Fields, WC2A 3BP
Architectural cabinet of curiosities and classical fragments, like a Grand Tour in one building, left to the nation by visionary architect Sir John Soane, in his own house.

Tate Britain
Millbank, SW1P 4RG
Worth visiting just for Richard Dadd's insane masterpiece *The Fairy Feller's Master Stroke*, but it is packed with blue-chip British art: Pre-Raphaelites, Modernists, Turner and the rest. Magnificent restaurant with Rex Whistler's mural *The Pursuit of Rare Meats*.

Pollock's Toy Museum
1 Scala Street, W1T 2HL
Tin toys, teddy bears and especially Victorian miniature theatres, all housed in a ramshackle, happily unmodernized warren of rooms with a shop on the ground floor.

The Cinema Museum
2 Dugard Way, SE11 4TH
Brainchild of Ronald Grant and Martin Humphries, this former workhouse is full of salvaged decor and equipment from the golden age of cinema. It also screens rare films, sometimes with live piano accompaniment. Worth checking what's on.

The Wallace Collection

Hertford House, Manchester Square, W1U 3BN
A treasure house in a quiet Marylebone backwater, with seemingly
disparate collections unified by nineteenth-century aristocratic taste.
Knights in armour, oriental weapons, and seriously great paintings
including Poussin's *A Dance to the Music of Time*.

Museum of Brands

111–17 Lancaster Road, W11 1QT
Showcasing the Robert Opie Collection, this is a cornucopia
of commercial graphics, packaging and advertising through the
nineteenth and twentieth centuries.

Handel and Hendrix in London

23 and 25 Brook Street, W1K 4HB
Formerly the Handel House Museum in Handel's eighteenth-century
house, with his red four-poster bed, this now encompasses the flat
next door where Jimi Hendrix lived during 1968 and 1969.

The Viktor Wynd Museum of Curiosities, Fine Art and Natural History

11 Mare Street, E8 4RP
Formerly going by the more evocative name of Viktor Wynd's Little
Shop of Horrors, this is an eccentric basement collection with dodo
bones, shrunken heads, strange things in bottles, vintage sleaze,
taxidermy and much more. Absinthe bar upstairs on ground floor.

British Museum

Great Russell Street, WC1B 3DG
Obligatory, but crowded and can be tiring. Not a knockout aesthetic
experience like the Louvre, the V&A or the National Gallery, but still
full of world-class exhibits. The ground-floor Enlightenment gallery
is a curating masterpiece; after that, you need to know what you want
to see – Asian, Islamic, Egyptian and so on – and not try to trek around
the whole thing.

Entertainment Venues

Curzon Mayfair

38 Curzon Street, W1J 7TY

Plush cinema, close to the tucked-away Mayfair pleasure zone of Shepherd's Market, with its pubs and restaurants. Emphasis on indie and foreign films. The Regent Street Cinema, with its cocktail bar, is also excellent.

Brick Lane Music Hall

433 North Woolwich Road, E16 2DA

No longer in Brick Lane but further out in a neon-lit former church; well worth traversing the futuristic wastelands east of Canary Wharf. Pantos, cockney camp and an enjoyably no-nonsense three-course dinner with no options (except for vegetarians). Sit there and eat what you're given, before the performance begins.

The Troxy

490 Commercial Street, E1 0HX

Formerly an Art Deco cinema in Stepney, now a venue for gigs and more. Jarvis Cocker, Patti Smith and the Jesus and Mary Chain (blastingly loud, with a totally immersive strobe) have all played here. Just the right size for the right intensity.

Globe Theatre

21 New Globe Walk, SE1 9DT

Shakespeare in a recreated Shakespearean theatre, with gallery and half-timbering.

Albert Hall

Kensington Gore, SW7 2AP

Spectacular domed Victorian venue, across the road from the Albert Memorial. Great auditorium, famous for the Last Night of the Proms and 'Land of Hope and Glory', but has much wider programming; the last thing I saw here was a film about Iggy Pop.

Wiltons Music Hall

1 Graces Alley, E1 8JB

A music hall since 1859, but time-patinated like something out of Venice, this warmly decayed Whitechapel building narrowly escaped demolition in the 1960s. Less of a full-on auditorium than the name suggests, it is more like a large galleried room behind a pub, with cast iron pillars. Good Victorian bar, and great theatrical and spoken word events.

The Illusioneer

19 Half Moon Lane, SE24 9JU

The novelty of the venue – which gets larger, like the Tardis, behind a tiny frontage in Herne Hill – is part of the magic in this close-up conjuring theatre for an audience of twenty or so. Done with immense charm, it manages to enchant even if you don't care for card tricks.

Old Red Lion

418 St John Street, EC1V 4NJ

Top-class fringe theatre above a good straightforward pub near the Angel; a number of shows have transferred to the West End.

The Lexington

96–8 Pentonville Road, N1 9JB

Transatlantic lounge bar, specializing in bourbon, in a former Victorian pub – DJs and live bands upstairs.

Ronnie Scott's

47 Frith Street, W1D 4HT

Legendary jazz club – open to non-members – started by saxophonist Scott in 1959. Smooth, classy and part of what made Soho into Soho, still going strong.

Restaurants and Cafes

St John

26 St John Street, EC1M 4AY
Fergus Henderson's 'nose to tail' menus, specializing in offal and unusual
game. Roasted marrow bones are a signature dish, with woodcock
in season, and even squirrel.

C&R Cafe

4–5 Rupert Court, W1D 6DY
Worth queueing for this superb Malaysian, down a Soho alley
on the edge of Chinatown. The Singapore laksa soup is magnificent.

Regency Cafe

17–19 Regency Street, SW1P 4BY
Doing the Full English since 1946, this white-tiled cafe has been in
demand as a film set. Claudia belts out the orders in what must be an
opera-trained voice, and they do breakfasts, liver and bacon, steak
pie and everything else you'd hope for, all washed down with proper
mahogany-colour tea. Shuts at 2.30 p.m. and reopens at 4 for the early
evening.

M. Manze's

87 Tower Bridge Road, SE1 4TW
Pie and mash with 'liquor' (a parsley sauce) is the original London
comfort food; you can just eat it with a spoon. Jellied eels are also
available but they are an acquired taste, to put it mildly. Sadly
pie-and-mash shops are becoming a thing of the past – the first
one I went to had the cutlery chained to the table, and they cleaned
it by taking a bucket round – so if you're curious don't wait too long.
The Manze's in Islington's Chapel Market has just gone.

The Troubadour Cafe

236–7 Old Brompton Road, SW5 9JA
Dark wood and enamel advertising give this oddly comforting
Kensington institution an eternally 1960s feel. Known for poetry

and live music, it does good simple food including breakfast, burgers and not-too-fancy cocktails. Garden at the back.

Mien Tay

106 Shoreditch Road, E2 8DP

Not much to choose between several excellent and good value Vietnamese restaurants in Hoxton's Vietnamese strip: Mien Tay, Cay Tre, Song Que and the rest. Pho, beef wrapped in betel, superb galangal goat and more.

The Bleeding Heart

Bleeding Heart Yard, EC1N 8SJ

Hidden away in this Dickensian yard near Hatton Garden, the Bleeding Heart has a restaurant, a more specifically French bistro and a pub. Atmospheric, romantic and nurturing.

Maramia Cafe

48 Golborne Road, W10 5PR

Not an old-school caff but a Palestinian restaurant. Friendly service and top quality, good value Middle Eastern food: tabbouleh, halloumi, falafel, good salads and grilled meats, with chips and pickles available on the side for extra comfort.

Mangal 2 Ockabasi

4 Stoke Newington Road, N16 7XN

Good, basic, meat-heavy Turkish kebab house, much loved by artists Gilbert and George. One of a number of good Turkish restaurants in the area.

Andrew Edmunds

46 Lexington Street, W1F 0LP

A bit of old – or at least 1980s – Soho: small, excellent candlelit restaurant in an eighteenth-century townhouse with old prints on the walls.

Pubs

City of London Distillery (COLD)

22–4 Bride Lane, EC4Y 8DT

Downstairs bar in the shadow of St Bride's Church, with a working gin distillery. You can drink and admire great copper stills with alchemical things going on, behind a big window.

The Duke

7 Roger Street, WC1N 2PB

Some of the better pubs are hard to find, preserved down alleys and time warps, and this is a classic example. Not far from busy Holborn, off Doughty Street, it is on a street you'd probably never visit. Strong 1930s feel, this pub makes me think of George Orwell, flat caps and greyhound racing (no logic to the last two). Bar staff come and go, but I've always found it friendly. No spectacular interior or novelty: just a good ordinary pub.

The Nag's Head

53 Kinnerton Street, SW1X 8ED

Tucked away down a secret mews, this is a gem of a pub. The landlord seems to like it quiet, but high prices, occasional rudeness and a more recent smell of drains still don't keep the public out. Do not under any circumstances let your mobile go off in here, or you'll find out how it stays so picturesque. Nearby pubs (including the Grenadier and the Star Tavern) also excellent.

Ye Olde Cheshire Cheese

Wine Office Court, 145 Fleet Street, EC4 2BU

Rebuilt in 1667, after the Fire. Supposedly a haunt of Dr Johnson, and definitely visited by Boswell, Dickens, Mark Twain, W. B. Yeats and more unexpectedly Picasso, who overdid it with the steak-and-oyster pudding and jokingly accused his friend André Derain of trying to poison him. A large building inside, with several bars, it somehow manages to keep some atmosphere and not be totally swamped with heritage-trailers.

Ye Olde Mitre

1 Ely Court, Ely Place, EC1N 6SJ

A little of 'ye olde' goes a long way, but this place is entitled to it: it goes back to 1546. Leaded windows and wood-panelled walls keep things looking suitably old. Not only a hidden destination worth seeking out, down an alley off Hatton Garden, but very much a functional pub for people working in the area.

The Black Friar

174 Queen Victoria Street, EC4V 4EG

Bizarrely ornate and opulent Art Nouveau pub, the only one in London, on a Flat Iron Building-style corner. Marble and copper frieze work give the interior an amber warmth. Gets crowded: probably best seen in the day, avoiding lunchtime, or late at night.

The Eagle

159 Farringdon Road, EC1R 3AL

So-called 'gastro-pubs' have been a mixed blessing, but this was the first – back in the early '90s, in what was then the quiet backwater of Clerkenwell – and it is still one of the best. Classic steak sandwiches.

The Salisbury

90 St Martin's Lane, WC2N 4AP

Beautiful pub in London's book and theatre district, with candelabras, etched glass and mirrors, like a gin palace. One of several good Victorian pubs, including the outstanding Princess Louise in Holborn (dark wood and majolica tilework; gets crowded) and the much smaller Red Lion on Duke of York Street, St James's, with its bevelled mirror interior.

The French House

49 Dean Street, W1D 5BG

The one and only 'French Pub', going back to the Bohemian Soho days of Francis Bacon and before that Charles de Gaulle and the Free French. After several changes of hands the interior still survives, and a little of the vibe. No pints, only the French-style half, to discourage the British riff-raff. Restaurant upstairs.

Shops

Liberty's
Regent Street, W1B 5AH
Upmarket Tudorbethan department store – made with wood from
two warships, HMS *Hindustan* and HMS *Impregnable* – with furniture,
stationery and fabrics. Originally associated with oriental goods and
Art Nouveau, it has a tradition of distinguished collaborations, from
William Morris to Vivienne Westwood.

Book Art Bookshop
17 Pitfield Street, N1 6HB
Not-for-profit Hoxton outlet showcasing artist's books and small press
publications.

Notting Hill Book and Comic Exchange
30–32 Pembridge Road, W11 3HN
'This is not the shop from the rubbish film *Notting Hill*, so don't ask!',
says a notice in this shop; 'We don't know where it is either.' Top marks
for attitude (matched only by Blackman's Shoes off Brick Lane, which
displays a long list of languages not spoken) and some interesting
second-hand books and magazines, tending to the hip rather than
the mainstream or antiquarian.

L. Cornellisen and Son, Artists' Colourmen
105 Great Russell Street, WC1B 3RY
Beautifully fitted-out emporium of art supplies, full of numbered
drawers and multicoloured jars. Pigments, papers, brushes and
more specialized materials for restoration and gilding.

Paxton & Whitfield
93 Jermyn Street SW1Y 6JE
The world of cheese since 1797, in a top-quality specialist shop
also offering kindred products such as pie and ham.

John Sandoe Books

10 Blackheath Terrace, SW3 2SR

Well-chosen books in this quietly classy bookshop just off the King's Road. The only new bookshop that feels as good as a second-hand bookshop.

The Algerian Coffee Stores

52 Old Compton Street, W1D 4PB

Founded by Mr Hassan in 1887, this is like a sweetshop for coffee. Great range of house blends, coffee-making equipment, tea bricks and more, with takeaway espressos at £1 a shot.

The Spice Shop

1 Blenheim Crescent, W11 2EE

This tiny shop, with its distinctive yellow packaging, began as a street stall and now stocks over 2,500 products. The emphasis really is on spice, diversifying a little into such things as tea, chia seeds and macca root. It's in the ever-interesting area of Portobello Road, with its market and exceptionally good charity shops – a British institution.

London Architectural Salvage Supply Company (LASSCO)

30 Wandsworth Road, SW8 2LG

Like an oasis in the bleak area at the southern end of Vauxhall Bridge, this eighteenth-century mansion is one of the wonders of London. Filled with ever-changing architectural antiques – rococo mirrors, neon signs, shopfittings and advertising, along with old prints – it also has a good bar and restaurant.

House of Hackney

131 Shoreditch High Street, E1 6JE

Proclaiming itself 'The future of the past', this maximalist wallpaper and furniture shop gives a funky edge to trad design. Founded in 2011 by Frieda Gormley and Javvy Royle, they have since collaborated with Zuber and have a prominent place in Liberty's, as well their flagship on the transfigured Shoreditch High Street.

Chronology

200,000 BC	There were hippopotami where Trafalgar Square is now, and Britain was connected to Europe by land
AD 43	The Roman settlement of Londinium comes after the Roman invasion
AD 60	Londinium is sacked and burned in the Iceni revolt led by Boudicca
AD 410	The Romans leave Britain. The Romanized Britons are pushed aside by another wave of invaders, the Saxons
1014	The likely year for the event in the nursery rhyme 'London Bridge is Falling Down', from an earlier Norse poem. Norwegians and Danes fight each other for London, with the Norwegians in alliance with the Saxon king Aethelred. Norwegian men destroy the bridge
1066	Norman invasion. Work begins on the Tower of London by around 1078
1348	The Black Death kills around half of London's 80,000 population
1381	Peasants' Revolt
1388	Gallows set up at Tyburn, near present-day Marble Arch. Public hangings become part of London's popular culture for the next 500 years, moving to Newgate in 1783
1397	Dick Whittington becomes mayor

1420	There is a tavern on the site of the present-day Cittie of Yorke pub, giving it a strong claim in the complicated business of 'London's oldest pub'
1476	Caxton sets up the first English printing press, at Westminster, having studied printing in Cologne, and publishes *The Canterbury Tales* (1478)
1484	The College of Arms, the nation's heraldic authority, is founded
1485	Richard III dies in battle, ending the 'Wars of the Roses'. Henry VII is crowned, bringing in the Tudors and with them the end of the mediaeval period. It is something of a golden age for London, remembered as the time of pageantry, half-timbered building, Shakespeare and the English Renaissance
1509	Henry VIII comes to the throne, in a reign that will break with Roman Catholicism, bringing the English Reformation and the dissolution of the monasteries
1535	Executions of Charterhouse monks (the Carthusian Martyrs) begin, the earliest of over 100 Catholic martyrs
*c.*1543	Wyngaerde's *Panorama of London*; one of several extraordinary depictions and maps by Continental artisans, including the Copperplate Map (*c.* 1560)
1553	The Catholic Mary I comes to the throne, and now Protestants are martyred
1558	Elizabeth I, 'Gloriana', becomes queen. Religious persecution switches back to Catholics. English Renaissance culture reaches its height during her reign
1599	Globe Theatre built

1605   Gunpowder Plot

1625   Charles I becomes king. His reign will be ended by the English
        Civil War (1642–45), leading to his execution in 1649

1652   First coffee house, Pasqua Rosée's, in St Michael's Alley, off
        Cornhill. The first Chocolate House follows in 1657

1658   Cromwell dies. Diarist John Evelyn notes 'the joyfullest funerall
        that I ever saw'

1660   Charles II, invited back from exile, comes to the throne.
        The Restoration begins, and theatres reopen

1665   The Great Plague (largest and last of many outbreaks since
        the fourteenth century)

1666   Great Fire of London

1673   Wren's Temple Bar (monumental gateway) across Fleet Street
        is completed

1685   Huguenots arrive, fleeing persecution in France

1702   The *Daily Courant* is published in Fleet Street, and now
        generally taken to be the first regular 'daily newspaper'

1712   Handel moves to London from Germany. *Water Music* is
        performed on a barge on the Thames, 1717, and *Music for
        the Royal Fireworks* is performed in Green Park, 1749

1714   George I comes from Germany to become king. He never learns
        to speak English
        Nicholas Hawksmoor designs Christ Church, Spitalfields.
        It is completed in 1729

1720   The South Sea Bubble

1724   Jack Sheppard, petty criminal and serial escaper, is hanged
        at Tyburn. Around 200,000 people turn out

1725   Jonathan Wild, supposedly 'Thief-Taker General' but in fact
        running the underworld, is finally hanged

1750   Hogarth, *Gin Lane*

1753   Horace Walpole remodels Strawberry Hill in Gothic style with
        fake battlements

1755   Dr Johnson's *Dictionary*, including 'Grub Street'

1770   Viewing the mad at Bedlam ceases to be public entertainment

1780   Gordon Riots

1793   The top hat, an iconic part of nineteenth-century London's
        image, is invented by Middlesex hatter George Dunnidge.
        There is an apocryphal story that it was invented and worn by
        a John Hetherington in 1797, and attracted such a crowd that
        he was fined £50 for causing a public nuisance, but it seems
        to be a spoof originating in the London of the 1890s

1794   Blake publishes *Songs of Experience*, including 'London'

1802   Madame Tussaud arrives in London from France, with
        35 waxworks. By the time of her death in 1850, her permanent
        show on Baker Street has become a national institution

1807   British Slave Trade Act ends British involvement in the slave
        trade. The Society for Effecting the Abolition of the Slave
        Trade had been founded in 1787

1810   Britain's first Indian restaurant, Dean Mahomet's Hindostanee Coffee House

1811   Ratcliff Highway murders in east London

1812   Gas street lighting, demonstrated on Pall Mall in 1807, is adopted. Westminster Bridge is lit by gas the following year

1815   Napoleon is defeated at Waterloo on 18 June; news reaches London on horseback on the 21st

1818   Royal Opera Arcade, London's first. Burlington Arcade opens the following year

1820   Cato Street conspiracy

1828   London Zoo opens
        Sir Robert Peel starts the Metropolitan Police ('Peelers' or 'Bobbies')

1833   Kensal Green Cemetery, the first of the 'Magnificent Seven', including Highgate (1839) and Brompton

1834   Houses of Parliament burn
        Harrods begins as a grocer in the East End

1837   *Oliver Twist* begins as a serial in *Bentley's Miscellany*

1840   Foundation stone laid for the new Palace of Westminster (Parliament), designed in meticulous Gothic. Over the next twenty years it is completed

1842   Fleet and Marshalsea debtors' prisons closed

1843   Trafalgar Square – named around 1830, laid out and paved around 1840 – is completed with Nelson's Column

1844   First known eel-and-mash shop in London, run by a Henry
        Blanchard at 101 Union Street, Southwark

1845   Penny dreadfuls: *Varney the Vampyre, or The Feast of Blood*,
        and the following year *The String of Pearls* (which launches
        'Sweeney Todd, the Demon Barber of Fleet Street')

1848   'Year of Revolutions' on the Continent; large Chartist rally on
        Kennington Common, demanding the vote for all adult men

1849   Karl Marx moves to London
        Lock & Co hatters make the first bowler hat

1851   The Great Exhibition
        Henry Mayhew's *London Labour and the London Poor*

1852   Following the Great Exhibition, the Museum of Manufactures,
        earliest predecessor of the Victoria and Albert Museum (or
        the South Kensington Museum) is opened by Queen Victoria
        in 1857; in 1899 she lays the foundation stone of the present
        museum, and it finally opens in 1907

1854   An epidemic of cholera kills 10,000. Dr John Snow traces the
        source of the Broad Street cholera outbreak (which killed 500)
        to a single water pump, validating his theory that cholera is
        waterborne, and forming the starting point for epidemiology.
        The London Necropolis Company begins operating Brookwood
        Cemetery; the London Necropolis Railway service has its own
        station beside Waterloo

1859   Clock Tower at the Palace of Westminster becomes operational.
        The bell, first installed in 1856, is nicknamed 'Big Ben'

1860   Battersea Dogs Home begins as Home for Lost and Starving
        Dogs

1863   First section of the London Underground (still not the deeper 'tube') opens: the Metropolitan Railway between Paddington and Farringdon Street, operated by steam

1867   Clerkenwell explosion ('Clerkenwell Outrage') at Clerkenwell House of Detention, to blow a hole in the wall for an escape: seventeen people are killed in nearby houses

1868   Last public hanging in Britain; Fenian bomber Michael Barrett is hanged for the Clerkenwell Outrage
        Smithfield Meat Market opens

1870   1870 Education Act makes schooling compulsory

1875   Liberty's

1878   Cleopatra's Needle
        Temple Bar is dismantled and moved to Theobalds Park in Hertfordshire

1879   Electric street lighting is introduced on the Thames Embankment.
        Fog descends in November and doesn't lift until March of the following spring

1881   1881 Anarchist Congress; international meeting in a pub behind Euston station

1885   Crusading journalist W. T. Stead shocks readers with a prostitution exposé in the *Pall Mall Gazette*, 'The Maiden Tribute of Modern Babylon' (1885)

1886   Stevenson, *The Strange Case of Dr Jekyll and Mr Hyde* (later filmed, 1920, 1931, 1941)

1887   Victoria's Golden Jubilee
        Sherlock Holmes and Dr Watson first appear in Conan Doyle's
        A Study in Scarlet, published in *Beeton's Christmas Annual*

1888   London matchgirls strike
        'Autumn of Terror': Jack the Ripper murders

1890   William Booth, *In Darkest England*
        Beginnings of deep tube, with a tunnelling machine
        (as opposed to the shallower 'cut and cover' method
        of the earlier underground)
        Oscar Wilde, *The Picture of Dorian Gray*

1893   Shaftesbury Memorial Fountain (popularly 'Eros') is
        unveiled at Piccadilly Circus

1896   The first tabloid paper, the *Daily Mail*, particularly aimed
        at women ('wives')
        Arthur Morrison's slum novel *A Child of the Jago*; in the same
        year the London County Council completes Boundary Estate,
        on the former Old Nichol slum where the novel is set

1900   The Relief of Mafeking
        Postman's Park, 'Memorial to Heroic Self-Sacrifice'

1903   Suffragettes adopt 'Deeds Not Words' policy

1911   The Siege of Sidney Street

1914   Outbreak of First World War; Lord Kitchener and 'Your
        Country Needs You' first appears on the cover of the *London
        Opinion* magazine, before becoming an iconic poster

1915   Zeppelin bombing begins; the first victim is a three-year-old
        girl, Elsie Leggatt, at Newington Green

1918	Vote given to women over thirty, subject to financial and educational status
1922	Radio 2LO, early incarnation of the BBC, begins broadcasting T. S. Eliot writes *The Waste Land* (published 1923) with its grey, dehumanized London commuter crowd in the 'Unreal City' passage: 'A crowd flowed over London Bridge, so many. / I had not thought death had undone so many'
1924	Classic red phone box appears: the model K2
1926	John Logie Baird demonstrates his invention of television at 22 Frith Street, Soho General Strike
1934	Battersea Power Station
1935	Green Belt scheme launched
1936	'Battle of Cable Street'; defeat for the British Union of Fascists in Jewish East End A to Z map of London first published
1939	Second World War begins
1940	The Blitz begins
1941	German spy Josef Jakobs becomes the last man executed at the Tower of London
1945	Street celebrations: 8 May, VE Day; 15 August, VJ Day
1948	The SS *Empire Windrush* arrives, bringing migrants from Jamaica

1952   Thick smog in December. Named in nineteenth-century style
       the Great Smog, it causes around 4,000 deaths. Parliament
       passes the Clean Air Act in 1956

1953   The first real Italian espresso coffee bar, the Moka in Soho's
       Frith Street, is opened by Gina Lollobrigida

1957   John Stephen's boutique His Clothes opens in Carnaby Street,
       a road behind Liberty's associated with the second-hand car trade

1958   Notting Hill race disturbances, after Teddy boys attack West
       Indian migrants
       The Campaign for Nuclear Disarmament is launched, with a
       rally in Trafalgar Square, followed by a march to Aldermaston

1964   First Biba boutique

1965   Post Office Tower
       Mary Quant introduces the miniskirt in her King's Road
       boutique, Bazaar

1966   Ronnie Kray shoots George Cornell dead in Whitechapel's
       Blind Beggar pub, the murder for which he is finally convicted
       in 1969
       Time magazine cover feature, 'Swinging London'
       Notting Hill Carnival

1967   'Summer of Love'
       The Beatles' *Sgt Pepper* LP

1968   Anti-Vietnam War demonstrations at Grosvenor Square,
       outside the US Embassy
       The IRA bomb the Post Office Tower; IRA bombing continues
       into the 1990s, with many public casualties

1973   Erno Goldfinger's Trellick Tower, a high-rise social housing
        block in run-down North Kensington
        Goodbye London by Lycett Green and Booker

1974   Britain's first McDonald's opens in Woolwich

1977   Silver Jubilee of Queen Elizabeth II
        The central year of punk

1979   Margaret Thatcher elected

1981   Brixton riots
        Wedding of Charles and Diana

1983   IRA bomb Harrods during Christmas shopping

1985   *New Georgian Handbook*
        Broadwater Farm riots

1986   Richard Rogers's Lloyd's Building opens

1987   Wapping dispute: News International papers including
        The Times are suspended by a strike over new technology
        and the move to Wapping, as the newspaper industry moves
        out of Fleet Street and into Docklands

1990   Poll tax riots

1994   Eurostar
        Terry Farrell's SIS building for the Secret Intelligence Service
        (more popularly 'the MI6 building') becomes operational in
        Vauxhall on the site of the old Vauxhall Pleasure Gardens
        Finsbury Park mosque

1997   New British Library building at St Pancras

2003   Demonstration against the Iraq War, with Trafalgar Square the focal point: largest demonstration in British history, with estimates of up to two million people

2004   30 St Mary Axe, 'The Gherkin', opens
Temple Bar comes back to London: it is reinstalled at Paternoster Square beside St Paul's

2005   '7/7' London bombings

2008   Boris Johnson becomes mayor; he relaxes controls on high building, seriously altering the skyline

2015   Population reaches record high of 8.6 million and is forecast to reach 11 million by 2050

2016   The first Muslim mayor, Sadiq Khan
Brexit: London votes to remain, but is defeated by poorer areas across the UK

2019   Extinction Rebellion campaigns against ecological disaster

References

p. 17 John T. Appleby, ed., *The Chronicle of Richard of Devizes* (London, 1963), p. 65.

p. 19 Widely syndicated, for example in the *New York Evening Post*, XXX/10 (July 1885). It later appears in Baedeker.

p. 19 Robert Hichens, *The Green Carnation* (London, 1894), p. 9.

p. 19 William Makepeace Thackeray in *Punch* (9 March 1850), p. 93.

p. 20 Heather Creaton, ed., *Bibliography of Printed Works on London History to 1939* (London, 1994).

p. 23 Caesar, *The Conquest of Gaul*, trans. S. A. Handford (Harmondsworth, 1963), p. 135.

p. 25 Tacitus, *Annals*, XIV, ed. C. J. Woodford (Indianapolis, IN, 2004), p. 291.

p. 26 Tacitus, *Agricola*, section 21.

p. 28 'The Ruins' (the city is Bath), in *Three Old English Elegies*, ed. R. F. Leslie (Manchester, 1961), pp. 23–7.

p. 31 Quoted in Peter Ackroyd, *London: The Biography* (London, 2000), p. 54.

p. 37 Quoted ibid., p. 291.

p. 37 Privy Council order of 1591, quoted in R. Chambers, ed., *The [Chambers] Book of Days* (Edinburgh, 14 July 1869).

p. 42 According to witness Philip Henry, *The Diaries and Letters of Philip Henry*, ed. M. H. Lee (London, 1882), p. 12.

p. 45 Quoted in Roy Porter, *London: A Social History* (London, 2000), p. 105.

p. 45 Esmond de Beer, ed., *The Diary of John Evelyn* (Oxford, 1959), p. 496.

p. 54 Walpole quoted in *The London Encyclopaedia*, ed. Ben Weinreb and Christopher Hibbert (London, 1993), p. 216; Henry Fielding, 'An Enquiry into the Causes of the Late Increase of Robbers', quoted in Roy Porter, *London: A Social History* (London, 2000), p. 183.

p. 54 Quoted in *The London Encyclopaedia*, p. 563.

p. 55 Quoted in David Nokes, *Samuel Johnson: A Life* (London, 2009), p. 141.

p. 55 James Boswell, *London Journal*, ed. G. Turnbull (London, 2010), p. 182.

p. 61 Christopher Hibbert, *London: The Biography of a City* (London, 1980), p. 162.

p. 61 Quoted in Andrew Hussey, *The Game of War: The Life and Death of Guy Debord* (London, 2001), p. 315.

p. 63 Henry James, *Complete Notebooks*, ed. Leon Edel (Oxford, 1987).

p. 63 Dean Mahomet, in *The Travels of Dean Mahomet*, ed. Michael Fisher (Berkeley, CA, 1997), p. 150.

p. 64 Thomas De Quincey, *Collected Writings*, ed. David Masson (Edinburgh, 1889), vol. I, p. 178.

p. 65 Thomas Lamb, *The Letters of Thomas Lamb*, ed. E. V. Lucas (London, 1935), vol. I, p. 241.

p. 69 Ian Nairn, *Nairn's London* (London, 1967), p. 57.

p. 70 Quoted in Rick Allen, ed., *The Moving Pageant: A Literary Sourcebook on London Street-Life, 1700–1914* (London, 1998), p. 138.

p. 71 Quoted in Roy Porter, *London: A Social History* (London, 2000), p. 326.

p. 71 Mary Kelynack of Newlyn, reported in *The Times* (as Mrs Callinack [*sic*]), 24 September 1851, p. 5. It took her five weeks.

p. 73 H. V. Morton, *The Heart of London* (London, 1925), p. 108.

p. 73 'The Greatest City in the World', *New York Evening Post*, XXX/10 (July 1885).

p. 73 Henry James, *English Hours*, (London, 1905).

p. 74 Quoted in Frank Kermode, *The Uses of Error* (Cambridge, MA, 1991), p. 183.

p. 74 *The Times*, 5 July 1849, p. 5.

p. 74 Quoted in Iain Bamforth, *A Doctor's Dictionary: Writings on Culture and Medicine* (Manchester, 2015), p. 29.

p. 75 Discussed by Simon Young, 'Sewer Hogs and Crocs', *Fortean Times*, CCCXXXI (September 2015), p. 23.

p. 77 French visitor quoted in Gillian Tindall, *The House by the Thames* (London, 2006), p. 149.

p. 78 Quoted in Christine Corton, *Fog: The Biography* (Cambridge, MA, 2015), p. 161.

p. 78 Ibid.

p. 78 Ibid., p. 184.

p. 79 George Gissing, *The Immortal Dickens* (London, 1925), p. 496.

p. 80 *Dickens' Journalism*, vol. II: *The Amusements of the People and Other Papers*, ed. Michael Slater (London, 1997), p. 82.

p. 81 Quoted in Philip Ward, *The Life and Times of Cardinal Wiseman* (London, 1897), vol. I, p. 568.

p. 81 William Makepeace Thackeray in *Punch*, 9 March 1850, p. 93.

p. 81 Henry Mayhew, 'Street-sellers of Green Stuff', in *London Labour and the London Poor* (London, 1851), vol. I, pp. 151–2.

p. 81 The London Diocesan Building Society, quoted in Porter, *London: A Social History*, p. 335.

p. 81 George Sims, *How the Poor Live; and, Horrible London* (London, 1889), p. 1.

p. 82 William Booth, *In Darkest England* (London, 1890), p. 13.

p. 83 Fyodor Dostoyevsky, *Winter Notes on Summer Impressions* (London, 1955), pp. 61–6.

p. 85 Blanchard Jerrold, *London: A Pilgrimage*, illus. Gustave Doré (London, 1872), p. 138.

p. 85 J. H. Mackay, *The Anarchists* (New York, 1891), p. 153.

p. 86 Quoted in *The Moving Pageant: A Literary Sourcebook on London Street-Life, 1700–1914*, ed. Rick Allen (London, 1998), p. 193.

p. 88 C. H. Rolph, *The Police and the Public* (London, 1962), p. 52.

p. 89 Quoted in Fiona McCarthy, *William Morris* (London, 1994), p. 466.

p. 89 *Punch*, 10 January 1863.

p. 90 Quoted in Kermode, *The Uses of Error*, p. 184.

p. 90 Fenning's patent medicine advert, quoted in Julia Jones, *Fifty Years in the Fiction Factory: The Working Life of Edward Allingham* (Pleshey, 2012), p. 47.

p. 91 Jacob Middleton, 'Of Empire and Eels', *Fortean Times*, CXCIV (March 2005), p. 51.

p. 92 Gordon Grimley, ed., *Walter: My Secret Life* (London, 1972), p. 8.

p. 93 Robert Mighall, *A Geography of Victorian Gothic Fiction* (Oxford, 1999), p. 45.

p. 94 J. G. Millais, *The Life of John Everett Millais*, quoted in *The Small Oxford Book of London*, ed. Benny Green (Oxford, 1984), p. 164.

p. 94   Raymond Williams, *The Country and the City* (London, 1975), p. 227.

p. 94   Arthur Conan Doyle, 'The Red-headed League', in *The Adventures of Sherlock Holmes* (1892)

p. 94   Quoted in John Andrews and Teresa Stoppani, eds, *Foundation of Exotic Studies: London Book* (London, 2002), unpaginated ['Introduction'].

p. 99   Quoted in Anthony Lejeune, *The Gentleman's Clubs of London* (London, 1979), p. 295.

p. 100 Arthur Symons, *London: A Book of Aspects*, quoted in *The Moving Pageant*, ed. Rick Allen (London, 1998), p. 212.

p. 103 LSE Booth Archive, George H. Duckworth's notebooks, 'An Opium Den in Jamaica Street', Booth/B/346, pp. 119–27.

p. 105 Quoted in Robert Wainwright, *Miss Muriel Matters* (London, 2017), p. 72.

p. 106 John Carey, *The Intellectuals and the Masses* (London, 1992), p. 49.

p. 110 Geoffrey Dennis, *Coronation Commentary* (New York, 1937) p. 40.

p. 111 Quoted on the dustjacket of 'The Man Who Dined With the Kaiser' [pseud.], *My Secret Service* (London, 1916).

p. 112 Graham Greene, 'The Poker Face', in *Collected Essays* (London, 1969), pp. 156–7.

p. 113 Marista Leishman, *My Father, Reith of the BBC* (Edinburgh, 2006), p. 148.

p. 116 Iain Nairn, *Nairn's London* (London, 1967), p. 193.

p. 118 Julie Burchill, *The Face*, 18 (March 1990), p. 62.

p. 119 Quoted in Richard Griffiths, *Fellow Travellers of the Right* (London, 1980), p. 164.

p. 119 *Daily Mail*, 15 January 1934.

p. 121 Harold Nicolson, *Diaries and Letters, 1939–1945* (London, 1967), p. 114.

p. 122 Quoted in, for example, D. J. Taylor, *The New Book of Snobs* (London, 2016), p. 190.

p. 123 Elizabeth Bowen, *The Collected Stories of Elizabeth Bowen* (London, 1980), p. 728.

p. 123 Rose Macaulay, *The World My Wilderness* (London, 1950), pp. 121–2.

p. 123 Graham Greene, 'At Home', in *Collected Essays*, p. 450.

p. 125 George Orwell, *Complete Works*, vol. XVI: *I Have Tried To Tell the Truth 1943–1944*, ed. Peter Davison (London, 1998), p. 230.

p. 127 *Illustrated News London*, 23 June 1945, pp. 678–9.

p. 127 Graham Greene, *Journey without Maps* (London, 1936), p. 7; *The Lawless Roads* (London, 1939), p. 79.

p. 128 Ian Cox, *The South Bank Exhibition: A Guide to the Story It Tells* (London, 1951), p. 7.

p. 129 Ray Davies, 'My London', *Evening Standard ES Magazine* 1 February 2013.

p. 130 Evelyn Waugh in *The Letters of Evelyn Waugh and Nancy Mitford*, ed. Charlotte Mosley (London, 1996), p. 336.

p. 130 Quoted in John Baxter, *A Pound of Paper* (London, 2002), p. 61.

p. 131 Roy Porter, *London: A Social History* (London, 2000), p. 419.

p. 132 Quoted in 'Sayings of 1954', *The Observer*, 2 January 1955, p. 8.

p. 132 Jeffrey Bernard, 'Low Life', *The Spectator*, 22 February 1997, p. 46.

p. 133 Jake Arnott, *He Kills Coppers* (London, 2001), p. 265.

p. 135 Michael Bracewell, in *London: From Punk to Blair*, ed. Joe Kerr and Andrew Gibson (London, 2003), p. 305.

p. 135 George Orwell, *Collected Works*, vol. XI: *Facing Unpleasant Facts, 1937–1939* (London, 1998), p. 360.

p. 138 Johnny Gunnell, sleeve notes to Georgie Fame and the Blue Flames, *Rhythm and Blues at the Flamingo* (RSO SLELP-80).

p. 138 Richard Weight, *Patriots* (London, 2002), p. 304.

p. 138 Henry Fairlie, 'Political Commentary', *The Spectator*, 23 September 1955, pp. 379–81.

p. 140 Pete Townsend, *Melody Maker*, 3 July 1965.

p. 141 *Time*, 15 April 1966.

p. 142 Quoted in Robert Greenfield, *A Day in the Life* (Cambridge, MA, 2009), p. 116.

p. 143 Benny Green, *Small Oxford Book of London* (Oxford, 1984), p. 99.

p. 143 Robert Irwin, *Satan Wants Me* (Sawtry, 1999), pp. 110–11.

p. 143 David Widgery, 'Against Grown-up Power', *New Statesman*, 4 August 1967, p. 141.

p. 144 Ian Fleming, *Casino Royale* (London, 1953), p. 61.

p. 144 *Oxford Dictionary of Quotations*, ed. Elizabeth Knowles (Oxford, 1999), p. 822.

p. 145 Vidal Sassoon, quoted in *Huffington Post*, 9 May 2012.

p. 145 *The Ipcress File*, dir. Sidney J. Furie (1965).

p. 150 Patrick Wright, *A Journey through Ruins* (London, 2001), p. 14.

p. 152 Quoted in Roy Porter, *London: A Social History* (London, 2000), p. 469.

p. 154 *Newsweek*, 3 November 1996.

p. 154 Geri Halliwell, 'Spice Girls Back Sceptics on Europe', *The Spectator*, XIV/21, December 1996, p. 14.

p. 156 Quoted in 'Feral Children Bring Fear to our Streets', *Evening Standard*, 15 May 2002.

p. 157 Comedy by Ashok Patel, Bloomsbury Theatre and Watermans Theatre.

p. 158 Laura Thompson, *A Different Class of Murder: The Story of Lord Lucan* (London, 2014), p. 18.

p. 158 Mark Eason, 'Why Have the White British Left London?', www.bbc.co.uk, 20 February 2013.

p. 159 Boris Johnson, quoted in 'Boris Brags about London's Exotic Army of Millionaires', *The Times*, 28 November 2014.

p. 159 Theo Crosby, quoted in Wright, *A Journey through Ruins*, p. 216.

p. 160 Peter York talk at Sohemian Society, The Wheatsheaf, Rathbone Place W1, 12 April 2017.

p. 161 'Up to 75% of Babies are Born to Migrant Mothers in Parts of UK', *The Times*, 9 May 2019.

p. 162 Quoted in 'Pass Notes: Michael Gove', *The Guardian*, 7 April 2014.

p. 163 Iain Sinclair, 'The Last London', *London Review of Books*, 30 March 2017.

p. 163 William Blake, 'Jerusalem, Emanation of the Giant Albion', in *The Poems of William Blake*, ed. W. H. Stevenson and David V. Erdman (London, 1971), p. 699.

p. 171 Quoted in 'Walkie Talkie Architect "Didn't Realise it Was Going to Be so Hot"', *The Guardian*, 13 September 2013.

p. 174 Peter Rees in *Evening Standard*, 11 March 2015.

p. 174 Rees in *Evening Standard*, 11 April 2014.

p. 175 Alexander Jan, *Evening Standard*, 12 March 2014.

p. 179 Henry James, 'London', in *Essays in London and Elsewhere* (London 1893), pp. 21–2.

p. 183 George Orwell, *Collected Works*, vol. XVI: *I Have Tried to Tell the Truth, 1943–1944* (London, 1988), p. 202.

p. 187 Quoted in Peter Vansittart, ed., *London: A Literary Companion* (London, 1992), p. 28.

p. 189 To borrow the title of a classic book on the cemetery, Felix Barker, *Highgate Cemetery: Victorian Valhalla* (London, 1984).

p. 191 William E. Fredeman, ed., *The Correspondence of Dante Gabriel Rossetti*, vol. IV (Woodbridge, 2004), p. 303.

p. 193 'Court Told of Naked Girl Dancing amongst Coffins', *The Times*, 12 June 1974, p. 5.

p. 195 Peter Ackroyd, *London: The Biography* (London, 2000), p. 581.

p. 196 Ibid., p. 580.

p. 196 Ben Weinreb and Christopher Hibbert, *The London Encyclopaedia* (rev. edn, 1993), p. 400.

p. 207 William Boyd, 'The Vanishing Game', in *The Dreams of Bethany Mellmoth* (London, 2017).

p. 210 Quoted on the back cover of *Viktor Wynd's Cabinet of Wonders* (London, 2014).

p. 213 John Tradescant, quoted in Jennifer Potter, *Strange Blooms: The Curious Lives and Adventures of the John Tradescants* (London, 2006), p. 168.

p. 219 Matthew Collings, 'Cult Watch', *Modern Painters* (Autumn 2001), p. 90.

p. 221 Iain Sinclair quoted in Henry Eliot and Matt Lloyd-Rose, eds, *Curiosity* (London, 2018), p. 405.

p. 226 Tessa Norton quoted in 'Fight to Save Iconic Hoxton Pub Begins', *Hackney Gazette*, 27 September 2010.

Reading and Viewing

Books

Ackroyd, Peter, *London: The Biography* (2000)
> Ackroyd's 'mystorical' faith in an eternal London is not to
> everyone's taste, but he is superb with detail.

Clunn, Chris, *Eels, Pie and Mash* (1995)
> Atmospheric photos from the vanishing world of the
> pie-and-mash shop.

Collins, Michael, *The Likes of Us: A Biography of the White Working
Class* (2004)
> Rooted in the author's own south London family, this is
> a no-nonsense and often moving history of the only group
> everyone seems to feel comfortable looking down on.

Cruickshank, Dan, *The Secret History of Georgian London: How the
Wages of Sin Shaped the Capital* (2009)
> Scholarly but evocative book on the ever-popular subject of
> London vice; does for the Georgians what Ronald Pearsall's
> *The Worm in the Bud* (1969) did for the Victorians.

Decharné, Max, *King's Road: The Rise and Fall of the Hippest Street
in the World* (2005)
> Solidly researched, and narrated with a suitably cool relish.

Del Rivo, Laura, *The Furnished Room* (1961)
> Young Irishman in a Notting Hill bedsit makes a pact to commit
> murder: moral melodrama filmed by Michael Winner as
> *West 11* (1963).

Dunn, Nell, *Up the Junction* (1963)
> Women looking for a good time in pre-gentrified Battersea.

Farson, Daniel, *Soho in the Fifties* (1987)
> Superb photos, with text by a writer who was there.

Fletcher, Geoffrey, *The London Nobody Knows* (1962)
> One of several classic books by the great Geoffrey Fletcher:
> deeply affectionate explorations, illustrated with his own
> drawings.

Gattrell, Vic, *City of Laughter: Sex and Satire in Eighteenth Century
London* (2006)

Incisive and colourful social history through the graphic prints and caricatures of the day.

Maddox, Adrian, *Classic Cafes* (2003)
Like pie-and-mash shops, the classic caff is disappearing, and this memorial celebration has become a cult book.

Mayhew, Henry, *London Labour and the London Poor* (1851)
The one and only Mayhew: his gigantic survey exists in numerous selections and abridgements such as *Mayhew's London*, *London's Underworld* and an Oxford World's Classics edition. The most entertaining of the original volumes is number four, *Those That Will Not Work*.

Nairn, Ian, *Nairn's London* (1966)
Informal, opinionated, wears its learning lightly and packed with interest: Nairn was a great writer, miles away from the worthwhile but slightly stuffier world of Pevsner.

Petit, Chris, 'Newman Passage; or, J. Maclaren-Ross and the Case of the Vanishing Writers', in *The Time Out Book of London Short Stories* (1993)
Intriguing, consummately done short-story-cum-essay on rediscovered fiction writer Julian Maclaren-Ross and the world of Fitzrovia.

Porter, Roy, *London: A Social History* (1994)
Sane, sound, reliable.

Quindlen, Anna, *Imagined London: A Tour of the World's Greatest Fictional City* (2004)
A London of the mind, as seen by an American reader.

Selvon, Samuel, *The Lonely Londoners* (1956)
Highly anecdotal novel of the West Indian experience in London, loosened up with a groundbreaking use of dialect.

Sinclair, Iain, *Lights Out for the Territory: Nine Excursions in the Secret History of London* (1997)
An inspired, baroque stylist with a taste for mixing arcana and lowlife, Sinclair virtually reinvented London writing.

Sinclair, Iain, ed., *London: City of Disappearances* (2006)
Compendium of pieces celebrating and commemorating a changing, vanishing city.

Stevenson, Robert Louis, *The Strange Case of Dr Jekyll and Mr Hyde* (1886)
> One of a clutch of late Victorian classics that set the image of a foggy, gaslit London.

Taylor, Craig, *Londoners* (2011)
> A brilliant collection of interviews.

Taylor, Terry, *Baron's Court, All Change* (1961)
> Suburban teenager discovers Soho: the title comes from Baron's Court as the tube station where the line suddenly goes underground, like a magic portal into 'London proper'.

Walkowitz, Judith, *City of Dreadful Delight: Narratives of Sexual Danger in Late-Victorian London* (1992).
> A feminist take on the Ripper case and other Victorian scares and scandals, seeing them – or their media coverage – as an attempt to frighten women into respectability. Exaggerated in places, but some real insight.

Weinreb, Ben, and Christopher Hibbert, *The London Encyclopaedia* (1983, rev. edn 1993)
> A monumental achievement, this is a work of reference but readable enough for dipping.

Films

Blackfriars Bridge, dir. Robert W. Paul (1896)
> Half a minute long, this has a good claim to be London's first – certainly very early – street scene on film. Currently available on YouTube.

Blow-up, dir. Michelangelo Antonioni (1966)
> Absurdly cool photographer (David Hemmings) thinks he's accidentally snapped a murder scene in a park; the mystery stays unsolved, but the take on Swinging Sixties London makes the film a magnificent period piece.

Dirty Pretty Things, dir. Stephen Frears (2002)
> Documentary-style drama of illegal immigrants managing to survive, with Nigerian Okwe and Turkish Senay encountering an organ-smuggling operation at the hotel where they work.

The Filth and the Fury, dir. Julien Temple (2000)
> Sex Pistols documentary using contemporary footage: the voice of Sid Vicious ('Girls like me, 'cos I've got a good body . . .') is what the yoof sounded like before the rise of 'multicultural London English'.

The Lodger: A Story of the London Fog, dir. Alfred Hitchcock (1927)
> Early Hitchcock silent, inspired by Jack the Ripper, with matinee idol Ivor Novello as the unlikely suspect.

London, dir. Patrick Keiller (1994)
> Highly idiosyncratic and quietly funny quasi-documentary with the voice of actor Paul Scofield discussing the journeys of fictitious researcher 'Robinson'.

The London Nobody Knows, dir. Norman Cohen (1967).
> James Mason in the footsteps of London explorer Geoffrey Fletcher and his classic book of the same title: there are a couple of dubious flights into wacky Sixties surrealism, but the documentary material and interviews are haunting.

London: The Modern Babylon, dir. Julien Temple (2012)
> Inspired, time-travelling use of archive footage from the last hundred years, coming together to make an epic of a diverse and endlessly resurgent city.

The Long Good Friday, dir. John Mackenzie (1980)
> The charm of 'Cockney Cagney' Bob Hoskins, playing a gangster boss, carries this crime flick with a spread of real, run-down London locations.

Naked England, dir. Vittorio De Sisti (1969)
> Largely naked London, this rare Italian exploitation documentary, in the 'Mondo' genre, goes where *The London Nobody Knows* might fear to tread: from pubs, guardsmen and cops chases to Happenings, sexual perversity and trepanation (drilling a hole in your head for enlightenment). Unexpectedly beautiful soundtrack by Piero Piccioni.

Night and the City, dir. Jules Dassin (1950)
> London film noir, based on Gerald Kersh's 1938 cult novel, with Richard Widmark as the unlovable protagonist. American

director Dassin had shot *Naked City* in Manhattan a year or
two earlier, and the film shows his feel for real urban locations.

Notting Hill, dir. Roger Michell (1999)

Feelgood movie with bookshop owner (Hugh Grant) falling in
love with world-famous actress (Julia Roberts) – it underlined
Notting Hill's transition from bedsitter land to Bohemia to one
of the world's most desirable, expensive (and now romantic)
neighbourhoods.

Passport to Pimlico, dir. Henry Cornelius (1949)

The inhabitants of Pimlico – artfully faked, just south and
not north of the river – declare independence. Typically
warm-hearted version of Englishness from Ealing Studios,
as Britain tried to rebuild psychologically after the war.
Other Ealing comedies include *The Ladykillers* (King's Cross)
and *The Lavender Hill Mob* (south London), although the
best – *Kind Hearts and Coronets* – is less London-y.

Peeping Tom, dir. Michael Powell (1960)

Creepy photographer murders women on camera, in this
now-classic study of cinematic voyeurism; hated on release,
it virtually ended the director's career. Fitzrovia's 'Jekyll and
Hyde Alley' (Newman Passage) figures as a location.

Performance, dir. Nicholas Roeg (1970)

Violent, druggy, overblown extravaganza, as a gangster
(James Fox) and a rock star (Mick Jagger) fuse and exchange
identities in a mansion-like Notting Hill house. Glamorous
and disturbing.

Piccadilly, dir. E.A. Dupont (1929)

Daringly cosmopolitan love affair between a West End club
owner (Jameson Thomas) and the incomparable Anna May
Wong as a girl from Limehouse. The simple, tragic storyline
is a vehicle for almost German Expressionist-style sets and
direction.

Sammy and Rosie Get Laid, dir. Stephen Frears (1987)

Ambitious if flawed, Hanif Kureishi's comic screenplay was
as much about the state and possibilities of Thatcher-era
London as the title's promiscuous couple.

Scrooge, dir. Brian Desmond Hurst (1951)
> One of the best of the many Dickens adaptations – they blur together in the memory, with studio street scenes like Christmas cards come to life – starring Alastair Sim in the title role.

The Small World of Sammy Lee, dir. Ken Hughes (1963)
> Anthony Newley plays a Soho strip-club compère, from Whitechapel, who has only a few desperate hours to pay back a debt to the Soho underworld. Real street shots.

The Sorcerers, dir. Michael Reeves (1967)
> Highly watchable mash-up of horror film and Swinging London, as evil Professor Monserrat (Boris Karloff) and his wife Estelle practise mind control – more sci-fi than supernatural – so they can direct and experience the life of a young man.

Withnail and I, dir. Bruce Robinson (1987)
> Enormously charming comedy of a recently bygone Bohemia, with Richard E. Grant as the charismatic but ultimately tragic Withnail.

Wonderful London, dir. Harry Parkinson and Frank Miller (1924)
> Priceless silent footage, with captions and piano music. Airing the perennial theme that London has an alarming number of foreigners, it could almost be retitled 'Xenophobic London': occasionally wince-inducing but still wonderful.

Online

Closed Pubs – closedpubs.co.uk
Londonist – Londonist.com
The Lost Byway – thelostbyway.com
Secret London – secretldn.com
Spitalfields Life – spitalfieldslife.com
Simons Walks – athomeinchelsea.com/simons-walks.html
Time Out – timeout.com

Acknowledgements

I've lived in London over thirty years, and although I know what I like I've probably grown blasé, so I want to thank Nancy Strouse for bringing such a fresh enthusiastic eye to the place, and showing it to me as I showed it to her.

I have had invaluable readerly advice from Mark Watson, Sheena Joughin and Simon Beesley, and I'm grateful to Malcolm Hopkins for his sharp-eyed take on Agatha Christie. 'Gratitude is heaven itself,' in the words of William Blake, and other people I'm grateful to, usually for much less specific things – talking, eating, drinking, walking around and exploring generally, as well as information and loan of books – include the late Mark Allan, Nish Chaturvedi, Allison Crawbuck, Deborah Dawkin, Geoffrey Elborn, Christopher Fowler, Nina Hathway, Ian Hunt, Rick Hutton, Patrick Matthews, Liz Parratt, Mark Pilkington, Ian Pindar, Jane Robins, Su Rose, Michele Slung, Phil Smith, Scott Wood and Viktor Wynd. A few errors creep into virtually all non-fiction, so although I've tried to root them out, there will inevitably be a couple lurking; they are of course entirely my own responsibility.

I'm also grateful to the staff of the British Library Rare Books Room – the best place to work, whether your books are rare or not – and to the wonderful staff of the London Library, one of London's great treasures in itself, along with the staff of Westminster Reference Library and Westminster Archives.

Photo Acknowledgements

The author and publishers wish to express their thanks to the below sources of illustrative material and/or permission to reproduce it:

Alamy: pp. 10 (Simon Turner), 13 top (agefotostock), 13 bottom (adam eastland), 22, 120 (Heritage Image Partnership), 67 (Garden Photo World), 84 (Antiqua Print Gallery), 122 , 128 (Chronicle), 126 (Trinity Mirror/Mirrorpix), 134 (CAMimage), 151 (David Seacombe), 172 (A.P.S. (UK), 188 (Lightworks Media), 197 (Gregory Wrona), 200 (Jeff Gilbert), 202 (Peter Schickert), 206 (RGB Ventures/Superstock), 207 (Roberto Herett), 224 (Kumar Sriskandan), 225 (Grant Rooney), 230 (Jordi Salas); © The Trustees of the British Museum, London: pp. 27, 46; Flickr: pp. 42 (It's No Game), 169 (Michael Clegg Photography CC), 190 (seanbjack), 204 (duncanc), 214 (mendhak CC BY-SA 2.0), 215 (Matt Brown); Getty Images: pp. 115, 124 (Kurt Hutton/Picture Post/Hulton Archive), 131 (Popperfoto), 136 (Charlie Phillips), 139 (Rick Hardy), 142 (Michael Putland), 145 (Harry Dempster), 148 (Janette Beckman), 154 (Howard Davies); iStockphoto: pp. 7 (Simon Bradfield), 8 top (thehague), 11 (greycloud), 12 top (BrasilNut1), 13 bottom (Jean Cuomo), 14 bottom (Fatima Luna), 15 top (oversnap), 15 bottom (stockinasia), 181 (sparhawk4242), 183 (tirc83), 184 (fotolupa); Library of Congress, Washington, D.C.: pp. 104, 108, 182; Mayflower Media Ltd: pp. 14 top, 166, 167 (Susannah Jayes); © Metropolitan Archives: p. 97; The Metropolitan Museum of Art, New York: p. 58; © Oskar Proctor: p. 212; Shutterstock: pp. 6, 8 bottom (Philip Bird LRPS CPAGB photographer), 51, 66, 96 (Chris Dorney), 164 (DrimaFilm), 170 (Miroslav Cik), 173 (Aerial Motion), 179 (Ron Ellis), 180 (asiastock), 185 (Kiev.Victo), 201 (LoisGoBe), 233 (Alex Segre); © TfL from the London Transport Museum collection (www.ltmuseum.co.uk): p. 118; The Wallace Collection, London: p.219; The Wellcome Library, London: pp. 49, 70; Wikipedia: pp.9 (Prioryman CC BY-SA 4.0), 28 (Carole Raddato CC BY-SA 2.0), 30 (thewub CC BY-SA), 109 (Christoph Braun), 192 (JohnArmagh), 195 (Passikivi CC BY-SA 4.0); Yale Center for British Art, New Haven, CT: p. 43.

Index